Pascal's Triangle

Thomas M. Green

Charles H. Hamberg

DALE SEYMOUR PUBLICATIONS

Pascal's Triangle Answer Key *is available as a separate book.*
Contact the publisher for ordering information.

Technical Art: Pat Rogondino

ISBN 0-86651-306-X

Order Number DS01603

bcdefghij-MA-89321098

DALE
SEYMOUR
PUBLICATIONS
P.O. BOX 10888
PALO ALTO, CA 94303

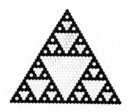

Contents

CHAPTER 4   **HIGHER DIMENSIONAL FIGURATE NUMBERS**   **159**

CHAPTER 5   **COUNTING PROBLEMS**   **203**

Preface

Pascal's Triangle is an intriguing array of numbers. Not only are there seemingly boundless patterns and relationships within the triangular array itself, but also there are many mathematical topics in which these numbers play a role.

This textbook has been designed to provide a vehicle to the discovery of mathematics related to Pascal's Triangle. The level of most of the exercises is the same or below that of high school algebra. However, the more advanced reader may extend the patterns and discussions by attempting to prove certain formulas or to generalize given patterns. For example, if T represents the nth triangular number and S represents the nth square number, an advanced reader could prove the following relationships:

$$T_{n+m} = T_n + T_m + (1) \cdot n \cdot m$$
$$S_{n+m} = S_n + S_m + (2) \cdot n \cdot m$$

Notice that $S_{n+m} = (n + m)^2$.

Another exercise for the advanced reader would be to extend the pattern made by pentagonal numbers or other figurate numbers. Our exercises suggest many patterns such as these.

One of our goals for this textbook has been to motivate the young beginning researcher by including many exercises that ask for verification of a pattern by testing a few specific cases. It is worth the time for students to ponder and explore some of these ideas before seeking out a specific answer. It has been our experience that students can gain true insight by exploring patterns. In this sense the actual process of the exercise is the answer.

Another one of our goals was to offer intriguing source materials for mathematics teachers to use in their classes, including many topics suitable for introducing students to discrete mathematics.

We have been exploring Pascal's Triangle for more than two decades and we're still amazed when we find new patterns and situations where these numbers can be applied. We hope you will find your favorite patterns in the pages that follow. We've also presented some new ideas we hope you will enjoy exploring as much as we have.

Thomas M. Green

Charles L. Hamberg

"... I leave out many more [uses of the Arithmetic Triangle] than I include; it is extraordinary how fertile in properties this triangle is. Everyone can try his hand."

Blaise Pascal
"Treatise on the
Arithmetic Triangle," 1653

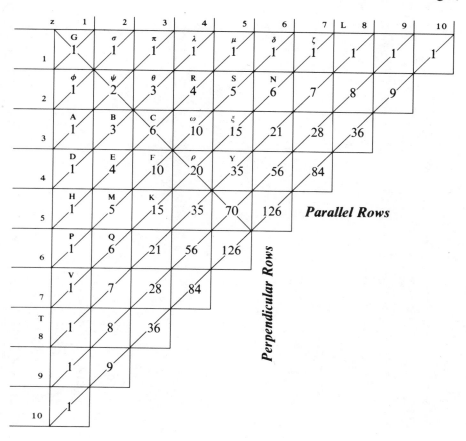

1 Pascal's Triangle and Where You Find It

1.1 THE PATTERN OF PASCAL'S TRIANGLE

Pascal's Triangle is an arrangement of certain whole numbers in a triangular pattern. In 1653, Blaise Pascal wrote "A Treatise on the Arithmetic Triangle," which described many of the properties of this triangular pattern.

The first few rows of Pascal's Triangle are:

Zeroth row					1			
First row				1		1		
Second row			1		2		1	
Third row		1		3		3		1
Fourth row	1		4		6		4		1
Fifth row	1	5		10		10		5		1

Each row can be formed from the previous row.

---

1. What is the rule for forming successive rows? What numbers are in the sixth row?

The numbers in the sixth row are: 1, 6, 15, 20, 15, 6, 1. Each row begins and ends with the number 1. The other numbers are found by adding consecutive pairs of numbers from the previous row. For example, the sixth row is formed from the fifth row.

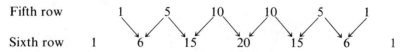

Check this rule for each of rows zero through five.

2. Complete the next three rows of Pascal's Triangle.

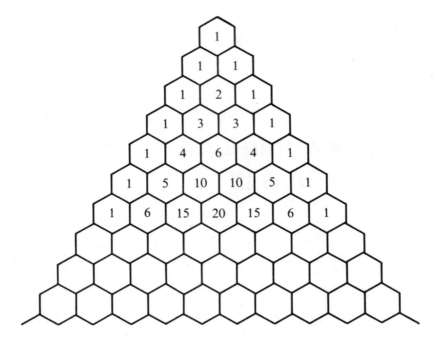

Pascal's Triangle provides solutions to many problems from several branches of mathematics. Four examples are presented in the succeeding sections of this chapter. These examples come from number theory, algebra, geometry, and probability.

This arrangement of numbers was known long before Pascal wrote about it. The triangle was used by Omar Khayyam about 1100. Another early reference to Pascal's Triangle appears in a Chinese manuscript by Chu Shih-Chieh in the year 1303. The mathematicians of Europe worked with the triangle for over one hundred years before Pascal, during the development of the science of algebra. Pascal's treatise on the arithmetic triangle contained many new properties. He was able to generalize earlier treatments using new methods, such as mathematical induction. Pascal also applied the triangle to probability theory.

In addition to the diverse problems that can be solved using Pascal's Triangle, the triangle contains many interesting numerical relationships. In Chapter 2, we shall explore several of these relationships and you may discover an interesting pattern by yourself.

1.2 PROBABILITIES OF TOSSING COINS

Consider the following probability example. If you flip a coin, it will come up either heads or tails. There are only two possibilities, and the probability of the coin coming up heads is 1 chance out of 2, or $\frac{1}{2}$. The same probability exists for a single coin to come up tails. The probability of any event is expressed as a fraction between 0 and 1 inclusive.

Suppose you toss two coins. What are the possible outcomes? We can arrange the outcomes using a tree diagram.

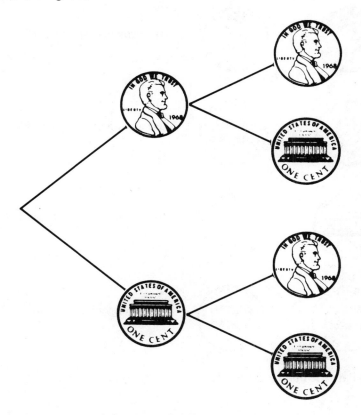

Using "*H*" for heads and "*T*" for tails, we can simplify this tree diagram.

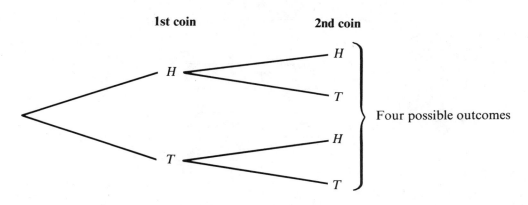

The four possible outcomes are:

   1st arrangement — 2 heads

   2nd arrangement — 1 head, 1 tail

   3rd arrangement — 1 tail, 1 head

   4th arrangement — 2 tails

Now we can tabulate the number of heads in these arrangements.

	1st coin	2nd coin
2 heads	H	H
1 head	H	T
	T	H
0 heads	T	T

Number of heads	Number of arrangements
2 heads	1
1 head	2
0 heads	1
Total	4

The probability of obtaining exactly two heads when two coins are tossed is 1 chance out of 4, or $\frac{1}{4}$. The probability of obtaining exactly one head is 2 chances out of 4, or $\frac{2}{4}$, which is equal to $\frac{1}{2}$. The probability of obtaining zero heads (two tails) is 1 chance out of 4, or $\frac{1}{4}$.

Suppose you toss three coins. The following tree diagram represents the possible outcomes.

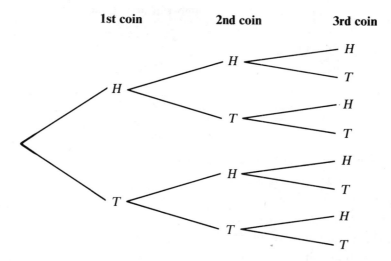

	1st coin	2nd coin	3rd coin

Now we can tabulate the number of heads in these arrangements.

	1st coin	2nd coin	3rd coin
1st arrangement	H	H	H
2nd arrangement	H	H	T
3rd arrangement	H	T	H
4th arrangement	H	T	T
5th arrangement	T	H	H
6th arrangement	T	H	T
7th arrangement	T	T	H
8th arrangement	T	T	T

Number of heads	Number of arrangements
3 heads	1
2 heads	3
1 head	3
0 heads	1
Total	8

The probability of obtaining exactly three heads when three coins are tossed is 1 chance out of 8, or $\frac{1}{8}$. The probability of obtaining exactly two heads is 3 chances out of 8, or $\frac{3}{8}$.

1. Calculate the probability of obtaining exactly one head when three coins are tossed.

2. Calculate the probability of obtaining exactly three tails when three coins are tossed.

3. Suppose four coins are tossed. Construct a tree diagram for this situation and tabulate the possible arrangements. Then complete the following table.

Number of heads	Number of arrangements
4 heads	____
3 heads	____
2 heads	____
1 head	____
0 heads	____
Total	____

Calculate the probability of obtaining exactly:

4. 4 heads when four coins are tossed.

5. 3 heads when four coins are tossed.

6. 2 heads when four coins are tossed.

7. 1 head when four coins are tossed.

8. 4 tails when four coins are tossed.

In summary:

Number of coins	Number of heads	Number of arrangements
1 coin	1 head	1
	0 heads	1
2 coins	2 heads	1
	1 head	2
	0 heads	1
3 coins	3 heads	1
	2 heads	3
	1 head	3
	0 heads	1
4 coins	4 heads	1
	3 heads	4
	2 heads	6
	1 head	4
	0 heads	1

Did you notice that the numbers of arrangements are the same as the numbers in the rows of Pascal's Triangle? For example, if four coins are tossed, then the numbers of arrangements are the numbers

1	4	6	4	1

which are also the numbers in the fourth row of Pascal's Triangle.

9. Assume that the fifth row of Pascal's Triangle contains the number of arrangements for 5, 4, 3, 2, 1, and 0 heads when 5 coins are tossed. Complete the following table by referring only to Pascal's Triangle (do not make a tree diagram or other tabulation).

Number of heads	Number of arrangements
5 heads	_____
4 heads	_____
3 heads	_____
2 heads	_____
1 head	_____
0 heads	_____
Total	_____

10. What is the probability of obtaining exactly 5 heads?   4 heads?   3 heads?   2 heads?   1 head?   0 heads (5 tails)?

Another way to show the distribution of the number of heads obtained when three coins are tossed is by using a **histogram**. The height of each column represents the number of arrangements containing the number of heads specified at the bottom of the column.

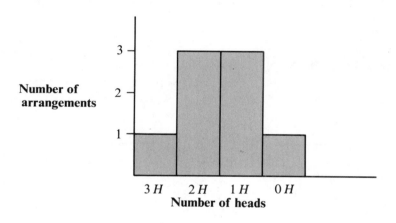

11. Construct histograms showing the distribution of the number of heads obtained when 4 coins are tossed and when 5 coins are tossed.

When three coins are tossed, we have the following probabilities:

Number of heads	Number of arrangements	Probability	Percent equivalent
3	1	$\frac{1}{8}$	12.5%
2	3	$\frac{3}{8}$	37.5%
1	3	$\frac{3}{8}$	37.5%
0	1	$\frac{1}{8}$	12.5%

Try this experiment. Toss three coins 80 times and tally each time you get 3 heads, 2 heads, 1 head, or 0 heads. Then total each set of tally marks and give the probability and percent equivalent of your experimental outcomes. Use the following chart.

Number of heads	Tally	Total	Probability	Percent equivalent
3				
2				
1				
0				

How do the percent equivalents from your experiment compare to those in the completed chart for three coins?

1.3 POWERS OF TWO AND ELEVEN

Suppose a living cell divides into two cells.

Next suppose the two cells undergo a second stage of cell division to form four cells.

Start	◯	1 Cell
Mitosis	◯◯	Cell-splitting
Stage 1	◯ ◯	2 Cells
Mitosis	◯◯ ◯◯	Cell-splitting
Stage 2	◯ ◯ ◯ ◯	4 Cells

The arrangement of the number of cells at each stage can be represented in a tree diagram.

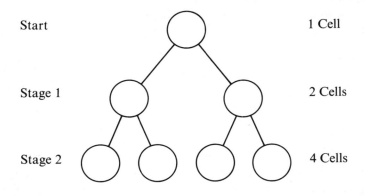

Start   1 Cell

Stage 1   2 Cells

Stage 2   4 Cells

---

1. Suppose each of the four cells of stage 2 divide. How many cells will there be in stage 3?
2. Draw a diagram showing stage 3 and stage 4, and record the number of cells at each stage.

The sequence of numbers of cells at each of the above stages is 1, 2, 4, 8, 16. What is your prediction for the next number in the sequence? If you predicted 32, you are correct. The numbers in this sequence are called "powers of two." The expression 2^3 is called the "third" power of two and is evaluated by using the base, two, as a factor three times.

$2^3 = 2 \cdot 2 \cdot 2 = 8$

Other powers of two are:

the first power of $2 = 2^1 = 2$
the second power of $2 = 2^2 = 2 \cdot 2 = 4$
the fourth power of $2 = 2^4 = 2 \cdot 2 \cdot 2 \cdot 2 = 16$

We also define the zeroth power of 2 to be: $2^0 = 1$.

---

3. Find the fifth and sixth powers of two.
4. Look at the sequence of the powers of two.

$2^0 = 1$
$2^1 = 2$
$2^2 = 4$
$2^3 = 8$
$2^4 = 16$
$2^5 = 32$
$2^6 = 64$

What number comes next in the sequence?
5. Compute these powers of two: $2^7, 2^8, 2^9, 2^{10}$.

Do you see that the powers of two describe the number of cells at each stage of the subdivision starting with one cell? And that the number of cells at the third stage is 2^3; the number of cells at the fourth stage is 2^4; and so on?

Now add the numbers in each row of Pascal's Triangle.

$$1 = 1$$
$$1 + 1 = 2$$
$$1 + 2 + 1 = 4$$
$$1 + 3 + 3 + 1 = 8$$
$$1 + 4 + 6 + 4 + 1 = 16$$

---

6. Find the sum: $1 + 5 + 10 + 10 + 5 + 1 =$ _____.

7. Is the sum of the numbers in the 6th, 7th, 8th, 9th, and 10th rows of Pascal's Triangle the same as 2^6, 2^7, 2^8, 2^9, and 2^{10}, respectively?

In general, the sum of the numbers in the nth row of Pascal's Triangle is equal to the nth power of two, 2^n. This result is a part of a more comprehensive mathematical concept called binomial expansion.

The sum of two numbers is a **binomial**. Thus, $a + b$, $x + 1$, $1 + 1$, and $10 + 1$ are examples of binomials. The numbers in Pascal's Triangle are also known as binomial coefficients. When a binomial is raised to a power, the result is an expansion of the binomial known as a **polynomial**. These polynomials utilize the numbers in Pascal's Triangle as coefficients. For example, the number 2 expressed as the binomial $1 + 1$ can be raised to the third power.

$$2^3 = (1 + 1)^3$$

The expansion of $(1 + 1)^3$ is

$$(1 + 1)^3 = 1 + 3 + 3 + 1$$

This can be checked by showing that $(1 + 1)^3 = 2^3 = 8$ and $1 + 3 + 3 + 1 = 8$. The numbers 1, 3, 3, 1 are from the third row of Pascal's Triangle and are called the binomial coefficients for the third power of $1 + 1$.

The expansion of the second power of $1 + 1$ is

$$(1 + 1)^2 = 1 + 2 + 1$$

---

8. Write the expansion for the fourth power of $1 + 1$.

9. Expand $(1 + 1)^5$.

Technically, the expansion for $(1 + 1)^3$ should be

$$(1 + 1)^3 = 1 \cdot 1^3 + 3 \cdot 1^2 + 3 \cdot 1^1 + 1 \cdot 1^0$$

but because $1^3 = 1^2 = 1^1 = 1^0 = 1$, that is, the powers of one equal 1, the final result is still $1 + 3 + 3 + 1$. The powers of one are included in the expansion since one is the first number in the binomial $1 + 1$. If the binomial to be expanded is $2 + 1$, then the powers of two should be present, as shown below.

$$(2 + 1)^3 = 1 \cdot 2^3 + 3 \cdot 2^2 + 3 \cdot 2^1 + 1 \cdot 2^0$$

Notice the binomial coefficients are 1, 3, 3, 1, just as in the previous example, but each one is multiplied by a power of 2, beginning with the third and ending with the zeroth power of two.

The previous equality can be verified by showing that $(2 + 1)^3 = 3^3 = 27$ and

$$1 \cdot 2^3 + 3 \cdot 2^2 + 3 \cdot 2^1 + 1 \cdot 2^0 = 1 \cdot 8 + 3 \cdot 4 + 3 \cdot 2 + 1 \cdot 1$$
$$= 8 + 12 + 6 + 1$$
$$= 27$$

---

10. Write the expansion for $(2 + 1)^4$ and check to see that the value of the expansion is $3^4 = 81$.

Now let's study the powers of 11 and look for a familiar pattern.

$11^0 = 1$

$11^1 = 11$

$11^2 = 121$

Look at the third power of 11.

$$11^3 = 11 \cdot 11 \cdot 11$$
$$= 121 \cdot 11$$
$$= 1331$$

Notice the digits of this and the other powers of 11. Do you recognize the digits as the numbers in successive rows of Pascal's Triangle?

---

11. What do you predict for $11^4 = ?$
Check to see that the fourth power of 11 is equal to 14641.

The reason the numbers of Pascal's Triangle are in the powers of 11 is that 11 is equal to the binomial $10 + 1$. For example, the binomial expansion for $(10 + 1)^3$ is:

$$(10 + 1)^3 = 1 \cdot 10^3 + 3 \cdot 10^2 + 3 \cdot 10^1 + 1 \cdot 10^0$$
$$= 1 \cdot 1000 + 3 \cdot 100 + 3 \cdot 10 + 1 \cdot 1$$
$$= 1000 + 300 + 30 + 1$$
$$= 1331$$

Therefore, $1 \cdot 10^3 + 3 \cdot 10^2 + 3 \cdot 10^1 + 1 \cdot 10^0$ is the expanded form of the number 1331.

---

12. Expand $(10 + 1)^4$ using the fourth row of Pascal's Triangle. Check to see that the value of the expansion is $11^4 = 14641$.

13. Find the value of 11^5 in two ways:
(a) $(10 + 1)^5 = $ _____
(b) $11 \cdot 11 \cdot 11 \cdot 11 \cdot 11 = $ _____

1.4 BINARY CODES AND PASCAL'S TRIANGLE

The binary number system is a positional number system like our base ten system, but place values are determined by powers of two instead of ten. Thus, the binary number 1101_{two} has a value in base ten determined by the powers of two.

Powers of two	$2^3 = 8$	$2^2 = 4$	$2^1 = 2$	$2^0 = 1$
Binary number	1	1	0	1
Place value base 10	8	4	0	1
Sum	8 +	4 +	0 +	1 = 13

Thus, $1101_{two} = 13$ in base ten notation.

Every binary number is written using only the digits "zero" and "one." Depending on its position, when a "one" occurs in the numeral, it represents a particular power of two. To compute the numeral's equivalent in base ten, add the values of the powers of two together. The powers of two are:

$2^0 = 1$	$2^6 = 64$	$2^{12} = $ _____
$2^1 = 2$	$2^7 = 128$	$2^{13} = $ _____
$2^2 = 4$	$2^8 = 256$	$2^{14} = $ _____
$2^3 = 8$	$2^9 = 512$	$2^{15} = $ _____
$2^4 = 16$	$2^{10} = 1024$	
$2^5 = 32$	$2^{11} = 2048$	

1. Complete the above table.
2. Change these base two numbers to base ten.

    (a) 111111_{two} (b) 111000_{two}

Each of the digits in a binary number is called a "bit." Some minicomputers use a sixteen bit representation of each piece of information they process. Thus, a base ten integer would be coded for the computer as a binary numeral. Each bit is represented by a magnetized core within the computer's memory. The largest 16 bit integer is $1\ 111\ 111\ 111\ 111\ 111_{two}$; however, one bit is usually reserved for the sign of the number, either positive or negative. Omitting this bit, the largest integer is $111\ 111\ 111\ 111\ 111_{two}$. To compute the base ten value of this number we need to find the sum of the powers of two from the zeroth to the fourteenth.

2^{14}	2^{13}	2^{12}	2^{11}	2^{10}	2^9	2^8	2^7	2^6	2^5	2^4	2^3	2^2	2^1	2^0
1	1	1	1	1	1	1	1	1	1	1	1	1	1	1

3. Show that the sum of the powers of two from the zeroth to the fourteenth is equal to $2^{15} - 1$.

The following table shows the first few numbers in base two.

Base 10	Base 2	Base 10	Base 2	Base 10	Base 2	Base 10	Base 2
0	0	10	1010	20	10100	30	_____
1	1	11	1011	21	10101	31	_____
2	10	12	1100	22	10110	32	_____
3	11	13	1101	23	10111	33	_____
4	100	14	1110	24	11000	34	_____
5	101	15	1111	25	11001	35	_____
6	110	16	10000	26	11010	36	_____
7	111	17	10001	27	11011	37	_____
8	1000	18	10010	28	11100	38	_____
9	1001	19	10011	29	11101	39	_____

4. Complete the last column of the previous chart.

How many base two numbers consist of just four digits? Looking at the chart, we find eight binary numbers (those from 8 through 15 in base ten):

1000   1100
1001   1101
1010   1110
1011   1111

5. In how many of these binary numbers is the bit "1" used just once? twice? three times? four times? See the chart on p. 42.

6. Do you recognize the pattern of numbers in the totals?

7. Fill in the chart on p. 42 for five-digit binary numbers.

8. Without listing them, predict the totals for all six-digit binary numbers and fill in the chart on p. 42.

Consider a string of two light bulbs represented by

Let an "x" inside of the circle represent a light bulb that is lit. Thus, the diagram will represent the situation where the first light bulb is "on" and the second light bulb is "off."

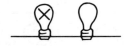

How many different arrangements with the lights "on" and "off" are possible? Since there are two ways of drawing the bulb (either 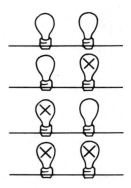 or) and since there are two bulbs, there are $2 \cdot 2$ or $2^2 = 4$ arrangements. They are easily drawn as indicated:

Consider the arrangements for a string of three bulbs. Since there are two ways of drawing each bulb and there are three bulbs, there are $2 \cdot 2 \cdot 2 = 2^3 = 8$ arrangements, as shown below.

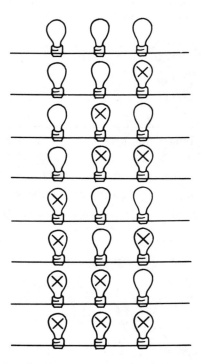

Suppose we have a panel of four lights.

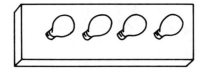

A lit bulb will represent the binary digit "1," and an unlit bulb will represent the binary digit "0." If we light all the bulbs, this will represent the number 1111_{two}. If all the lights are off, this will represent 0000_{two}, or simply 0_{two}.

---

9. How many binary numbers can be represented by the panel of lights above? Fill in the chart on p. 42.

10. How many binary numbers can be represented by adding one more light bulb to the panel?

11. Without listing them, predict the totals for a five-light panel.

12. Complete the table on p. 43.

13. How many arrangements would there be if a panel of six lights is examined?

14. In the arrangement of six lights, what is the number of ways three bulbs are lit and three are not?

15. How many arrangements would there be if a panel of seven lights were examined?

The Morse Code is a system of dots and dashes used in telegraphy to represent letters of the alphabet, digits, and other symbols. If we call the dots and dashes bits, then using only one bit, we can only represent two different letters, one with a dot and one with a dash.

---

16. How many letters can be represented by two bits? three bits? four bits? Complete the tables on p. 43.

The American Standard Code for Information Interchange (ASCII) is a code using binary numbers to represent the letters of the alphabet, numerals, and other symbols. This code is used to transmit information from teletype terminals to a computer. The code numbers for A, B, C, and D are 65, 66, 67, and 68 in base ten. The binary representation of 65, the code for the letter A, is the seven-digit numeral 1000001.

---

17. What are the binary representations for the letters B, C, and D?

18. How many seven-digit binary numerals are possible?

19. What is the word transmitted by the code:
1010000, 1000001, 1010011, 1000011, 1000001, 1001100?

Information transmitted to a computer is usually accomplished directly from a terminal keyboard, similar to a typewriter keyboard. The codes are automatically produced when the keys are stroked. However, other types of media are also available for input and output. These consist of punched cards, punched paper tape, magnetic tape or disks, magnetic-inked characters, and optically scanned characters. The following diagram shows how punched paper tape is used to represent data. A punched hole represents the digit "1," and the lack of a punched hole represents the digit "0." There are eight channels on the paper tape, seven of which are used to represent the alphabet and other symbols on the keyboard. The eighth channel is used by the particular computer being operated and may be either a "0" or a "1" depending on that computer. It is called the "high order bit."

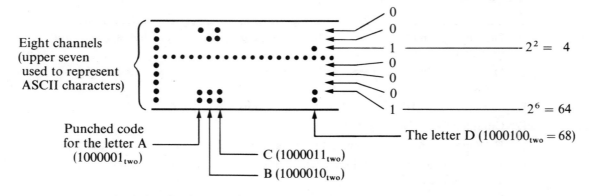

Eight channels (upper seven used to represent ASCII characters)

Punched code for the letter A (1000001_{two})

C (1000011_{two})

B (1000010_{two})

$2^2 = 4$

$2^6 = 64$

The letter D ($1000100_{two} = 68$)

---

20. For the digit 1, how many seven-digit binary numbers have exactly: one occurrence? two occurrences? three? four? five? six? seven?

21. Total number of seven-digit numbers = _____.

22. What word is punched on the paper tape shown?

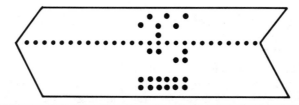

1.5 SHADING SECTORS OF A PIE GRAPH

Consider the following figure. We want to find the number of different ways the sectors can be shaded when either one, two, three, etc., sectors are to be shaded at a given time.

For example, if one sector is to be shaded, then there are six different ways to shade just that one sector.

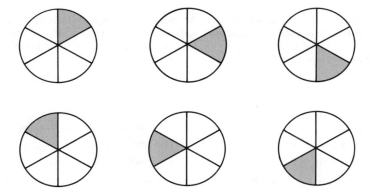

If two sectors are to be shaded at one time, there are considerably more ways to shade just two sectors. Also, there are many patterns possible if three, four, or five sectors are to be shaded. Notice that there is only one pattern possible if all six sectors are to be shaded.

To determine the total number of each type of shading pattern, start with fewer sectors and look for a predictable pattern. Suppose there are only three sectors.

When only one sector is shaded, there are three different patterns.

  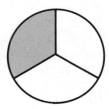

There are also three different patterns when only two sectors are shaded.

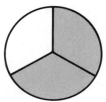 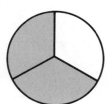 

Finally, there is one pattern when all three sectors are shaded and one pattern when no sector is shaded. In summary:

Number of ways when no sector is shaded	Number of ways when one sector is shaded	Number of ways when two sectors are shaded	Number of ways when three sectors are shaded
1	3	3	1
Total number of ways to shade the sectors = 1 + 3 + 3 + 1 = 8.			

1. Do you recognize the numbers in the chart above?

2. Make a chart showing the different ways of shading a circle with just two sectors.

3. Suppose a circle has four sectors. Shade the different patterns when just one of the sectors is shaded. Then, shade the different patterns when just two of the sectors are shaded... then when just three of the sectors are shaded. Use the sectors on p. 44 for shading your patterns. Finally, count all of the different patterns and enter the results into the chart on p. 45.

4. Enter the results from exercise 3 into the chart on p. 45. What pattern of numbers is emerging?

5. Predict the number of different patterns of each type for the circle with six sectors.

1.6 GOLD BRICK STACKING PROBLEM

In the fictional Land of Oro there lived a ruler by the name of King Tut. The king spent the better part of each day in the Royal Mint counting his bricks of gold. It was often his habit to stack his bricks in groups of two, three, four, or five and count by twos, threes, fours, or fives. One afternoon while stacking his gold bricks in groups of four, the king became curious as to the total number of different ways that he could stack just four bricks.

King Tut knew he could make one stack that would be four bricks high and four stacks so each stack would be one brick high. But, he didn't know how many ways he could arrange the four bricks into two stacks or three stacks. The king soon set about stacking four bricks in as many different ways as he could. The results of his efforts are shown in the table on the next page.

Then, King Tut tabulated the total number of different ways two gold bricks and three gold bricks could be stacked. As soon as he looked at the results, he suspected a pattern was developing and predicted the number of different ways five gold bricks could be stacked. The king was so excited about his discovery he decided to conduct a contest throughout the kingdom. He would offer one gold brick to anyone who could correctly find the pattern he had found and predict the number of different ways five gold bricks could be stacked.

The stacking had to be done according to the following rules:

1. The bricks had to be stacked directly on top of each other.

The Different Ways of Stacking 4 Gold Bricks

1 Stack	2 Stacks	3 Stacks	4 Stacks
1 way	3 ways	3 ways	1 way

Total = 8 ways

This was not allowed.

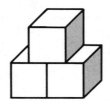

2. The bricks had to be in a single file, adjacent to each other, left and right faces, but not front and back.
This was not allowed.

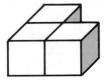

1. Do you recognize the pattern discovered by King Tut?
2. Make a chart showing the different ways of stacking 3 gold bricks; 2 gold bricks.
3. Make a chart showing the different ways of stacking 5 gold bricks.
4. Predict the number of ways that 6 gold bricks can be stacked.

1.7 CHECKERBOARD PATHS

Starting with a checker (not "kinged") as shown, how many ways can the player move to arrive at the square marked with an X?

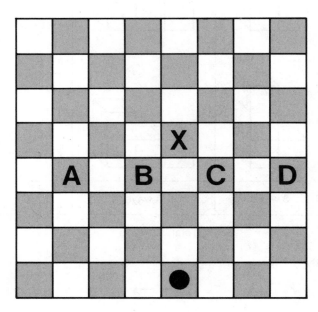

The following diagrams show the six different paths.

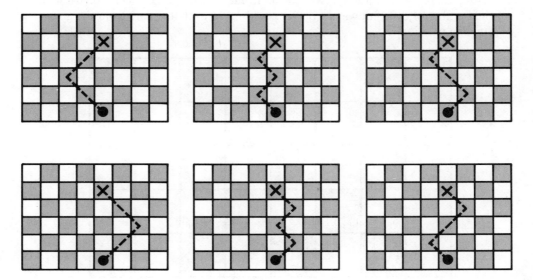

Find the number of different paths to:

1. The square labeled A.
2. The square labeled B.
3. The square labeled C.
4. The square labeled D.

Notice that the player can get to the square labeled X only by arriving there from either the square labeled B or C. If there are three ways to get to square B and three ways to get to square C, then there are $3 + 3 = 6$ ways to get to square X. In general, if there are n ways to get to square B and m ways to get to square C, then there are $n + m$ ways to get to square X.

5. Using the principle stated previously, fill in each circle on the checkerboard with the number of different ways a player could move to that square from the given starting position.

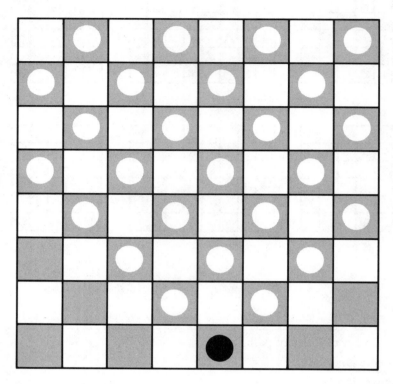

6. Do you see the beginning of a familiar pattern?

1.8 POINTS, LINES, PLANES, AND HIGHER SPACES OF GEOMETRY

The elements of geometry are points, lines, planes, and space.

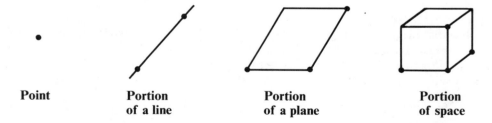

| Point | Portion of a line | Portion of a plane | Portion of space |

Space is 3-dimensional, a plane is 2-dimensional, a line is 1-dimensional, and a point is 0-dimensional. Each of these elements can be thought of as a space of a given dimension. Two distinct points determine a line. Three distinct points (not on the same line) determine a plane. Four distinct points (not in the same plane) determine space.

The simplest figure that can be drawn in any one of these dimensional spaces is called a **simplex**. In 0-dimensional space, the point is a simplex of order 0. In 1-dimensional space, the line segment is a simplex of order 1 and the point is a simplex of order 0. The triangle is a simplex of order 2 in 2-dimensional space. The line segment and the point exist in 2-dimensional space as simplexes of orders 1 and 0, respectively. The tetrahedron is a simplex of order 3 in 3-dimensional space and does not exist in lower-dimensional spaces. However, the point, the line segment, and the triangle all exist as simplexes of orders 0, 1, and 2, respectively, in 3-dimensional space.

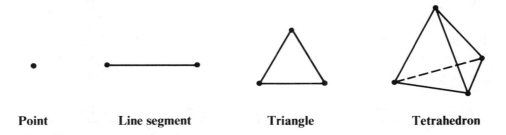

| Point | Line segment | Triangle | Tetrahedron |

Simplexes of the dimensional spaces 0−3

Each simplex of a given order is composed of elements that are simplexes of lesser orders. For example, a triangle is composed of 3 points (simplexes of order 0) and 3 line segments (simplexes of order 1).

---

1. How many simplexes of order 2 are found in a tetrahedron?

2. How many simplexes of order 1 are found in a tetrahedron?

3. How many simplexes of order 0 are found in a tetrahedron?

Also, the tetrahedron is made up of one simplex of order 3, that is, the tetrahedron itself. In summary, the composition of each simplex of a given order is given in the following table.

	Subspaces			
Simplex	**Points (Order 0)**	**Line segments (Order 1)**	**Triangles (Order 2)**	**Tetrahedrons (Order 3)**
Point	1	0	0	0
Line segment	2	1	0	0
Triangle	3	3	1	0
Tetrahedron	4	6	4	1

If you've recognized part of Pascal's Triangle in this table, you are right! Except for the leading 1, each row of Pascal's Triangle gives the number of subspaces contained in each simplex of order equal to the row number minus one.

Based on your knowledge of Pascal's Triangle and the assumption that 4-dimensional space can be defined, predict the number of subelements a simplex of order 4 would have. The simplex of order 4 is called a **pentatope**.

4. Complete the following table, and predict the number of subelements for the pentatope.

Simplex	Subspaces				
	Points (Order 0)	Line segments (Order 1)	Triangles (Order 2)	Tetrahedrons (Order 3)	Pentatopes (Order 4)
Point	1	0	0	0	0
Line segment	2	1	0	0	0
Triangle	3	3	1	0	0
Tetrahedron	4	6	4	1	0
Pentatope	_____	_____	_____	_____	1

5. Make a sketch of a pentatope containing the subelements listed.

In 1752, Leonhard Euler published his famous formula

$$V - E + F = 2$$

where V represents the number of vertices, E represents the number of edges, and F represents the number of faces of a polyhedron.

Consider the polyhedron known as a cube.

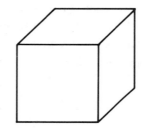

Count the vertices.

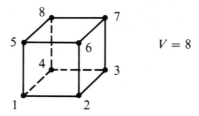

$V = 8$

Count the edges.

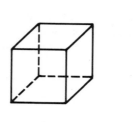
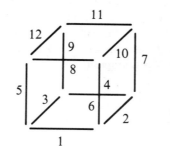

$E = 12$

Count the faces.

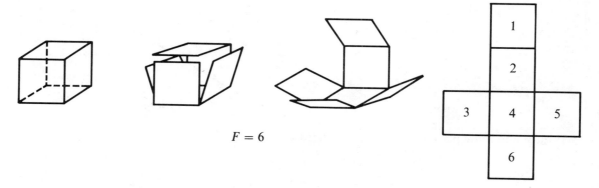

$$F = 6$$

Substituting these numbers into the expression $V - E + F$, we have

$$V - E + F = 8 - 12 + 6$$
$$= -4 + 6$$
$$= 2$$

As expected, the result is 2. The formula $V - E + F - 1 = 1$ is equivalent to the formula $V - E + F = 2$ and is useful for our purposes. If we restrict the discussion to simplexes and count the subelements used to make up the simplex, we have the following results:

Point	1 point = 1
Line segment	2 points − 1 edge = 1
Triangle	3 points − 3 edges + 1 triangle = 1
Tetrahedron	4 points − 6 edges + 4 faces − 1 tetrahedron = 1
	(V − E + F − 1 = 1)

---

6. Using the information for the pentatope in the previous table, check the formula similar to the pattern given.

1.9 DIVIDING SPACE

Just as a wall divides two rooms, we can think of dividing space with a plane. Two half-spaces exist, one on either side of the plane. Similarly, we can divide a plane with a line and a line with a point.

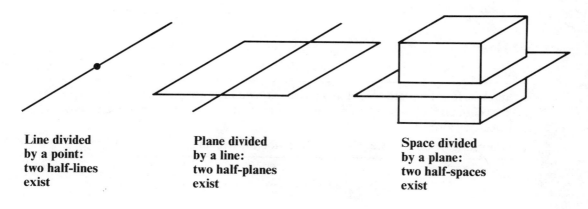

**Line divided
by a point:
two half-lines
exist**

**Plane divided
by a line:
two half-planes
exist**

**Space divided
by a plane:
two half-spaces
exist**

If two points are placed on a line, it is divided into three pieces.

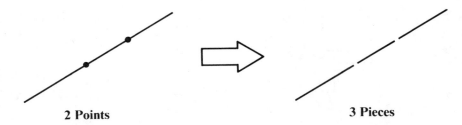

2 Points   **3 Pieces**

If three points are placed on a line, it is divided into four pieces, and so on.

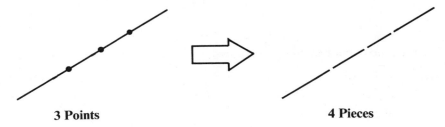

3 Points   **4 Pieces**

If two lines that are not parallel are placed in a plane, the plane is divided by the lines into four pieces.

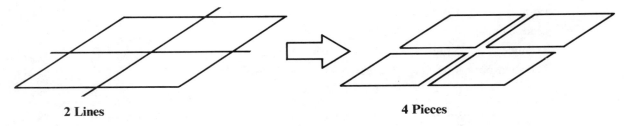

2 Lines   **4 Pieces**

Consider three lines that are placed in a plane. If no two are parallel and not all three pass through the same point, but intersect each of the other lines, the plane is divided into seven pieces.

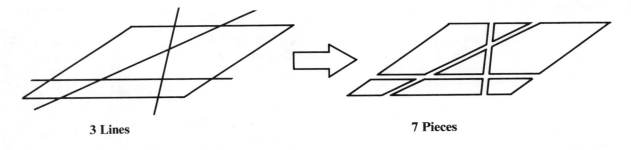

3 Lines   **7 Pieces**

1. Suppose four lines are placed in a plane. No two lines are parallel and no three lines contain the same point, but intersect each of the previous lines. How many pieces are formed?

2. Draw a figure and answer the same question for five lines.

Let's consider similar questions for space figures. These are more difficult to visualize as well as to draw. This will limit our exploration, but we hope to develop a pattern enabling us to predict how many pieces will be formed when space is divided by a given number of planes.

One plane divides space into two pieces.

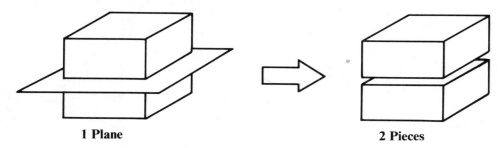

1 Plane   **2 Pieces**

Two planes that are not parallel divide space into four pieces.

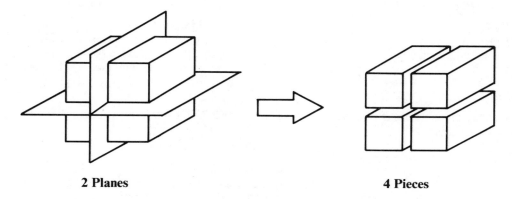

2 Planes   **4 Pieces**

Three planes, no two parallel and not all three containing the same line, divide space into eight pieces.

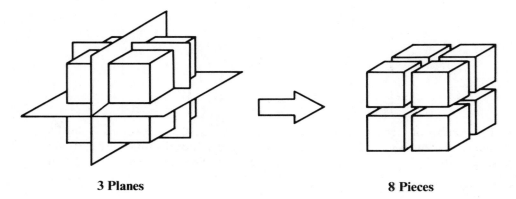

3 Planes   **8 Pieces**

It is not easy to see how many pieces are formed when space is divided by four planes, but an analogy with two-dimensional space may be helpful.

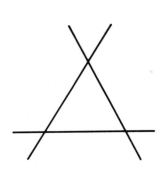

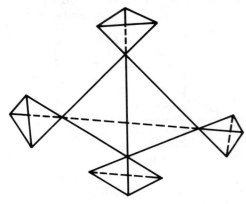

Plane cut by 3 lines

interior triangle = 1 piece
1 piece at each vertex = 3 pieces
1 piece at each edge = 3 pieces
total = 7 pieces

Space cut by 4 planes

interior tetrahedron = 1 piece
1 piece at each vertex = 4 pieces
1 piece at each edge = 6 pieces
1 piece at each face = 4 pieces
total = 15 pieces

How many pieces result if five planes are placed in space? To do this, let's collect the data we know into a table.

Number of dividing elements	Number of pieces formed when space is divided		
	Line by points	Plane by lines	Space by planes
0	1	1	1
1	2	2	2
2	3	4	4
3	4	7	8
4	5	11	15
5	6	16	?

The number of pieces of a line is an easy sequence: 1, 2, 3, 4, 5, 6, and so on. To understand the sequence for dividing the plane by lines, notice the following pattern that is suggested by the figure showing a plane divided by three lines and space divided by four planes.

$$1 = 1$$
$$2 = 1 + 1$$
$$4 = 1 + 2 + 1$$
$$7 = 1 + 3 + 3$$
$$11 = 1 + 4 + 6$$
$$16 = 1 + 5 + 10$$

These numbers are found in Pascal's Triangle as follows:

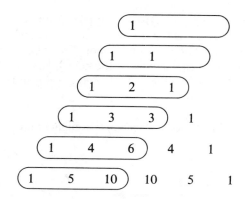

---

3. Predict the number of pieces formed if six lines are placed in a plane.

The subdivision of the line and of space can be associated with similar patterns.

Subdivision of a line	Subdivision of space
1 = 1	1 = 1
2 = 1 + 1	2 = 1 + 1
3 = 1 + 2	4 = 1 + 2 + 1
4 = 1 + 3	8 = 1 + 3 + 3 + 1
5 = 1 + 4	15 = 1 + 4 + 6 + 4
6 = 1 + 5	26 = 1 + 5 + 10 + 10

Subdivision of a line:

1 → (1)

2 → (1   1)

3 → (1   2)   1

4 → (1   3)   3   1

5 → (1   4)   6   4   1

6 → (1   5)   10   10   5   1

Subdivision of space:

1 → (1)

2 → (1   1)

4 → (1   2   1)

8 → (1   3   3   1)

15 → (1   4   6   4)   1

26 → (1   5   10   10)   5   1

Assuming the patterns are correct, we see that space is divided into 26 pieces by five planes.

---

4. Predict the number of pieces formed if six planes are placed in space.

Note: Assuming that four-dimensional space can be subdivided by three-dimensional space, predict a possible pattern that would determine the number of pieces resulting for a given number of three-dimensional space dividing elements?

1.10 GEOMETRIC DUPLICATION

In Section 1.3 we saw the process of cell division. Suppose a similar process is defined for geometric figures. This new process has the property that each newly duplicated figure is connected to the original by line segments called bonds. These bonds will all be in the same direction, that is, parallel and will become part of the new formation. For example, suppose we start with a triangle. Then, we duplicate the triangle and bond it to the original. See the following figure.

The process of geometric duplication

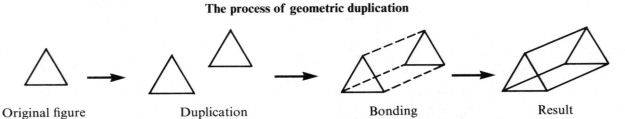

| Original figure | Duplication | Bonding | Result |

The resulting figure could be considered three-dimensional. It consists of 6 points, 9 line segments, 5 faces, and 1 solid or three-dimensional figure (a prism).

Let's continue this process of geometric duplication through several stages, starting with a single point.

	Original	Duplication	Bonding	Result
Start				•
Stage 1	•	• •	•‑ ‑ ‑•	•——•
Stage 2	•——•	•——• •——•	▢	▢

---

1. Continue the process for stage 3.

	Original	Duplication	Bonding	Result
Stage 3	▢			

Let's count the total number of geometric elements in the resulting figure of each stage.

2. Complete the table.

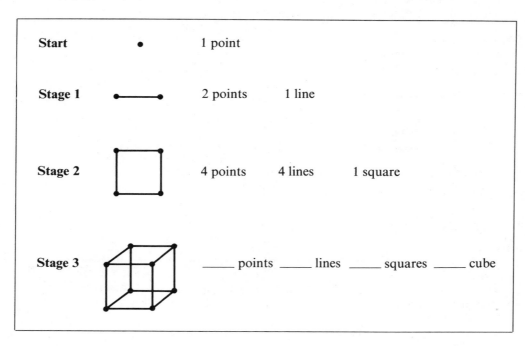

Start	•	1 point		
Stage 1	•——————•	2 points	1 line	
Stage 2	☐	4 points	4 lines	1 square
Stage 3	(cube)	___ points ___ lines ___ squares ___ cube		

The total elements at each stage are:

       Start   1 = 1
       Stage 1   3 = 2 + 1
       Stage 2   9 = 4 + 4 + 1
       Stage 3   27 = 8 + 12 + 6 + 1

To construct further stages, let's look for a pattern in the numbers of the previous table. Notice that the numbers 1, 3, 9, and 27 form a sequence of powers of three.

$$3^0 = 1$$
$$3^1 = 3$$
$$3^2 = 9$$
$$3^3 = 27$$

3. Find 3^4 and 3^5.

If we write the number 3 as the binomial $2 + 1$ and use the expansion (see Section 1.3), we find:

$$1 = (2 + 1)^0 = 1 \cdot 2^0 = 1$$
$$3 = (2 + 1)^1 = 1 \cdot 2^1 + 1 \cdot 2^0 = 2 + 1$$
$$9 = (2 + 1)^2 = 1 \cdot 2^2 + 2 \cdot 2^1 + 1 \cdot 2^0 = 4 + 4 + 1$$
$$27 = (2 + 1)^3 = 1 \cdot 2^3 + 3 \cdot 2^2 + 3 \cdot 2^1 + 1 \cdot 2^0 = 8 + 12 + 6 + 1$$

Thus, each term in these expansions represents the number of each type of geometric element present in the resulting figures of each stage. (Notice that the binomial coefficients of the powers of two in the expansions are the numbers from Pascal's Triangle.)

From this pattern we can predict the number of elements present if we duplicate the cube and bond it. The resulting figure is called a hypercube.

---

4. Write the expansion for $(2 + 1)^4$.

5. Draw the fourth stage of the geometric duplication that starts with a single point.

6. Complete the following table:

	Total elements		Points		Lines		Squares		Cubes		Hypercube
Start	1	=	1								
Stage 1	3	=	2	+	1						
Stage 2	9	=	4	+	4	+	1				
Stage 3	27	=	8	+	12	+	6	+	1		
Stage 4	81	=	___	+	___	+	___	+	___	+	___

The following diagrams are formed by geometric duplication. At each level of the diagram, count the number of points.

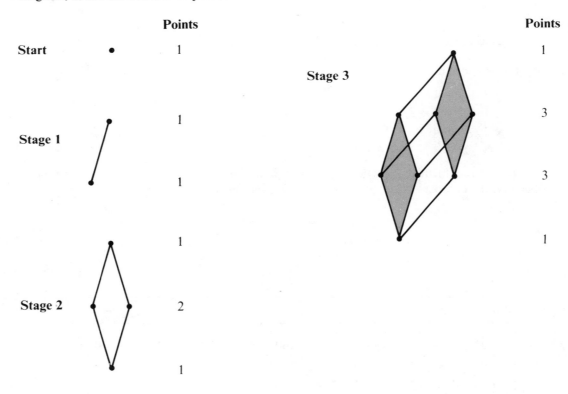

Points

Start   •   1

Stage 1   1   1

Stage 2   1   2   1

Stage 3

Points   1   3   3   1

Points

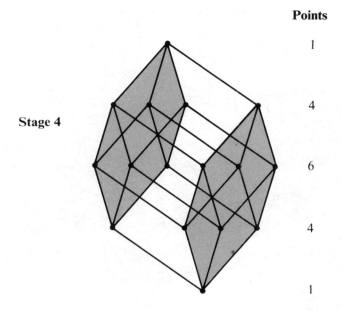

Stage 4

1

4

6

4

1

Notice that the numbers of points found at each level of these figures are the numbers from the rows of Pascal's Triangle.

---

7. Draw the figure for stage 5 (consisting of 32 points) by duplicating the figure given in stage 4 and then by bonding the two figures together. Label the number of points found at each level.

8. Connect the dots from 0 through 65.

9. Count the dots in each row of the figure for exercise 8 and compare the totals to the numbers in Pascal's Triangle.

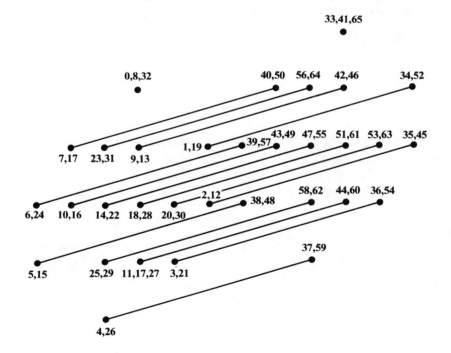

10. In the blanks at the right, enter the number of points at that level.

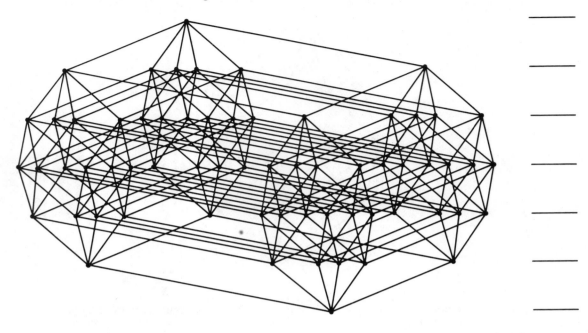

—————

—————

—————

—————

—————

—————

—————

11. To what row of Pascal's Triangle does the set of numbers found in exercise 10 correspond? What stage does this figure represent?

1.11 A NUMBER TREE, BINOMIAL EXPANSIONS, AND PASCAL'S RULE

Choose any three natural numbers, not necessarily different. For example, choose the numbers 4, 2, and 3. Let the first number, 4, be the "root" number and the numbers 2 and 3 be "left" and "right branch" numbers. The number tree formed is shown below.

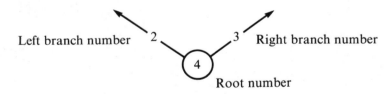

Left branch number   2   3   Right branch number

4

Root number

During the first season of growth, the root sends out two branches and forms a number "fruit" at the end of each branch. The number "fruits" are determined by multiplication of the root number with each branch number. Thus, the number fruit on the left branch is $4 \cdot 2 = 8$ and the number fruit on the right branch is $4 \cdot 3 = 12$.

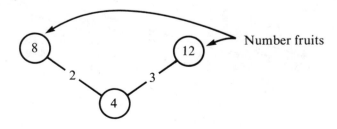

8   12   Number fruits

2   3

4

During the second season of growth, each "fruit" serves as a root and sends out a right and left branch. Furthermore, when two branches intersect, a number fruit is formed in a different way. Study the following picture of the second season number tree.

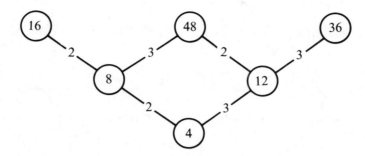

The number fruit 48 is formed by $8 \cdot 3 + 12 \cdot 2 = 24 + 24 = 48$.

---

1. Find the number "fruits" in the third and fourth seasons of growth as shown in the following diagram.

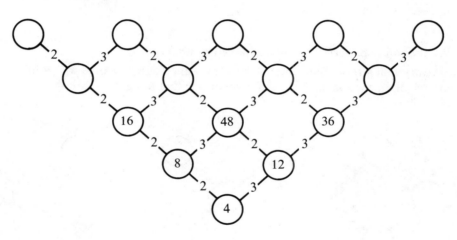

Now, let's draw another number tree by choosing the root number to be 1 and the right and left branch numbers to be 1.

2. Find the missing number fruits in the number tree below.

3. What number pattern is displayed in the tree above?
4. Starting with a root number equal to 1, left branch number equal to 1, and right branch number equal to 2, draw a number tree that has grown through 5 seasons.

Although various number trees can be drawn with different root and branch numbers, they are all related to Pascal's Triangle. The number fruits are formed according to Pascal's Rule, which is to add together the fruits of intersecting branches. An even more striking pattern can be seen if the number fruits are factored into a convenient form. For example, the number tree with root number 4 and branch numbers 2 and 3 can be represented as follows:

$$64 \quad 384 \quad 864 \quad 864 \quad 324$$
$$32 \quad 144 \quad 216 \quad 108$$
$$16 \quad 48 \quad 36$$
$$8 \quad 12$$
$$4$$

Each number fruit is factored as follows:

$$2^4(4) \qquad 2^3 \cdot 3^1(16) \qquad 2^2 \cdot 3^2(24) \qquad 2^1 \cdot 3^3(16) \qquad 3^4(4)$$
$$2^3(4) \qquad 2^2 \cdot 3^1(12) \qquad 2^1 \cdot 3^2(12) \qquad 3^3(4)$$
$$2^2(4) \qquad 2^1 \cdot 3^1(8) \qquad 3^2(4)$$
$$2^1(4) \qquad 3^1(4)$$
$$(4)$$

If each of the numbers in parentheses is divided by the root number 4 and the branch numbers are discarded, you get Pascal's Triangle. Also, there is an interesting pattern in the distribution of the branch numbers.

---

5. Predict the factored form of each of the number fruits found in the next season, the fifth season of growth.

6. Express the number fruits of the number tree formed with root number 1 and branch numbers 1 and 2 in a factored form that displays Pascal's Triangle.

If we use the same branch numbers but a different root number, the only changes in the factored forms are the numbers in parentheses.

$$2^4(\quad) \qquad 2^3 \cdot 3^1(\quad) \qquad 2^2 \cdot 3^2(\quad) \qquad 2^1 \cdot 3^3(\quad) \qquad 3^4(\quad)$$
$$2^3(\quad) \qquad 2^2 \cdot 3^1(\quad) \qquad 2^1 \cdot 3^2(\quad) \qquad 3^3(\quad)$$
$$2^2(\quad) \qquad 2^1 \cdot 3^1(\quad) \qquad 3^2(\quad)$$
$$2^1(\quad) \qquad 3^1(\quad)$$
$$(\quad)$$

Factored form of the number tree with branch numbers 2 and 3 and an undetermined root number

---

7. Starting with the root number 1, fill in the blanks of the previous number tree. What numbers are generated?

8. Erase the number found in exercise 7 and, starting with root number 2, fill in the blanks. What numbers are generated?

In general, starting with branch numbers x and y, the following pattern is formed:

$$x^4(\quad) \qquad x^3y^1(\quad) \qquad x^2y^2(\quad) \qquad x^1y^3(\quad) \qquad y^4(\quad)$$
$$x^3(\quad) \qquad x^2y^1(\quad) \qquad x^1y^2(\quad) \qquad y^3(\quad)$$
$$x^2(\quad) \qquad x^1y^1(\quad) \qquad y^2(\quad)$$
$$x^1(\quad) \qquad y^1(\quad)$$
$$(\quad)$$

---

9. Predict the factored form of the branch numbers x and y found in the next season, the fifth season of growth.

If we start with root number 1, the parentheses are filled with the numbers of Pascal's Triangle. In this arrangement, the number fruits are the **terms** in what is called a **binomial expansion**.

$$x^4(1) \qquad x^3y^1(4) \qquad x^2y^2(6) \qquad x^1y^3(4) \qquad y^4(1)$$
$$x^3(1) \qquad x^2y^1(3) \qquad x^1y^2(3) \qquad y^3(1)$$
$$x^2(1) \qquad x^1y^1(2) \qquad y^2(1)$$
$$x^1(1) \qquad y^1(1)$$
$$(1)$$

Factored form of the number tree with branch numbers x and y and root number 1

Rearranging the factors in the fourth season and adding the numbers together, we have the expansion of the binomial $(x + y)$ raised to the fourth power:

$$(x + y)^4 = 1x^4 + 4x^3y^1 + 6x^2y^2 + 4x^1y^3 + 1y^4$$

Similarly, the binomial expansion of $(x + y)$ raised to the third power is given by:

$$(x + y)^3 = 1x^3 + 3x^2y + 3xy^2 + 1y^3$$

In this expansion, the numbers in Pascal's Triangle are called **binomial coefficients**.

---

10. Find the binomial expansion of $(x + y)^2$.

11. What are the binomial coefficients in the expansion of $(x + y)^5$?

12. Find the binomial expansion of $(x + y)^5$.

13. Let $x = 2$ and $y = 3$ and verify that

$$(x + y)^4 = 1x^4 + 4x^3y + 6x^2y^2 + 4xy^3 + 1y^4$$

by showing that the left member of the equation has the same numerical value as the right member.

How many great-grandparents do you have? Let F represent your father and let M represent your mother. Let FF represent your father's father, FM represent your father's mother, MF represent your mother's father, and MM represent your mother's mother. This information is shown in the following family tree.

The first generation of your ancestors consists of your mother and father. The second generation consists of your grandparents, FF, FM, MF, and MM. The third generation of ancestors consists of your great-grandparents. These are shown in the following family tree.

---

14. How many great-grandparents do you have?

15. Construct a family tree going back to your great-great-grandparents.

16. Describe how Pascal's Triangle fits into this pattern.

To find the entries in successive rows of Pascal's Triangle, Pascal's Rule tells us to add adjacent elements in one row to generate an element in the next row. In the number tree, we used this rule when we added the number fruits on intersecting branches. We conclude this section with another rule for determining numbers that occur in Pascal's Triangle. For example, the 20th row of Pascal's Triangle starts with 1 and 20.

     1   20 ...?

If we use Pascal's Rule, to determine the next element would require that we know the entries in the 19th row. The following rule applies to adjacent numbers; that is, if we know any number in a given row, we can find the next number in that same row. To do this we need to refer to the row position and column position of the known number.

0th row	1	
1st row	1 1	
2nd row	1 2 1	
3rd row	1 3 3 1	
4th row	1 4 6 4 1	

0th column
1st column
2nd column
3rd column
4th column

1
1 1
1 2 1
1 3 3 1
1 4 6 4 1

The number 20 is thus in the 20th row and the 1st column. The formula for the next number is

$$N = P \cdot \frac{R - C + 1}{C}$$

where N = the next number to be found in a row, P = the previous number in the row (20 in our example), R = the number of the row (also 20 in our example), and C = the column position of N in the row (2 in our example). Thus,

$$N = 20 \cdot \frac{20 - 2 + 1}{2}$$

$$= 190$$

---

17. Find the number in the 20th row and 3rd column of Pascal's Triangle.

18. Using the formula, find all the numbers in the 10th row of Pascal's Triangle.

1
1 1   2nd column
1 2 1   3rd column
1 3 3 1
4th row ⟶ 1 4 ⑥ 4 1
5th row ⟶ 1 5 10 ⑩ 5 1

The number 6 is in the 4th row and 2nd column of Pascal's Triangle, and the number 10 is in the 5th row and 3rd column. Notice that $5 \cdot 6 = 3 \cdot 10$; that is, if 10 is in the 5th row and 3rd column, then 5 times the element in the 4th row and 2nd column equals 3 times 10. In general, pick any element in Pascal's Triangle (except in the 0th column) and say it is in the Rth row and the Cth column. Then R times the element in the $(R - 1)$ row and $(C - 1)$ column is equal to C times the given element.

---

19. Find the element in the 8th row and the 4th column. Show that 8 times the element in the 7th row and the 3rd column is equal to 4 times the given element.

20. Pick any element and show this property.

Let the element in the Rth row and Cth column be represented by the symbol $\binom{R}{C}$. Thus, $\binom{5}{3} = 10$ and $\binom{4}{2} = 6$. The property described previously can be represented as

$$R \cdot \binom{R - 1}{C - 1} = C \cdot \binom{R}{C}$$

21. Find the value of $\binom{6}{3}$.

22. Find the value of $\binom{5}{2}$.

23. Show that $6 \cdot \binom{5}{2} = 3 \cdot \binom{6}{3}$.

Using this notation, we can express Pascal's Rule as

$$\binom{R}{C-1} + \binom{R}{C} = \binom{R+1}{C}$$

For example, if $R = 4$ and $C = 3$, then

$$\binom{4}{2} + \binom{4}{3} = \binom{5}{3}$$

or, equivalently,

$$6 + 4 = 10$$

24. Verify Pascal's Rule for $R = 8$ and $C = 4$.

Because of the symmetry in Pascal's Triangle (the left half looks like the right half), we have the following property:

$$\binom{R}{C} = \binom{R}{R-C}$$

25. Show that

$$\binom{6}{2} = \binom{6}{6-2}$$

26. Choose several values for m and n and verify that

$$\binom{m+n}{m} = \binom{m+n}{n}$$

THE FOLLOWING CHARTS ARE TO BE USED WITH THE INDICATED EXERCISES.

Exercise 5, p. 13

<table>
<tr><th colspan="5">Four-Digit Binary Numbers</th></tr>
<tr><th></th><th>One occurrence of the digit 1</th><th>Two occurrences of the digit 1</th><th>Three occurrences of the digit 1</th><th>Four occurrences of the digit 1</th></tr>
<tr><td>Listing</td><td>1000</td><td>1001
1010
1100</td><td>1011
1101
1110</td><td>1111</td></tr>
<tr><td>Totals</td><td>1</td><td>3</td><td>3</td><td>1</td></tr>
</table>

Exercise 7, p. 13

<table>
<tr><th colspan="6">Five-Digit Binary Numbers</th></tr>
<tr><th></th><th>One occurrence of the digit 1</th><th>Two occurrences of the digit 1</th><th>Three occurrences of the digit 1</th><th>Four occurrences of the digit 1</th><th>Five occurrences of the digit 1</th></tr>
<tr><td>Listing</td><td></td><td></td><td></td><td></td><td></td></tr>
<tr><td>Totals</td><td></td><td></td><td></td><td></td><td></td></tr>
</table>

Exercise 8, p. 13

<table>
<tr><th colspan="6">Six-Digit Binary Numbers</th></tr>
<tr><th>One occurrence of the digit 1</th><th>Two occurrences of the digit 1</th><th>Three occurrences of the digit 1</th><th>Four occurrences of the digit 1</th><th>Five occurrences of the digit 1</th><th>Six occurrences of the digit 1</th></tr>
<tr><td></td><td></td><td></td><td></td><td></td><td></td></tr>
</table>

Exercise 9, p. 15

<table>
<tr><th colspan="6">Four-Light Panel</th></tr>
<tr><th></th><th>No lit bulbs</th><th>One lit bulb</th><th>Two lit bulbs</th><th>Three lit bulbs</th><th>Four lit bulbs</th></tr>
<tr><td>Listing of binary numbers</td><td></td><td></td><td></td><td></td><td></td></tr>
<tr><td>Totals</td><td></td><td></td><td></td><td></td><td></td></tr>
</table>

Exercise 12, p. 15

Number of bulbs	Number of ways when no bulbs are lit	Number of ways when one bulb is lit	Number of ways when two bulbs are lit	Number of ways when three bulbs are lit	Number of ways when four bulbs are lit	Number of ways when five bulbs are lit	Total number of arrange-ments
0	1						$2^0 = 1$
1	1	1					$2^1 = 2$
2	1	2	1				$2^2 = 4$
3	1	3	3	1			$2^3 = 8$
4							
5							

Exercise 16, p. 15

Two Bits			
No dash	One dash	Two dashes	
. .	. — — .	— —	
1	2	1	Sum =

Three Bits				
	No dash	One dash	Two dashes	Three dashes
Listing				
Totals				Sum =

Four Bits				
	No dash	One dash	Two dashes	Three dashes	Four dashes
Listing				
Totals				Sum =

Exercise 3, p. 18
Use this page to shade your patterns.

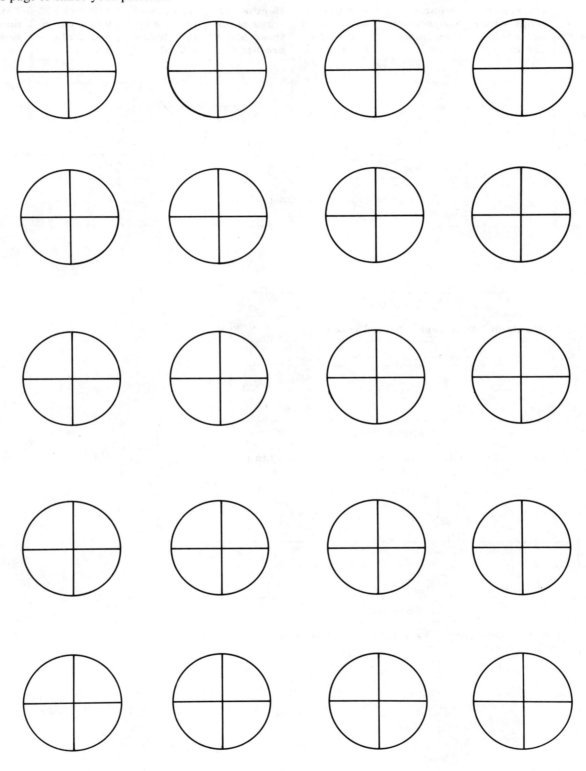

Exercise 3, p. 18, continued.

Number of ways when no sector is shaded	Number of ways when one sector is shaded	Number of ways when two sectors are shaded	Number of ways when three sectors are shaded	Number of ways when four sectors are shaded

Total number of ways to shade the sectors = _____.

Exercise 4, p. 18

Number of sectors	Patterns	No sector shaded	One sector shaded	Two sectors shaded	Three sectors shaded	Four sectors shaded	Total
1		1	1				2
2		1	2	1			4
3		1	3	3	1		8
4							

2 Number Patterns Within Pascal's Triangle

2.1 SUMS OF ROW ELEMENTS

In Chapter 1 we saw that the sum of a row of elements in Pascal's Triangle is equal to a power of 2.

$$1 = 1 = 2^0$$
$$1 + 1 = 2 = 2^1$$
$$1 + 2 + 1 = 4 = 2^2$$
$$1 + 3 + 3 + 1 = 8 = 2^3$$
$$1 + 4 + 6 + 4 + 1 = 16 = 2^4$$
$$1 + 5 + 10 + 10 + 5 + 1 = 32 = 2^5$$

The sum of the elements in the nth row is equal to 2^n. This can be shown by using the binomial expansion of the binomial $(1 + 1)$.

$$2^0 = (1 + 1)^0 = 1$$
$$2^1 = (1 + 1)^1 = 1 + 1$$
$$2^2 = (1 + 1)^2 = 1 + 2 + 1$$
$$2^3 = (1 + 1)^3 = 1 + 3 + 3 + 1$$
$$2^4 = (1 + 1)^4 = 1 + 4 + 6 + 4 + 1$$
$$2^5 = (1 + 1)^5 = 1 + 5 + 10 + 10 + 5 + 1$$

Consider the number trees of the previous chapter. For example, consider the tree with root number 1 and branch numbers 1 and 2:

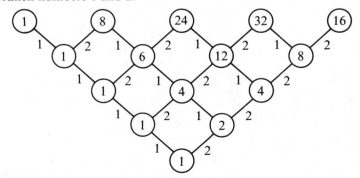

Now flip this number tree over to form the following number triangle.

$$
\begin{array}{ccccccccc}
& & & & 1 & & & & \\
& & & 1 & & 2 & & & \\
& & 1 & & 4 & & 4 & & \\
& 1 & & 6 & & 12 & & 8 & \\
1 & & 8 & & 24 & & 32 & & 16
\end{array}
$$

---

1. Add the elements in each row of this triangle. What powers are generated?
2. Extend the triangle two more rows and add the elements in each of these rows. What do you notice?

Suppose we write each of the number fruit in a factored form.

$$
\begin{array}{ccccccccc}
& & & & 1(1) & & & & \\
& & & 1(1) & & 1(2) & & & \\
& & 1(1) & & 2(2^1) & & 1(2^2) & & \\
& 1(1) & & 3(2^1) & & 3(2^2) & & 1(2^3) & \\
1(1) & & 4(2^1) & & 6(2^2) & & 4(2^3) & & 1(2^4)
\end{array}
$$

---

3. Extend the factored form of the number triangle two more rows.

In the factored form we see the binomial coefficients, that is, the numbers of Pascal's Triangle. The binomial is $(1 + 2)$. Thus,

$(1 + 2)^0 = 1$

$(1 + 2)^1 = 1(1) + 1(2)$

$(1 + 2)^2 = 1(1) + 2(2^1) + 1(2^2)$

$(1 + 2)^3 = 1(1) + 3(2^1) + 3(2^2) + 1(2^3)$

$(1 + 2)^4 = 1(1) + 4(2^1) + 6(2^2) + 4(2^3) + 1(2^4)$

The value of the binomial is $1 + 2$, or 3, and so we have a row sum equal to a power of 3.

---

4. Construct a number triangle with root number 1 and branch numbers 2 and 3 with at least 5 rows. Add the row elements. Express the sum of each row as a binomial expansion.

Suppose instead of adding the elements of each row in Pascal's Triangle we alternately add and subtract the elements.

---

5. Complete the following table.

$$
\begin{array}{l}
1 \; = \; 1 \\
1 \; - \; 1 \; = \; 0 \\
1 \; - \; 2 \; + \; 1 \; = \; 0 \\
1 \; - \; 3 \; + \; 3 \; - \; 1 \; = \; \underline{\quad} \\
1 \; - \; 4 \; + \; 6 \; - \; 4 \; + \; 1 \; = \; \underline{\quad} \\
1 \; - \; 5 \; + \; 10 \; - \; 10 \; + \; 5 \; - \; 1 \; = \; \underline{\quad} \\
1 \; - \; 6 \; + \; 15 \; - \; 20 \; + \; 15 \; - \; 6 \; + \; 1 \; = \; \underline{\quad} \\
1 \; - \; 7 \; + \; 21 \; - \; 35 \; + \; 35 \; - \; 21 \; + \; 7 \; - \; 1 \; = \; \underline{\quad}
\end{array}
$$

Except for the first row, the sum of each of the preceding rows represents the binomial expansion of $(1 - 1)^n = 0$.

---

6. Complete the following table.

$$1 = 1$$
$$1 + 1 = 2$$
$$1 + 2 - 1 = \underline{\hspace{1cm}}$$
$$1 + 3 - 3 + 1 = \underline{\hspace{1cm}}$$
$$1 + 4 - 6 + 4 - 1 = \underline{\hspace{1cm}}$$
$$1 + 5 - 10 + 10 - 5 + 1 = \underline{\hspace{1cm}}$$
$$1 + 6 - 15 + 20 - 15 + 6 - 1 = \underline{\hspace{1cm}}$$
$$1 + 7 - 21 + 35 - 35 + 21 - 7 + 1 = \underline{\hspace{1cm}}$$

In exercises 7–9, perform the indicated computations, not including the elements enclosed in the rectangle. In each case describe the sequence of resulting numbers.

7.

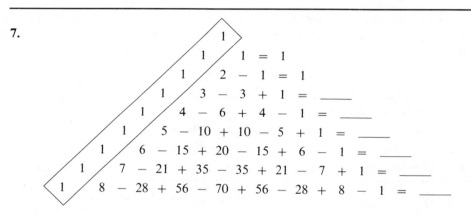

$$1 = 1$$
$$2 - 1 = 1$$
$$3 - 3 + 1 = \underline{\hspace{1cm}}$$
$$4 - 6 + 4 - 1 = \underline{\hspace{1cm}}$$
$$5 - 10 + 10 - 5 + 1 = \underline{\hspace{1cm}}$$
$$6 - 15 + 20 - 15 + 6 - 1 = \underline{\hspace{1cm}}$$
$$7 - 21 + 35 - 35 + 21 - 7 + 1 = \underline{\hspace{1cm}}$$
$$8 - 28 + 56 - 70 + 56 - 28 + 8 - 1 = \underline{\hspace{1cm}}$$

8.

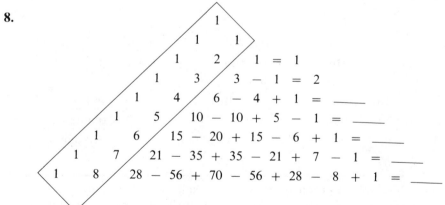

$$1 = 1$$
$$3 - 1 = 2$$
$$6 - 4 + 1 = \underline{\hspace{1cm}}$$
$$10 - 10 + 5 - 1 = \underline{\hspace{1cm}}$$
$$15 - 20 + 15 - 6 + 1 = \underline{\hspace{1cm}}$$
$$21 - 35 + 35 - 21 + 7 - 1 = \underline{\hspace{1cm}}$$
$$28 - 56 + 70 - 56 + 28 - 8 + 1 = \underline{\hspace{1cm}}$$

9.

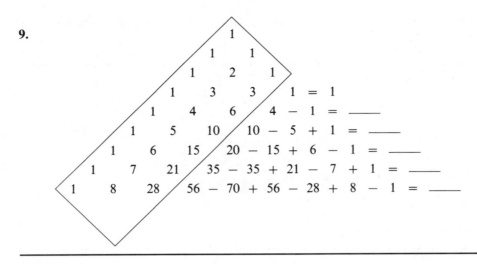

$$1 = 1$$
$$4 - 1 = \underline{\hphantom{xxx}}$$
$$10 - 5 + 1 = \underline{\hphantom{xxx}}$$
$$20 - 15 + 6 - 1 = \underline{\hphantom{xxx}}$$
$$35 - 35 + 21 - 7 + 1 = \underline{\hphantom{xxx}}$$
$$56 - 70 + 56 - 28 + 8 - 1 = \underline{\hphantom{xxx}}$$

The 11th row of Pascal's Triangle is

| 1 | 11 | 55 | 165 | 330 | 462 | 462 | 330 | 165 | 55 | 11 | 1 |

and these numbers are also the binomial coefficients for the expansion of $(x + y)^{11}$. Let the coefficient in the 0th column be C_0, the coefficient in the 1st column be C_1, the 2nd column be C_2, and so on. Then

$$C_0 + C_2 + C_4 + C_6 + C_8 + C_{10} = C_1 + C_3 + C_5 + C_7 + C_9 + C_{11}$$

10. (a) Verify the preceding formula.

(b) Verify a similar formula for the 1st, 3rd, 5th, 7th, and 9th rows.

11. (a) Verify that $C_1 + C_3 + C_5 + C_7 + C_9 + C_{11} = 2^{10}$.

(b) Verify that a similar formula holds for the 1st, 3rd, 5th, 7th, and 9th rows.

The following is Pascal's Triangle with each element being multiplied by its column number.

				1(0)			Column 0
			1(0)	1(1)			Column 1
		1(0)	2(1)	1(2)			Column 2
	1(0)	3(1)	3(2)	1(3)			Column 3
1(0)	4(1)	6(2)	4(3)	1(4)			Column 4
1(0)	5(1)	10(2)	10(3)	5(4)	1(5)		Column 5
1(0)	6(1)	15(2)	20(3)	15(4)	6(5)	1(6)	Column 6

12. Multiply each of the products and add the results in each preceding row. Verify that the sum of the 6th row is $6 \cdot 2^5$, the sum of the 5th row is $5 \cdot 2^4$, the sum of the 4th row is $4 \cdot 2^3$, the sum of the 3rd row is $3 \cdot 2^2$, and the sum of the 2nd row is $2 \cdot 2^1$.

13. Predict a formula for the sum in the *n*th row.

14. Perform the following computations.

$$1(0) = 0$$
$$1(0) + 1(1) = 1$$
$$1(0) + 2(1) - 1(2) = \underline{\quad}$$
$$1(0) + 3(1) - 3(2) + 1(3) = \underline{\quad}$$
$$1(0) + 4(1) - 6(2) + 4(3) - 1(4) = \underline{\quad}$$
$$1(0) + 5(1) - 10(2) + 10(3) - 5(4) + 1(5) = \underline{\quad}$$
$$1(0) + 6(1) - 15(2) + 20(3) - 15(4) + 6(5) - 1(6) = \underline{\quad}$$

15. The 7th row of Pascal's Triangle is

$$1 \quad 7 \quad 21 \quad 35 \quad 35 \quad 21 \quad 7 \quad 1$$

If we call these numbers $C_0, C_1, C_2, C_3, C_4, C_5, C_6,$ and C_7, then verify that

$$C_1 + 2C_2 + 3C_3 + 4C_4 + 5C_5 + 6C_6 + 7C_7 = 7 \cdot 2^6$$

and that

$$C_1 - 2C_2 + 3C_3 - 4C_4 + 5C_5 - 6C_6 + 7C_7 = 0$$

16. Suppose $C_0, C_1, C_2, C_3,$ and C_4 are the binomial coefficients in the 4th row of Pascal's Triangle. Verify that

$$C_0 + \frac{1}{2}C_1 + \frac{1}{3}C_2 + \frac{1}{4}C_3 + \frac{1}{5}C_4 = \frac{1}{5}(2^5 - 1)$$

17. Choose your own value for *n* and verify that

$$C_0 + \frac{1}{2}C_1 + \frac{1}{3}C_2 + \frac{1}{4}C_3 + \cdots + \frac{1}{n+1}C_n = \frac{1}{n+1}(2^{n+1} - 1)$$

Add the circled numbers in each row of Pascal's Triangle. What sequence of numbers is generated?

18.

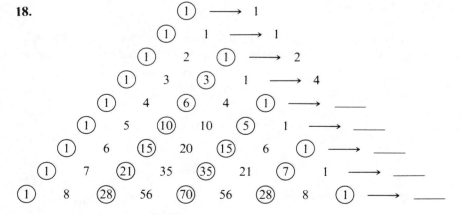

19.

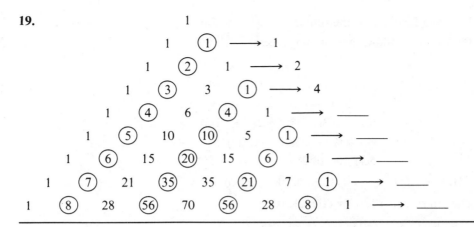

Choose any row of Pascal's Triangle; for example, the 6th row. Separate the row into 2 rows as shown.

$$
1 \quad 6 \quad 15 \quad 20 \quad 15 \quad 6 \quad 1 \quad \longrightarrow \quad
\begin{array}{cccc}
6 & 20 & 6 & \\
1 & 15 & 15 & 1
\end{array}
$$

Form a fraction with the numerator being the sum of the numbers in the top row and the denominator being the sum of the numbers in the bottom row.

$$
\frac{6 + 20 + 6}{1 + 15 + 15 + 1}
$$

The value of this fraction is 1.

20. Follow the process described previously for each of the first 8 rows of Pascal's Triangle. What are the values of these fractions?

2.2 SUMS OF COLUMN ELEMENTS

In this section we continue our investigation of number patterns within Pascal's Triangle. Consider the sums of successive column elements. For example, the 2nd column of elements is:

$$
\begin{array}{c}
1 \\
3 \\
6 \\
10 \\
15 \\
21
\end{array}
$$

Let's form a sequence of sums in the following way.

$$
\begin{aligned}
1 &= 1 \\
1 + 3 &= 4 \\
1 + 3 + 6 &= 10 \\
1 + 3 + 6 + 10 &= 20 \\
1 + 3 + 6 + 10 + 15 &= 35 \\
1 + 3 + 6 + 10 + 15 + 21 &= 56
\end{aligned}
$$

Observe the pattern of sums 1, 4, 10, 20, 35, and 56. These numbers are in the 3rd column of Pascal's Triangle. Note that the sum of the first 2 elements of column 2 equals the 2nd element of column 3. The sum of the first 3 elements of column 2 equals the 3rd element of column 3.

---

1. What is the sum of the first 4 elements of column 2?

We can diagram the sum of the first 4 elements of column 2 of Pascal's Triangle as follows:

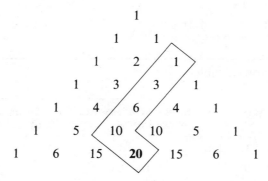

Similarly, the sum of the first 5 elements of column 2 can be diagrammed as follows:

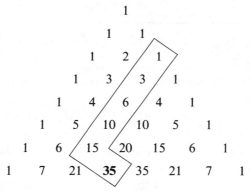

The shape of the figure in the diagrams resembles a "hockey stick." Let's call this the hockey stick property for adding column elements. Because of the symmetry in Pascal's Triangle, the hockey stick can also be formed in the other direction.

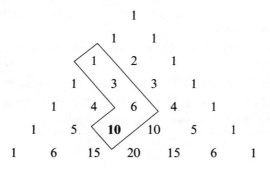

Does the hockey stick property work for other columns in Pascal's Triangle? Study the following table.

Sums of elements of column 0	Sums of elements of column 1	Sums of elements of column 2
$1 = 1$	$1 = 1$	$1 = 1$
$1 + 1 = 2$	$1 + 2 = 3$	$1 + 3 = 4$
$1 + 1 + 1 = 3$	$1 + 2 + 3 = 6$	$1 + 3 + 6 = 10$
$1 + 1 + 1 + 1 = 4$	$1 + 2 + 3 + 4 = 10$	$1 + 3 + 6 + 10 = 20$

2. Complete the following tables.

Sums of elements of column 3	Sums of elements of column 4	Sums of elements of column 5
$1 = 1$	$1 = \underline{\hspace{1cm}}$	$1 = \underline{\hspace{1cm}}$
$1 + 4 = 5$	$1 + 5 = \underline{\hspace{1cm}}$	$1 + 6 = \underline{\hspace{1cm}}$
$1 + 4 + 10 = \underline{\hspace{1cm}}$	$1 + 5 + 15 = \underline{\hspace{1cm}}$	$1 + 6 + 21 = \underline{\hspace{1cm}}$
$1 + 4 + 10 + 20 = \underline{\hspace{1cm}}$	$1 + 5 + 15 + 35 = \underline{\hspace{1cm}}$	$1 + 6 + 21 + 56 = \underline{\hspace{1cm}}$

By examining the previous sums, we see that the hockey stick pattern holds for those columns.

3. The sum of the first 4 elements of the 3rd column equals the _____ element of the _____ column.

4. The sum of the first 6 elements of the 8th column equals the _____ element of the _____ column.

5. The sum of the first _____ elements of the 12th column equals the 9th element of the _____ column.

6. The sum of the first r elements of the 6th column equals the _____ element of the _____ column.

7. The sum of the first 20 elements of the nth column equals the _____ element of the _____ column.

8. The sum of the first _____ elements of the _____ column equals the 17th element of the $(n + 1)$th column.

9. The sum of the first m elements of the nth column equals the _____ element of the _____ column.

10. Find the actual sum of the first 10 elements of the 1st column.

11. Find the actual sum of the first 8 elements of the 2nd column.

12. Find the sum of the first 8 elements of the 3rd column.

We will now focus on column 1. The numbers in this column are the natural numbers 1, 2, 3, 4, 5,.... Recall each of the sums is a number from the 2nd column of Pascal's Triangle.

$$\begin{array}{cccccc}
\underline{+\,1} & 1 & 1 & 1 & 1 & 1 \\
1 & \underline{+\,2} & 2 & 2 & 2 & 2 \\
 & 3 & \underline{+\,3} & 3 & 3 & 3 \\
 & & 6 & \underline{+\,\ 4} & 4 & 4 \\
 & & & 10 & \underline{+\,\ 5} & 5 \\
 & & & & 15 & \underline{+\,\ 6} \\
 & & & & & 21
\end{array}$$

---

13. Find the sum $1 + 2 + 3 + 4 + 5 + 6 + 7 + 8$ by using the hockey stick property and Pascal's Triangle.

To obtain the sum $1 + 2 + 3 + \cdots + 10$, we need to know the 10th number in the 2nd column. By observation this number is 55, but we can develop a formula for this number using the property of adjacent numbers in Pascal's Triangle. For example, the next number after 10 in column 1 is 11. The number for the sum of the first 10 numbers in column 1 is adjacent to 11. The number 11 is in the 11th row and 1st column. Thus, if N is the adjacent number, then

$$\begin{aligned}
N &= P \cdot \frac{R - C + 1}{C} \\
&= 11 \cdot \frac{11 - 2 + 1}{2} \\
&= 11 \cdot \frac{10}{2} \\
&= 55
\end{aligned}$$

Notice that $R - C + 1$ is equal to the last number in the sequence to be added and P is equal to the last number plus 1. Using this information we write

$$\begin{aligned}
1 + 2 + 3 + \cdots + n &= (n + 1) \cdot \frac{n}{2} \\
&= \frac{n(n + 1)}{2}
\end{aligned}$$

Thus, to find the sum $1 + 2 + 3 + \cdots + 50$, let $n = 50$; then

$$\begin{aligned}
\frac{n(n + 1)}{2} &= \frac{50(51)}{2} \\
&= \frac{2550}{2} \\
&= 1275
\end{aligned}$$

Therefore, $1 + 2 + 3 + \cdots + 50 = 1275$.

14. Use the previous formula to find the sum of the numbers $1 + 2 + 3 + \cdots + 100$.

15. Devise a plan to find the sum of the numbers $51 + 52 + 53 + \cdots + 100$.

16. Complete these computations.

$$1 \cdot 1 = \underline{1} \qquad 1 \cdot 2 = 2 \qquad 1 \cdot 3 = 3 \qquad 1 \cdot 4 = \underline{}$$
$$ 1 \qquad 2 \cdot 1 = \underline{2} \qquad 2 \cdot 2 = 4 \qquad 2 \cdot 3 = \underline{}$$
$$ 4 \qquad 3 \cdot 1 = \underline{3} \qquad 3 \cdot 2 = \underline{}$$
$$ 10 \qquad 4 \cdot 1 = \underline{}$$
$$\underline{}$$
$$\underline{}$$

$$1 \cdot 5 = \underline{}$$
$$2 \cdot 4 = \underline{}$$
$$3 \cdot 3 = \underline{}$$
$$4 \cdot 2 = \underline{}$$
$$5 \cdot 1 = \underline{}$$
$$\underline{}$$
$$\underline{}$$

The sums are 1, 4, 10, _____, _____ and these numbers are found in the _____ column of Pascal's Triangle.

17. Complete these computations.

$$\frac{1 \cdot 2}{2} = 1 \qquad \frac{2 \cdot 3}{2} = 3 \qquad \frac{3 \cdot 4}{2} = 6 \qquad \frac{4 \cdot 5}{2} = \underline{}$$

$$\frac{5 \cdot 6}{2} = \underline{} \qquad \frac{6 \cdot 7}{2} = \underline{}$$

The results are 1, 3, 6, _____, _____, and _____. These numbers are found in the _____ column of Pascal's Triangle.

18. Complete these computations.

$$\frac{1 \cdot 2 \cdot 3}{6} = 1$$

$$\frac{2 \cdot 3 \cdot 4}{6} = 4$$

$$\frac{3 \cdot 4 \cdot 5}{6} = 10$$

$$\frac{4 \cdot 5 \cdot 6}{6} = \underline{}$$

$$\frac{5 \cdot 6 \cdot 7}{6} = \underline{}$$

$$\frac{6 \cdot 7 \cdot 8}{6} = \underline{}$$

The results are 1, 4, 10, _____, _____, _____. These numbers are found in the _____ column of Pascal's Triangle.

19. Complete these computations.

$$\frac{1 \cdot 2 \cdot 3 \cdot 4}{24} = 1$$

$$\frac{2 \cdot 3 \cdot 4 \cdot 5}{24} = 5$$

$$\frac{3 \cdot 4 \cdot 5 \cdot 6}{24} = 15$$

$$\frac{4 \cdot 5 \cdot 6 \cdot 7}{24} = \underline{}$$

$$\frac{5 \cdot 6 \cdot 7 \cdot 8}{24} = \underline{}$$

$$\frac{6 \cdot 7 \cdot 8 \cdot 9}{24} = \underline{}$$

The results are 1, 5, 15, _____, _____, _____. These numbers are found in the _____ column of Pascal's Triangle.

Find the pattern for the numbers in each of the "T-sticks" shown.

20.

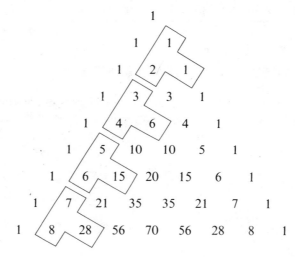

21.

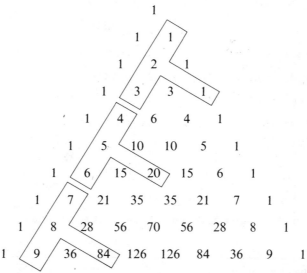

22.

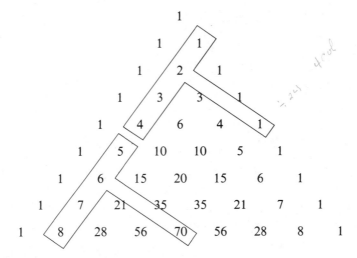

23. Do these "T-sticks" work for other numbers?

2.3 SUMS OF THE SQUARES OF THE ROW ELEMENTS

Pascal's Rule states that the sum of two consecutive elements in one row of the Triangle is equal to the element below them in the next row. An extension of this rule is shown in the triangle.

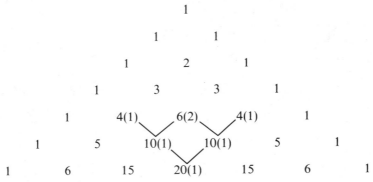

Not only does this show that $20 = 10 + 10$, but also that

$$20 = 4(1) + 6(2) + 4(1)$$

Furthermore, the numbers in parentheses form an inverted Pascal's Triangle. If we include one more row in this inverted triangle and multiply each element by the appropriate element in the first triangle, we obtain

$$20 = 1(1) + 3(3) + 3(3) + 1(1)$$
$$= 1^2 + 3^2 + 3^2 + 1^2$$

Notice that the sum of the squares of the 3rd row of Pascal's Triangle is equal to 20, the middle element of the 6th row.

1. Square the elements of the 2nd row and add the results. The sum is the middle element of the _____ row.

2. Square the elements of the 4th row and add the results. The sum is the middle element of the _____ row.

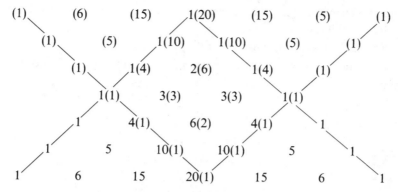

Two Pascal's Triangles—one inverted

Now let's focus our attention on the overlapping part of the two Pascal's Triangles.

```
                1(20)
            1(10)    1(10)
         1(4)    2(6)    1(4)
    1(1)    3(3)    3(3)    1(1)
        4(1)    6(2)    4(1)
           10(1)    10(1)
                20(1)
```

3. Multiply each pair of numbers as indicated. Add the results in each row. What do you find?

4. Add the results in each column (diagonal column). What do you find? Is this a number in Pascal's Triangle?

5. In the following diagram, fill in the numbers for two Pascal's Triangles with one triangle inverted.

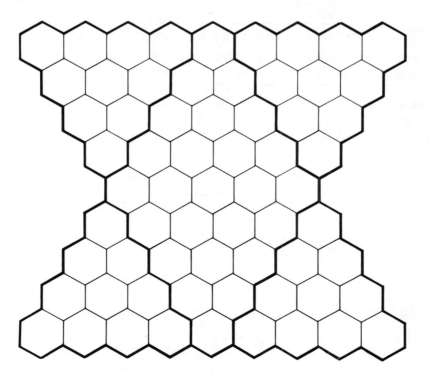

6. Where two elements share the same cell, multiply them together. Add the results in each row. What do you find?

7. Add the results in each column. What do you find?

8. Find the square of each of the elements in Pascal's Triangle and add the results in each row.

$$1^2 = 1$$
$$1^2 + 1^2 = 2$$
$$1^2 + 2^2 + 1^2 = \underline{\quad}$$
$$1^2 + 3^2 + 3^2 + 1^2 = \underline{\quad}$$
$$1^2 + 4^2 + 6^2 + 4^2 + 1^2 = \underline{\quad}$$
$$1^2 + 5^2 + 10^2 + 10^2 + 5^2 + 1^2 = \underline{\quad}$$
$$1^2 + 6^2 + 15^2 + 20^2 + 15^2 + 6^2 + 1^2 = \underline{\quad}$$

The numbers resulting from the previous computations can be found in Pascal's Triangle on a vertical line through the middle of the triangle.

```
                    (1)
                1       1
            1      (2)      1
          1     3       3     1
        1    4     (6)     4     1
      1    5    10     10    5     1
     1   6    15   (20)    15   6    1
    1   7   21   35    35   21   7   1
   1   8   28   56  (70)   56   28   8   1
  1   9   36   84  126  126   84  36   9   1
 1  10  45  120 210 (252) 210 120  45  10   1
```

9. Find the middle number of the 12th row of Pascal's Triangle.

10. The sum of the squares of the elements of the 6th row of Pascal's Triangle is equal to the middle element of the _____ row.

The middle element of the 4th row is 6 and 6 is in the 2nd column. The middle element of the 6th row is 20 and 20 is in the 3rd column. In general, the middle element of the $(2n)$th row is in the nth column. That is, if the row number is even, then the column number is half the row number.

11. The middle element of the 8th row is in the _____ column.

Using the notation introduced in Section 1.11, the middle element of the 4th row can be represented by $\binom{4}{2}$ and the middle element of the 6th row by $\binom{6}{3}$ and so on. The column number of the middle element is always $\frac{1}{2}$ of the row number.

---

12. Use the row-column notation to complete the following equations.

$$\binom{2}{1} = 1^2 + 1^2$$

$$\binom{4}{2} = 1^2 + 2^2 + 1^2$$

$$\binom{6}{3} = 1^2 + 3^2 + 3^2 + 1^2$$

$$\binom{}{} = 1^2 + 4^2 + 6^2 + 4^2 + 1^2$$

$$\binom{}{} = 1^2 + 5^2 + 10^2 + 10^2 + 5^2 + 1^2$$

$$\binom{}{} = 1^2 + 6^2 + 15^2 + 20^2 + 15^2 + 6^2 + 1^2$$

13. Perform the indicated operations.

$$1^2 = 1$$
$$1^2 - 1^2 = 0$$
$$1^2 - 2^2 + 1^2 = \underline{-2}$$
$$1^2 - 3^2 + 3^2 - 1^2 = \underline{}$$
$$1^2 - 4^2 + 6^2 - 4^2 + 1^2 = \underline{}$$
$$1^2 - 5^2 + 10^2 - 10^2 + 5^2 - 1^2 = \underline{}$$
$$1^2 - 6^2 + 15^2 - 20^2 + 15^2 - 6^2 + 1^2 = \underline{}$$
$$1^2 - 7^2 + 21^2 - 35^2 + 35^2 - 21^2 + 7^2 - 1^2 = \underline{}$$
$$1^2 - 8^2 + 28^2 - 56^2 + 70^2 - 56^2 + 28^2 - 8^2 + 1^2 = \underline{}$$

14. Without performing the computations, predict the results of the 9th and 10th rows of this pattern.

15. In the following diagram there are two Pascal's Triangles with one of them inverted, but they are not centered. Where two elements share the same cell, multiply them together. Add the results in each row of the overlap area. What do you find?

16. Add the results in each column of the overlap area. What do you find?

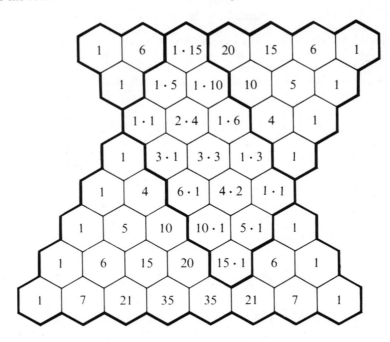

___

2.4 OTHER INTERESTING NUMERICAL RELATIONSHIPS

Recall that the sum of the elements in a row of Pascal's Triangle is equal to a power of 2. Now let's add up all the elements in all the rows through the nth row.

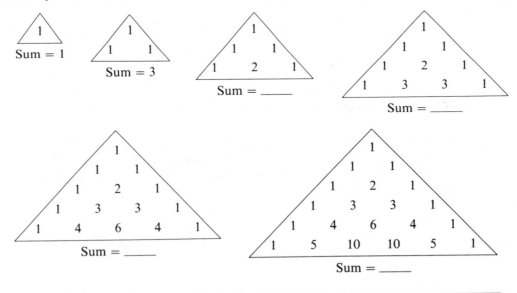

___

1. Find the sums of all the elements in Pascal's Triangle as shown.

___

The numbers you found fit the pattern in the following table.

n	2^{n+1}	$2^{n+1} - 1$
0	2	1
1	4	3
2	8	7
3	____	____
4	____	____
5	____	____

2. Complete the table above.

3. In each of the Pascal's Triangles, add all the numbers encircled in the top group, then add all the numbers encircled in the bottom group. Compare the two sums. What do you find?

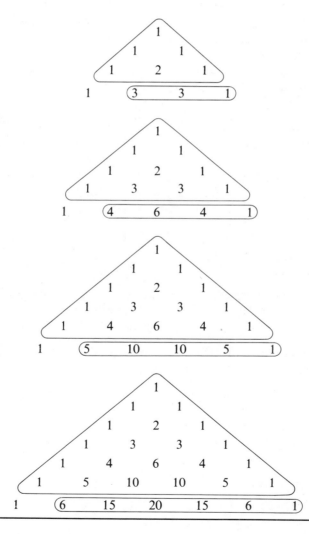

It seems that up through the nth row the sum of the numbers in Pascal's Triangle is equal to $2^{n+1} - 1$. We can show this is true by using the hockey stick property for adding the elements in the columns of Pascal's Triangle.

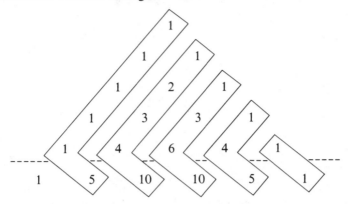

The sum of all of the elements up through the 4th row is equal to 1 less than the sum of the elements in the 5th row.

Since the sum of the elements in each row is 2^n, we have the following formula.

$$2^0 + 2^1 + 2^2 + 2^3 + 2^4 = 2^5 - 1$$

---

4. Complete this table.

$$2^0 = 2^1 \quad - 1 = 1$$
$$2^1 + 2^0 = 2^2 \quad - 1 = 3$$
$$2^2 + 2^1 + 2^0 = 2^3 \quad - 1 = \rule{1cm}{0.4pt}$$
$$2^3 + 2^2 + 2^1 + 2^0 = \rule{1cm}{0.4pt} - 1 = \rule{1cm}{0.4pt}$$
$$2^4 + 2^3 + 2^2 + 2^1 + 2^0 = \rule{1cm}{0.4pt} - 1 = \rule{1cm}{0.4pt}$$
$$2^5 + 2^4 + 2^3 + 2^2 + 2^1 + 2^0 = \rule{1cm}{0.4pt} - 1 = \rule{1cm}{0.4pt}$$
$$2^6 + 2^5 + 2^4 + 2^3 + 2^2 + 2^1 + 2^0 = \rule{1cm}{0.4pt} - 1 = \rule{1cm}{0.4pt}$$
$$2^7 + 2^6 + 2^5 + 2^4 + 2^3 + 2^2 + 2^1 + 2^0 = \rule{1cm}{0.4pt} - 1 = \rule{1cm}{0.4pt}$$
$$2^8 + 2^7 + 2^6 + 2^5 + 2^4 + 2^3 + 2^2 + 2^1 + 2^0 = \rule{1cm}{0.4pt} - 1 = \rule{1cm}{0.4pt}$$
$$2^n + 2^{n-1} + 2^{n-2} + \cdots + \cdots + 2^3 + 2^2 + 2^1 + 2^0 = \rule{1cm}{0.4pt} - 1$$

5. Use the formula in the last line of the previous table to find the sum of the powers of 2 from the 30th through the 0th. That is,
$$2^{30} + 2^{29} + 2^{28} + \cdots + 2^2 + 2^1 + 2^0 = ?$$

6. Add all the numbers to the right of the line in each row of Pascal's Triangle shown below. What sequence of numbers is formed?

$$1|$$
$$1|1 = \ 1$$
$$1|2 + \ 1 = \ 3$$
$$1|3 + \ 3 + \ 1 = \rule{1cm}{0.4pt}$$
$$1|4 + \ 6 + \ 4 + \ 1 = \rule{1cm}{0.4pt}$$
$$1|5 + 10 + 10 + \ 5 + \ 1 = \rule{1cm}{0.4pt}$$
$$1|6 + 15 + 20 + 15 + \ 6 + \ 1 = \rule{1cm}{0.4pt}$$
$$1|7 + 21 + 35 + 35 + 21 + \ 7 + 1 = \rule{1cm}{0.4pt}$$
$$1|8 + 28 + 56 + 70 + 56 + 28 + 8 + 1 = \rule{1cm}{0.4pt}$$

7. In each of the Pascal's Triangles shown, add all the numbers encircled in the top group, then add all the numbers encircled in the bottom group. Compare the two sums. What do you find in each case?

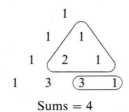

Sums = 4

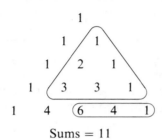

Sums = 11

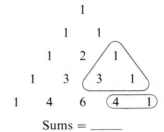

Sums = _____

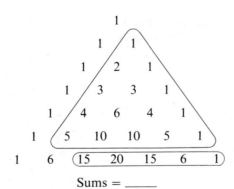

Sums = _____

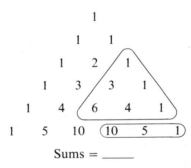

Sums = _____

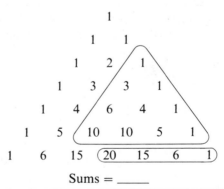

Sums = _____   Sums = _____

The sequence of numbers found in the previous exercise, 4, 11, 26, 57,... represent the partial sums of the sequence 1, 3, 7, 15,.... Also, the numbers in the sequence 1, 3, 7, 15,... are the partial sums of the sequence 1, 2, 4, 8,....

$$1 = 1$$
$$1 + 2 = 3$$
$$1 + 2 + 4 = 7$$
$$1 + 2 + 4 + 8 = 15$$
$$1 + 2 + 4 + 8 + 16 = 31$$

$$1 = 1$$
$$1 + 3 = 4$$
$$1 + 3 + 7 = 11$$
$$1 + 3 + 7 + 15 = 26$$
$$1 + 3 + 7 + 15 + 31 = 57$$

---

8. Extend the pattern of equations shown to include two more equations in each group.

These sequences of partial sums are formed by removing columns from the left side of Pascal's Triangle and adding the remaining elements in each row.

The following property is also a consequence of the hockey stick property. The sum of all the numbers in the parallelogram shown is one less than the number two rows down and pointed to by the lower corner of the parallelogram.

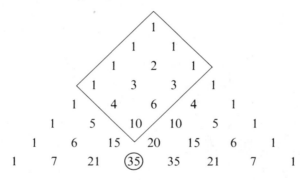

Add one to the sum of each of the indicated groups of numbers. Then, circle the number in Pascal's Triangle equal to the sum of all the numbers.

9.

10.

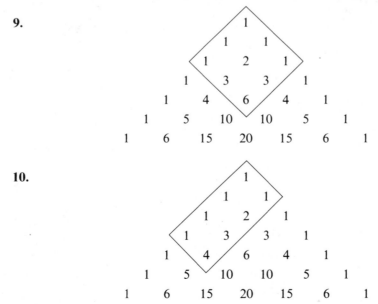

Now, consider a different form of Pascal's Triangle.

1	0	0	0	0	0	0
1	1	0	0	0	0	0
1	2	1	0	0	0	0
1	3	3	1	0	0	0
1	4	6	4	1	0	0
1	5	10	10	5	1	0
1	6	15	20	15	6	1
⋮	⋮	⋮	⋮	⋮	⋮	⋮

In this form, the column of 1's is called the 0th column. The column of numbers 0, 1, 2, 3, 4, 5, 6,... is called the 1st column. The column of numbers 0, 0, 1, 3, 6, 10, 15,... is called the 2nd column, and so on. Consider the following fractions formed from the numbers in the 2nd column.

$$\frac{0 + 0 + 1}{1 + 1 + 1} = \frac{1}{3}$$

$$\frac{0 + 0 + 1 + 3}{3 + 3 + 3 + 3} = \frac{4}{12} = \frac{1}{3}$$

$$\frac{0 + 0 + 1 + 3 + 6}{6 + 6 + 6 + 6 + 6} = \frac{10}{30} = \frac{1}{3}$$

$$\frac{0 + 0 + 1 + 3 + 6 + 10}{10 + 10 + 10 + 10 + 10 + 10} = \frac{20}{60} = \frac{1}{3}$$

---

11. Predict the form of the next fraction in the preceding sequence and compute its value.

12. Consider the elements in the 3rd column. Compute the value of each fraction below.

$$\frac{0 + 0 + 0 + 1}{1 + 1 + 1 + 1} = \underline{\qquad}$$

$$\frac{0 + 0 + 0 + 1 + 4}{4 + 4 + 4 + 4 + 4 + 4} = \underline{\qquad}$$

$$\frac{0 + 0 + 0 + 1 + 4 + 10}{10 + 10 + 10 + 10 + 10 + 10} = \underline{\qquad}$$

$$\frac{0 + 0 + 0 + 1 + 4 + 10 + 20}{20 + 20 + 20 + 20 + 20 + 20 + 20} = \underline{\qquad}$$

Predict the form of the next fraction in the preceding sequence and compute its value.

Notice the value of the fractions formed in this manner from the 1st column.

$$\frac{0 + 1}{1 + 1} = \frac{1}{2}$$

$$\frac{0 + 1 + 2}{2 + 2 + 2} = \frac{3}{6} = \frac{1}{2}$$

$$\frac{0 + 1 + 2 + 3}{3 + 3 + 3 + 3} = \frac{6}{12} = \frac{1}{2}$$

$$\frac{0 + 1 + 2 + 3 + 4}{4 + 4 + 4 + 4 + 4} = \frac{10}{20} = \frac{1}{2}$$

In general,

$$\frac{0 + 1 + 2 + 3 + 4 + \cdots + n}{n + n + n + n + n + \cdots + n} = \frac{1}{2}$$

therefore,

$$0 + 1 + 2 + 3 + 4 + \cdots + n = \frac{1}{2}(n + n + n + n + n + \cdots + n)$$

or, equivalently,

$$1 + 2 + 3 + 4 + \cdots + n = \frac{1}{2}n(n + 1)$$

since there are $(n + 1)$ n's in the parentheses on the right above.

---

13. Use this formula to find the sum of all the natural numbers from 1 to 100.

A hexagon is a plane figure with 6 sides. If you draw a hexagon around a group of 7 numbers in Pascal's Triangle, the sum of the numbers is 2 times the number directly below the hexagon.

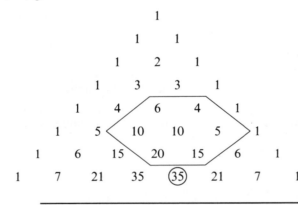

The sum of the numbers in the hexagon equals 2 times 35, the number directly below the hexagon.

---

14. Find the sum of the numbers in the hexagon shown below. Divide the sum by 2. Circle the result in Pascal's Triangle.

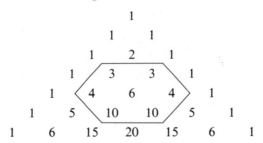

15. Draw several other hexagons and perform the same computations. Compare your results.

16. In the hexagons below, find the product of the three numbers that are circled and find the product of the three numbers in squares. Compare the two results. What do you find?

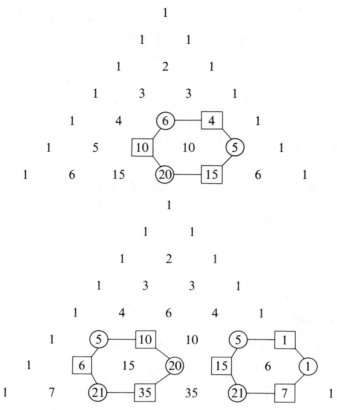

Choose your own hexagon and try the same procedure.

17. Study the pattern below and complete the two equations.

$$1 \cdot 1 = 1 \cdot 1$$
$$3 \cdot 2 = 2 \cdot 3$$
$$5 \cdot 6 = 3 \cdot 10$$
$$7 \cdot 20 = 4 \cdot 35$$
$$\underline{\quad} \cdot \underline{\quad} = \underline{\quad} \cdot \underline{\quad}$$
$$\underline{\quad} \cdot \underline{\quad} = \underline{\quad} \cdot \underline{\quad}$$

In the previous section we saw that the sum of the squares of the elements in the nth row of Pascal's Triangle was equal to the middle element of the $(2n)$th row. Now we will generalize this result to apply to the product of any two rows in Pascal's Triangle term by term. To describe this property, let's define a new kind of operation called "string multiplication." A string will be a sequence of numbers, such as the 3rd row of Pascal's Triangle $(1, 3, 3, 1)$. To multiply two strings together, such as the string $(1, 3, 3, 1)$ and the string $(1, 4, 6, 4)$, we write

$$
\begin{aligned}
(1, 3, 3, 1) \bullet (1, 4, 6, 4) &= 1 \cdot 1 + 3 \cdot 4 + 3 \cdot 6 + 1 \cdot 4 \\
&= 1 + 12 + 18 + 4 \\
&= 35
\end{aligned}
$$

Incidentally,

$$
\begin{aligned}
(1, 3, 3, 1) \bullet (1, 3, 3, 1) &= 1^2 + 3^2 + 3^2 + 1^2 \\
&= 20
\end{aligned}
$$

In order to discuss the string multiplication of different rows of Pascal's Triangle, let's assume that each row consists of its normal elements and as many additional zeros as necessary. Thus, to form the string product of the 3rd and 4th rows of Pascal's Triangle, we write

$$
\begin{aligned}
(1, 3, 3, 1, 0) \bullet (1, 4, 6, 4, 1) &= 1 \cdot 1 + 3 \cdot 4 + 3 \cdot 6 + 1 \cdot 4 + 0 \cdot 1 \\
&= 1 + 12 + 18 + 4 + 0 \\
&= 35
\end{aligned}
$$

The result of this string multiplication is 35, the element in the 7th row and 4th column of Pascal's Triangle: $\binom{7}{4} = 35$. In general, if we string multiply the nth and mth rows of Pascal's Triangle, we get the element in the $(n + m)$th row and the mth column (or the nth column). That is,

$$
\binom{n + m}{n} = \binom{n + m}{m}
$$

because of the symmetry in Pascal's Triangle and the fact that string multiplication is a commutative operation.

---

18. Compute this string multiplication.

$$(1, 4, 6, 4, 1) \bullet (1, 4, 6, 4, 1) = ?$$

19. Multiply the two strings shown in Pascal's Triangle below.

```
                    1
                 1     1
              1     2     1
         ┌  1     3     3     1     0     0  ┐
           1     4     6     4     1
         └  1     5    10    10     5     1  ┘
```

In what row and column can the result be found?

20. Multiply the 4th and 5th rows of Pascal's Triangle as strings using zeros where necessary. Verify that the result is $\binom{9}{4}$.

21. Multiply each circled string below by $(1, 2, 1)$. The results can all be found in Pascal's Triangle. Describe the resulting numbers.

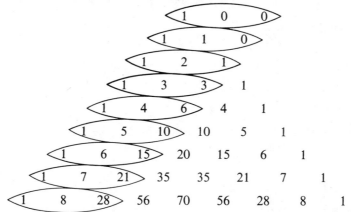

22. Several string products are formed below by using the numbers from the 1st and 2nd columns of Pascal's Triangle. Complete this table. Describe the resulting numbers, which can all be found in Pascal's Triangle.

$(1) \cdot (1) = 1$

$(1, 2) \cdot (3, 1) = 5$

$(1, 2, 3) \cdot (6, 3, 1) = $ _____

$(1, 2, 3, 4) \cdot (10, 6, 3, 1) = $ _____

$(1, 2, 3, 4, 5) \cdot (15, 10, 6, 3, 1) = $ _____

$(1, 2, 3, 4, 5, 6) \cdot (21, 15, 10, 6, 3, 1) = $ _____

23. In a similar manner, use the 1st and 3rd columns of Pascal's Triangle to form several string products. Describe the resulting numbers.

The string multiplication of $(1, 4, 6, 4, 1)$ and $(x^4, x^3, x^2, x^1, x^0)$ gives us $1 \cdot x^4 + 4 \cdot x^3 + 6 \cdot x^2 + 4 \cdot x^1 + 1 \cdot x^0$, which is the binomial expansion of $(x + 1)^4$.

---

24. Let $x = 2$ and verify that

$$(1, 4, 6, 4, 1) \cdot (x^4, x^3, x^2, x^1, x^0) = (x + 1)^4$$

Note: $2^0 = 1$.

25. String multiply

$$(1, 3, 3, 1) \cdot (x^3, x^2, x^1, x^0)$$

What binomial expansion is this result?

26. Suppose

$$S_0 = 1^0 + 2^0 + 3^0 = 1 + 1 + 1 = 3$$
$$S_1 = 1^1 + 2^1 + 3^1 = 1 + 2 + 3 = 6$$
$$S_2 = 1^2 + 2^2 + 3^2 = 1 + 4 + 9 = 14$$
$$S_3 = 1^3 + 2^3 + 3^3 = 1 + 8 + 27 = 36$$

then verify the following:

$$3^1 = 1 \cdot S_0$$
$$3^2 = 2 \cdot S_1 - 1 \cdot S_0$$
$$3^3 = 3 \cdot S_2 - 3 \cdot S_1 + 1 \cdot S_0$$
$$3^4 = 4 \cdot S_3 - 6 \cdot S_2 + 4 \cdot S_1 - 1 \cdot S_0$$

If $S_4 = 1^4 + 2^4 + 3^4$, use this quantity to predict the next formula in the sequence above. Verify your result.

27. Suppose

$$S_0 = 1^0 + 2^0 + 3^0 + 4^0 = 1 + 1 + 1 + 1 = 4$$
$$S_1 = 1^1 + 2^1 + 3^1 + 4^1 = 1 + 2 + 3 + 4 = 10$$
$$S_2 = 1^2 + 2^2 + 3^2 + 4^2 = 1 + 4 + 9 + 16 = 30$$
$$S_3 = 1^3 + 2^3 + 3^3 + 4^3 = 1 + 8 + 27 + 64 = 100$$

then verify the following:

$$4^1 = 1 \cdot S_0$$
$$4^2 = 2 \cdot S_1 - 1 \cdot S_0$$
$$4^3 = 3 \cdot S_2 - 3 \cdot S_1 + 1 \cdot S_0$$
$$4^4 = 4 \cdot S_3 - 6 \cdot S_2 + 4 \cdot S_1 - 1 \cdot S_0$$

If $S_4 = 1^4 + 2^4 + 3^4 + 4^4$, use this quantity to predict the next formula in the sequence above. Verify your result.

28. In general, if $S_i = 1^i + 2^i + 3^i + \cdots + n^i$, then

$$n = 1 \cdot S_0$$
$$n^2 = 2 \cdot S_1 - 1 \cdot S_0$$
$$n^3 = 3 \cdot S_2 - 3 \cdot S_1 + 1 \cdot S_0$$
$$n^4 = 4 \cdot S_3 - 6 \cdot S_2 + 4 \cdot S_1 - 1 \cdot S_0$$

Predict a formula for n^5.
Let $n = 2$ and verify your formula for n^5.

29. Suppose

$$S_0 = 1^0 + 2^0 + 3^0 = 1 + 1 + 1 = 3$$
$$S_1 = 1^1 + 2^1 + 3^1 = 1 + 2 + 3 = 6$$
$$S_2 = 1^2 + 2^2 + 3^2 = 1 + 4 + 9 = 14$$
$$S_3 = 1^3 + 2^3 + 3^3 = 1 + 8 + 27 = 36$$
$$S_4 = 1^4 + 2^4 + 3^4 = 1 + 16 + 81 = 98$$

then verify the following string multiplications:

$$(2) \cdot (S_1) = 4^2 - 4$$
$$(3, 3) \cdot (S_2, S_1) = 4^3 - 4$$
$$(4, 6, 4) \cdot (S_3, S_2, S_1) = 4^4 - 4$$
$$(5, 10, 10, 5) \cdot (S_4, S_3, S_2, S_1) = 4^5 - 4$$

If $S_5 = 1^5 + 2^5 + 3^5$, then use this quantity to predict the next formula in the sequence above. Verify your result.

2.5 FIBONACCI NUMBERS

A problem concerning population growth in a rabbit hutch was proposed by Leonardo Fibonacci in his book *Liber Abaci*, which was published in Pisa in A.D. 1202. His hypothetical problem asked for the number of pairs of rabbits in a hutch at the end of one year, if you begin with a single pair and it is assumed that every month a pair of rabbits produces another pair. It is also assumed that the rabbits begin to bear young two months after their own birth.

The first pair produces a second pair in the first month. Therefore, there are two pairs after one month. After two months, the first pair produce another pair making the total number of pairs equal to three. At the end of the next month, the first pair have again produced another pair. Also, the second pair that were born in the first month produce their first pair making the total equal to five pairs. This process continues throughout the year. In the following diagrams we can see how this population growth proceeds for the first seven months. Each hexagon in the diagram represents a pair of rabbits. The number in the hexagon represents the month in which that pair was first counted. Let's assume that a census is taken at the beginning of each month. Thus, ⟨1⟩ represents the original pair counted at the beginning of the first month. The symbol ⟨2⟩ represents the second pair born to the first pair and counted at the beginning of the second month, and so on. If one pair is born to another pair, this is indicated by a line segment connecting the hexagons. The smaller number corresponds to the parents and the larger number corresponds to the offspring. These births will be recorded month by month in a clockwise direction around each hexagon.

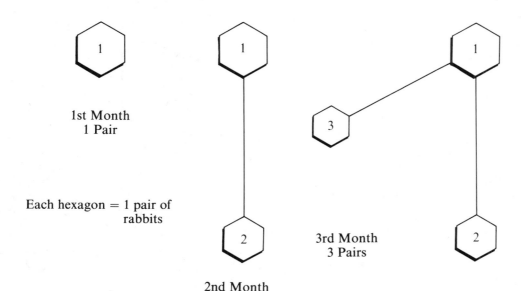

1st Month
1 Pair

Each hexagon = 1 pair of rabbits

2nd Month
2 Pairs

3rd Month
3 Pairs

Census is taken at the beginning of each month.

The number in the hexagon represents the month in which that pair is first counted.

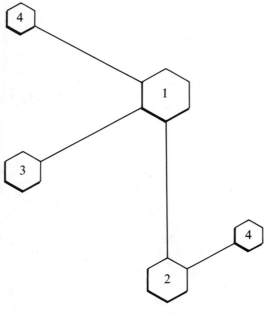

4th Month
5 Pairs

(This is the first time more than one new
pair of rabbits was born.)

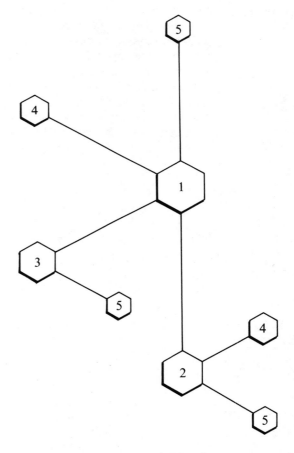

5th Month
8 Pairs

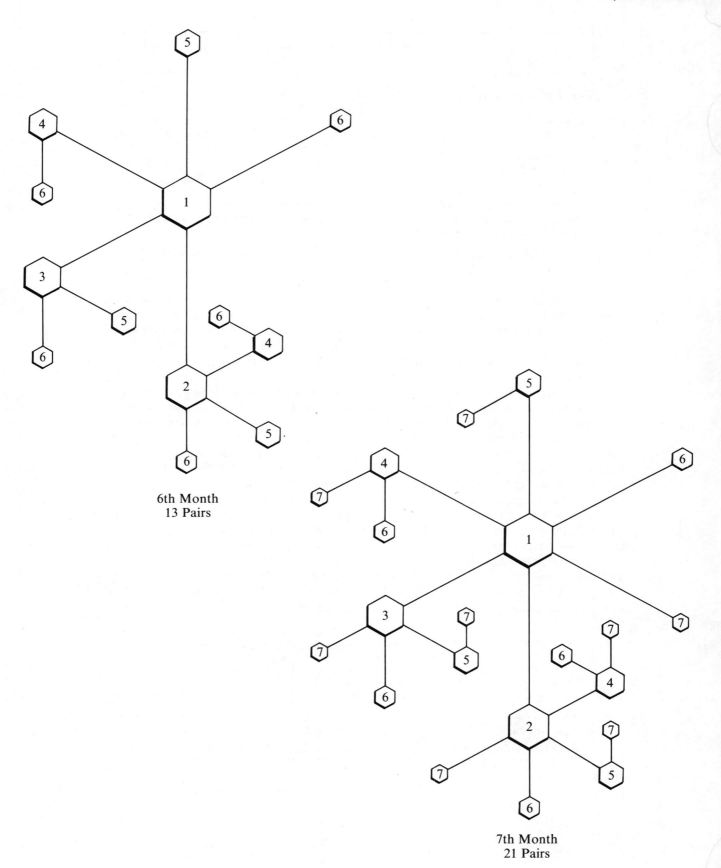

6th Month
13 Pairs

7th Month
21 Pairs

1. Extend the diagrams another month to produce a diagram showing the number of pairs of rabbits present at the beginning of the 8th month.

This chart summarizes the results of the rabbit population growth.

Month	1	2	3	4	5	6	7	8	9	10	11	12	13
Number of rabbit pairs	1	2	3	5	8	13	21						

2. Study the sequence of numbers in the chart to discover a rule that can be used to predict the next numbers in the sequence.

3. How many rabbit pairs are there at the beginning of the 13th month (after 12 months)?

The sequence of numbers above, 1, 2, 3, 5, 8, 13, 21, are part of the sequence known as **Fibonacci numbers**. Although these numbers were largely ignored for hundreds of years after the publication of *Liber Abaci*, there now exists an extensive amount of literature on Fibonacci numbers and their many ramifications in nature and mathematics. In the early 1960's, The Fibonacci Association was founded in California for the purpose of studying and promoting the research of this interesting sequence of numbers.

In the rest of this section and the next two sections, we will be studying a few of the properties of Fibonacci numbers, namely, their properties connected with Pascal's Triangle.

We will now re-examine the diagrams showing the number of rabbit pairs for each of the first 7 months of Fibonacci's problem. With these diagrams we will generate Pascal's Triangle. Instead of counting the number of rabbit pairs (hexagons), we will count the lines of ancestry. For example, in the diagram for the 5th month there are 7 lines drawn between the hexagons. Let's call these lines the "lines of ancestry." In this diagram there are two types of lines of ancestry: the longer lines connecting the larger hexagon with a "1" in it to the other hexagons representing "1's" offspring, and the shorter lines connecting the hexagons of these offspring to their own offspring. There are 4 longer lines and 3 shorter lines. Let's call the 4 longer lines first generation lines of ancestry and the 3 shorter lines second generation lines of ancestry. To these lines of ancestry let's add one more and call it the "prime" line of ancestry. It can be thought of as the line connecting the original pair of rabbits to their ancestors. Counting this line with the others, we have 8 lines of ancestry. Notice that this is the same number as the number of rabbit pairs at the beginning of the 5th month. The count is summarized below:

	Prime line	1st generation lines	2nd generation lines
5th Month	1	4	3

4. Examine the diagrams for the other months and verify the counts entered in the following table. Predict the numbers needed to complete the table.

Fibonacci's rabbit problem—lines of ancestry	Prime line	1st generation lines	2nd generation lines	3rd generation lines	4th generation lines	5th generation lines	6th generation lines	Total
1st month	1	0	0	0	0	0	0	1
2nd month	1	1	0	0	0	0	0	2
3rd month	1	2	0	0	0	0	0	3
4th month	1	3	1	0	0	0	0	5
5th month	1	4	3	0	0	0	0	8
6th month	1	5	6	1	0	0	0	13
7th month	1	6	10	4	0	0	0	21
8th month	1	7	15	10	1	0	0	34
9th month	___	___	___	___	___	___	___	___
10th month	___	___	___	___	___	___	___	___
11th month	___	___	___	___	___	___	___	___
12th month	___	___	___	___	___	___	___	___
13th month	___	___	___	___	___	___	___	___

The numbers in the previous table are the numbers of Pascal's Triangle. The column of 2nd generation lines is the same as the 2nd column in Pascal's Triangle. The other columns of numbers also correspond to columns in Pascal's Triangle. If we eliminate the zeros from the table and shift each column upward to fill the vacancies, we would have the following arrangement. Notice that this is Pascal's Triangle tipped up on one side.

```
1    1    1    1    1    1    1
1    2    3    4    5    6    7
1    3    6    10   15   21
1    4    10   20   35   56
1    5    15   35   70
1    6    21   56   126
1    7    28   84
1    8    36   120
1    9    45
1    10   55
1    11
1    12
1
```

Pascal's Triangle can also be used in its standard form to find the Fibonacci numbers. In the following diagram, the encircled groups of numbers are added together to form a Fibonacci number. Each group of numbers in Pascal's Triangle formed this way is called a **Fibonacci diagonal**. The Fibonacci diagonals are composed of the same numbers as the rows of numbers in the preceding table for the lines of ancestry.

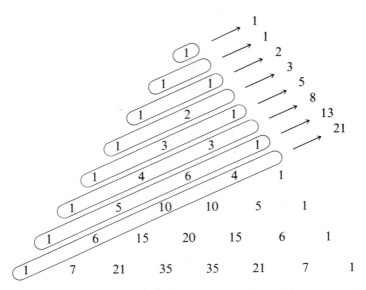

Fibonacci diagonals in Pascal's Triangle

5. Extend Pascal's Triangle in the above figure and encircle two more Fibonacci diagonals. Add the numbers in each encircled group. Verify that these are Fibonacci numbers.

2.6 FIBONACCI'S RULE AND PASCAL'S TRIANGLE

By now you have probably noticed a very simple rule for finding subsequent Fibonacci numbers. If you add two consecutive Fibonacci numbers, you get the next Fibonacci number. If you examine the Fibonacci diagonals and use Pascal's Rule, you can see why Fibonacci's Rule works.

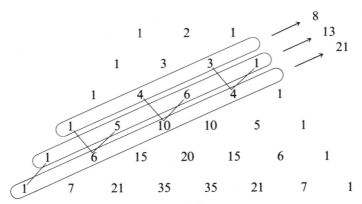

Using Pascal's Rule on Fibonacci diagonals to show that 8 + 13 = 21

---

1. Draw the Fibonacci diagonals for 13, 21, and 34 and show how Pascal's Rule works to verify that $13 + 21 = 34$.

If F_1 represents the 1st Fibonacci number, F_2 represents the 2nd Fibonacci number, F_3 represents the 3rd Fibonacci number, and so on, then the previous diagram shows that

$$F_8 = F_7 + F_6$$

where $F_6 = 8$, $F_7 = 13$, and $F_8 = 21$. In general, we write the nth Fibonacci number equals the sum of the $(n-1)$th Fibonacci number plus the $(n-2)$th Fibonacci number:

$$F_n = F_{n-1} + F_{n-2}$$

This formula, called the Fibonacci Rule, is an example of a **recursion formula**. Given the first two Fibonacci numbers, all the others are determined by the rule.

Given $F_1 = 1$ and $F_2 = 1$

then $F_3 = F_2 + F_1 = 1 + 1 = 2$

            $F_4 = F_3 + F_2 = 2 + 1 = 3$

            $F_5 = F_4 + F_3 = 3 + 2 = 5$

and so on.

---

2. Use the Fibonacci Rule to find the first 20 Fibonacci numbers given that $F_1 = 1$ and $F_2 = 1$.

3. Given that $F_{29} = 514{,}229$ and $F_{30} = 832{,}040$, find F_{31}.

The first 7 Fibonacci numbers are 1, 1, 2, 3, 5, 8, 13. Fibonacci's Rule states that $13 = 8 + 5$, or equivalently,

$$13 = 1 \cdot 8 + 1 \cdot 5$$

but $8 = 5 + 3$ and $5 = 3 + 2$. Therefore, by substituting these expressions into the above formula, we have

$$13 = 1 \cdot 5 + 2 \cdot 3 + 1 \cdot 2$$

and by further substitutions of equivalent expressions, we have

$$13 = 1 \cdot 3 + 3 \cdot 2 + 3 \cdot 1 + 1 \cdot 1$$

The right members of each of the above formulas can be expressed as the result of string multiplications.

$$13 = (1) \cdot (13)$$
$$13 = (1, 1) \cdot (8, 5)$$
$$13 = (1, 2, 1) \cdot (5, 3, 2)$$
$$13 = (1, 3, 3, 1) \cdot (3, 2, 1, 1)$$

---

4. Find these string products.

    _____ $= (1) \cdot (21)$

    _____ $= (1, 1) \cdot (13, 8)$

    _____ $= (1, 2, 1) \cdot (8, 5, 3)$

    _____ $= (1, 3, 3, 1) \cdot (5, 3, 2, 1)$

    _____ $= (1, 4, 6, 4, 1) \cdot (3, 2, 1, 1, 0)$

5. Perform these computations.

$$1(55) = 55$$
$$1(34) + 1(21) = 55$$
$$1(21) + 2(13) + 1(8) = \underline{\hspace{1cm}}$$
$$1(13) + 3(8) + 3(5) + 1(3) = \underline{\hspace{1cm}}$$
$$1(8) + 4(5) + 6(3) + 4(2) + 1(1) = \underline{\hspace{1cm}}$$
$$1(5) + 5(3) + 10(2) + 10(1) + 5(1) + 1(0) = \underline{\hspace{1cm}}$$

In general, we have the following formulas, which are the Pascal extensions of Fibonacci's Rule.

$$F_n = 1 \cdot F_n$$
$$= 1 \cdot F_{n-1} + 1 \cdot F_{n-2}$$
$$= 1 \cdot F_{n-2} + 2 \cdot F_{n-3} + 1 \cdot F_{n-4}$$
$$= 1 \cdot F_{n-3} + 3 \cdot F_{n-4} + 3 \cdot F_{n-5} + 1 \cdot F_{n-6}$$
$$= 1 \cdot F_{n-4} + 4 \cdot F_{n-5} + 6 \cdot F_{n-6} + 4 \cdot F_{n-7} + 1 \cdot F_{n-8}$$
$$= 1 \cdot F_{n-5} + 5 \cdot F_{n-6} + 10 \cdot F_{n-7} + 10 \cdot F_{n-8} + 5 \cdot F_{n-9} + 1 \cdot F_{n-10}$$

etc.

6. (a) Let $n = 14$ and write the first 14 Fibonacci numbers. Substitute these numbers into the above formulas and verify their sum to be F_{14}.

(b) Repeat for $n = 11$.

7. Verify the following string products.

$$F_5 = (1, 2, 1) \bullet (1, 1, 2)$$
$$F_7 = (1, 3, 3, 1) \bullet (1, 1, 2, 3)$$
$$F_9 = (1, 4, 6, 4, 1) \bullet (1, 1, 2, 3, 5)$$
$$F_{11} = (1, 5, 10, 10, 5, 1) \bullet (1, 1, 2, 3, 5, 8)$$

Predict a string product for F_{13} and verify the result.

8. Perform these computations.

$$1 \cdot F_1 = \underline{\hspace{1cm}}$$
$$1 \cdot F_1 + 1 \cdot F_2 = \underline{\hspace{1cm}}$$
$$1 \cdot F_1 + 2 \cdot F_2 + 1 \cdot F_3 = \underline{\hspace{1cm}}$$
$$1 \cdot F_1 + 3 \cdot F_2 + 3 \cdot F_3 + 1 \cdot F_4 = \underline{\hspace{1cm}}$$
$$1 \cdot F_1 + 4 \cdot F_2 + 6 \cdot F_3 + 4 \cdot F_4 + 1 \cdot F_5 = \underline{\hspace{1cm}}$$
$$1 \cdot F_1 + 5 \cdot F_2 + 10 \cdot F_3 + 10 \cdot F_4 + 5 \cdot F_5 + 1 \cdot F_6 = \underline{\hspace{1cm}}$$

Describe the sequence of numbers resulting from the above computations.

9. Verify these string products.

$$F_4 = (2, 1) \cdot (1, 1)$$
$$F_6 = (3, 3, 1) \cdot (1, 1, 2)$$
$$F_8 = (4, 6, 4, 1) \cdot (1, 1, 2, 3)$$
$$F_{10} = (5, 10, 10, 5, 1) \cdot (1, 1, 2, 3, 5)$$

Predict a string product for F_{12} and verify the result.

10. Perform the following computations.

$$1 \cdot 0 = 0$$
$$1 \cdot 0 + 1 \cdot F_1 = \underline{\quad}$$
$$1 \cdot 0 + 2 \cdot F_1 + 1 \cdot F_2 = \underline{\quad}$$
$$1 \cdot 0 + 3 \cdot F_1 + 3 \cdot F_2 + 1 \cdot F_3 = \underline{\quad}$$
$$1 \cdot 0 + 4 \cdot F_1 + 6 \cdot F_2 + 4 \cdot F_3 + 1 \cdot F_4 = \underline{\quad}$$
$$1 \cdot 0 + 5 \cdot F_1 + 10 \cdot F_2 + 10 \cdot F_3 + 5 \cdot F_4 + 1 \cdot F_5 = \underline{\quad}$$

Describe the sequence of numbers resulting from the above computations.

Now let's explore another interesting relationship between the Fibonacci numbers and Pascal's Triangle. This relationship involves powers of 5. We will demonstrate this relationship for the 5th Fibonacci number F_5. Start with the 5th row of Pascal's Triangle.

$$1 \quad 5 \quad 10 \quad 10 \quad 5 \quad 1 \longrightarrow \begin{array}{ccc} 5 & 10 & 1 \\ 1 & 10 & 5 \end{array}$$

Form the string product of the top row of numbers on the right $(5, 10, 1)$ and the powers of 5 $(5^0, 5^1, 5^2)$. This product forms the numerator of a fraction. The fraction's denominator is equal to the sum of the bottom row of numbers left over from the 5th row of Pascal's Triangle. This fraction is equal to F_5.

$$F_5 = \frac{5 \cdot 5^0 + 10 \cdot 5^1 + 1 \cdot 5^2}{1 + 10 + 5}$$
$$= \frac{5 + 50 + 25}{16}$$
$$= \frac{80}{16}$$
$$= 5$$

Let's demonstrate this again, this time for F_6.

Step 1	
Write down the 6th row of Pascal's Triangle.	1 6 15 20 15 6 1

Step 2	
Separate these numbers into 2 rows.	6 20 6 1 15 15 1

Step 3	
Form the string product of the top row with $(5^0, 5^1, 5^2)$. (Use as many powers of 5 as needed.)	$6 \cdot 5^0 + 20 \cdot 5^1 + 6 \cdot 5^2$ 1 15 15 1

Step 4	
Add the numbers in the bottom row and form a fraction.	$\dfrac{6 \cdot 5^0 + 20 \cdot 5^1 + 6 \cdot 5^2}{1 + 15 + 15 + 1}$

Step 5	
Evaluate this fraction and verify that it is equal to F_6.	$F_6 = \dfrac{6 \cdot 5^0 + 20 \cdot 5^1 + 6 \cdot 5^2}{1 + 15 + 15 + 1}$ $= \dfrac{6 + 100 + 150}{32}$ $= \dfrac{256}{32} = 8$

11. Form the fractions for F_4 and F_7 in the manner demonstrated and verify their values.

2.7 SUMS OF FIBONACCI NUMBERS AND PASCAL'S TRIANGLE

We have seen that the sum of the numbers in a Fibonacci diagonal of Pascal's Triangle is equal to a Fibonacci number. Now let's add all the elements in all the Fibonacci diagonals through the nth diagonal.

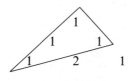

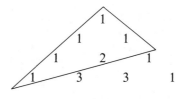

Sum = 1   Sum = 2   Sum = 4   Sum = ____

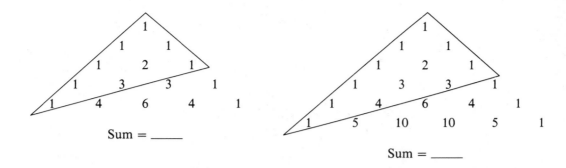

Sum = _____   Sum = _____

---

1. Find the sums of all the numbers in each triangle shown above.

The numbers you found fit into the following table.

n	F_{n+2}	$F_{n+2} - 1$
1	2	1
2	3	2
3	5	4
4	8	7
5	____	____
6	____	____
7	____	____

Note: If $n = 4$, then $F_{n+2} = F_6$ and this is the 6th Fibonacci number, $F_6 = 8$.

---

2. Complete the table above.

3. In each of the Pascal's Triangles below and at the top of the next page, add all the numbers in the top group, then add all the numbers in the bottom group. Compare the two sums in each case. What do you find?

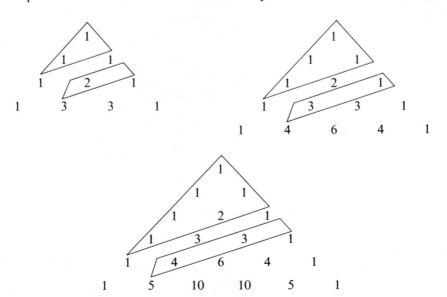

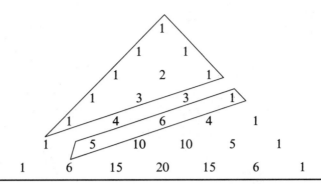

The numbers we've been examining are closely related to the Fibonacci numbers. It seems that the sum of the Fibonacci numbers up through the nth Fibonacci diagonal is equal to $F_{n+2} - 1$.

4. Complete this table.

$$F_1 = F_3 \quad -1 = 2 \quad -1 = 1$$
$$F_1 + F_2 = F_4 \quad -1 = 3 \quad -1 = 2$$
$$F_1 + F_2 + F_3 = F_5 \quad -1 = 5 \quad -1 = 4$$
$$F_1 + F_2 + F_3 + F_4 = \underline{\quad} -1 = \underline{\quad} -1 = \underline{\quad}$$
$$F_1 + F_2 + F_3 + F_4 + F_5 = \underline{\quad} -1 = \underline{\quad} -1 = \underline{\quad}$$
$$F_1 + F_2 + F_3 + F_4 + F_5 + F_6 = \underline{\quad} -1 = \underline{\quad} -1 = \underline{\quad}$$
$$F_1 + F_2 + F_3 + F_4 + F_5 + F_6 + F_7 = \underline{\quad} -1 = \underline{\quad} -1 = \underline{\quad}$$
$$F_1 + F_2 + F_3 + \cdots + F_{n-2} + F_{n-1} + F_n = \underline{\quad} -1$$

5. Use the formula in the last line of the previous table to find the sum of the first 20 Fibonacci numbers.

$$F_1 + F_2 + F_3 + \cdots + F_{20} = ?$$

6. Add all the numbers encircled in each group. What sequence of numbers is formed?

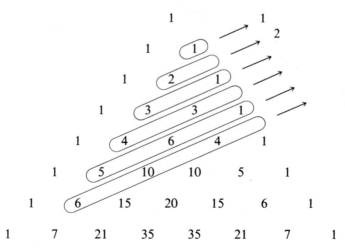

7. In each of the Pascal's Triangles below add all the numbers encircled in the top group of numbers, then add all the numbers encircled in the bottom group. Compare the two sums. What do you find in each case?

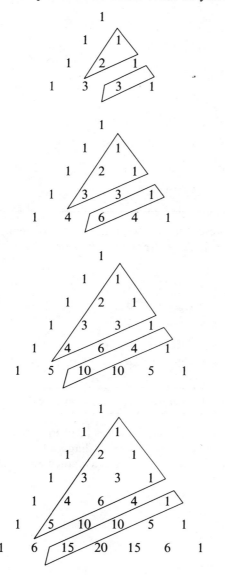

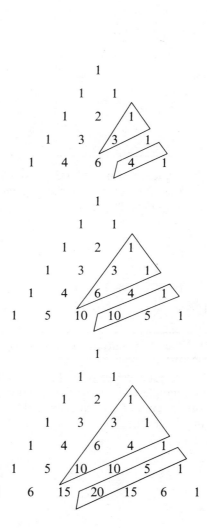

8. Add the numbers in each encircled group shown. What sequence of numbers is generated?

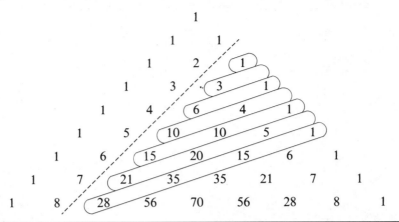

The sequence of numbers 3, 7, 14, 26,... represent the partial sums of the sequence 1, 2, 4, 7, 12,.... Also, the numbers in the sequence 1, 2, 4, 7, 12,... are the partial sums of the Fibonacci numbers, 1, 1, 2, 3, 5, 8,....

$$1 = 1 \qquad\qquad\qquad 1 = 1$$
$$1 + 1 = 2 \qquad\qquad 1 + 2 = 3$$
$$1 + 1 + 2 = 4 \qquad\qquad 1 + 2 + 4 = 7$$
$$1 + 1 + 2 + 3 = 7 \qquad\qquad 1 + 2 + 4 + 7 = 14$$
$$1 + 1 + 2 + 3 + 5 = 12 \qquad\qquad 1 + 2 + 4 + 7 + 12 = 26$$

9. Extend the pattern of equations to include two more equations in each group.

These sequences of partial sums are formed by removing columns from the left side of Pascal's Triangle and adding the remaining elements in each Fibonacci diagonal. These results are a consequence of the "hockey stick" property of Pascal's Triangle, as indicated in the following diagram.

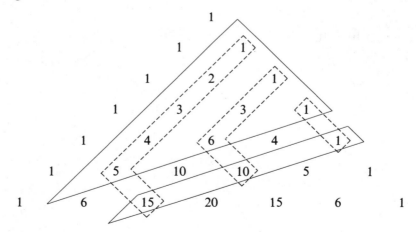

2.8 LUCAS NUMBERS AND OTHER NUMBER TRIANGLES

In this section, we are going to form a new number triangle. Let's start with two Pascal's Triangles as shown.

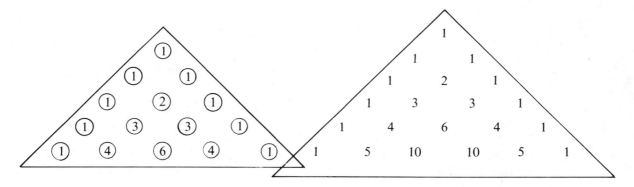

Imagine picking up the triangle on the left and putting it down partially over the other triangle as shown below.

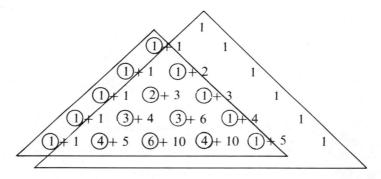

Now add the corresponding elements to form the following new number triangle.

```
              1
           2     1
        2     3     1
     2     5     4     1
  2     7     9     5     1
2    9    16    14    6     1
```

This new number triangle has properties similar to those that hold for Pascal's Triangle. For example, Pascal's Rule and the "hockey stick" property both work.

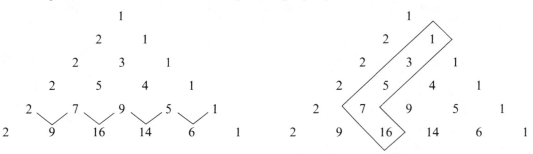

1. Develop the next 3 rows of the number triangle shown above.
2. Draw the "hockey stick" for the sum $1 + 3 + 5 + 7 + 9 + 11$ and determine the sum from the triangle.
3. Write down the 4th row of this number triangle. Then just below that write down that row again only in reverse order.

```
2    7    9    5    1
1    5    9    7    2
```

Now add each pair of corresponding elements.

```
    2    7    9    5    1
+   1    5    9    7    2
   ─────────────────────
    3   12   18   12    3
```

Finally, divide each sum by 3. What numbers do you obtain? Follow the same steps for the 5th row of this number triangle and for the 3rd row. What numbers do you obtain?

4. Add the numbers in each encircled group shown in the following new number triangle. What sequence of numbers is generated?

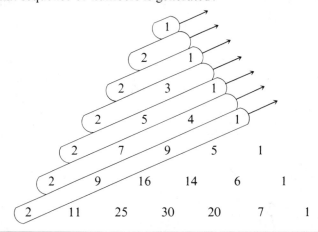

Now let's form a new sequence of numbers, called the Lucas numbers. Examine the sums of the numbers encircled in each group below.

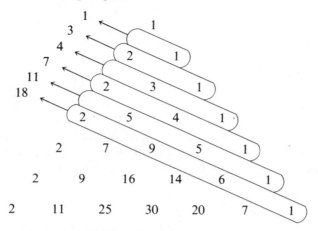

Lucas diagonals in this new number triangle

---

5. Extend the number triangle shown and encircle two more Lucas diagonals. Add the numbers in each encircled group.

The sequence of numbers 1, 3, 4, 7, 11, 18,... are called Lucas numbers. If L_1 represents the 1st Lucas number, $L_1 = 1$, and L_2 represents the 2nd Lucas number, $L_2 = 3$, and so on, we can show Lucas' Rule that

$$L_5 = L_4 + L_3$$

where $L_5 = 11$, $L_4 = 7$, and $L_3 = 4$. In general,

$$L_n = L_{n-1} + L_{n-2}$$

Thus, if $L_1 = 1$ and $L_2 = 3$, then

$$L_3 = L_2 + L_1 = 3 + 1 = \;\;4$$
$$L_4 = L_3 + L_2 = 4 + 3 = \;\;7$$
$$L_5 = L_4 + L_3 = 7 + 4 = 11$$

and so on.

---

6. Use Lucas' Rule to find the first 20 Lucas numbers.

7. Given that $L_{29} = 1,149,851$ and $L_{30} = 1,860,498$, find L_{31} and L_{28}.

8. The first 9 Lucas numbers are 1, 3, 4, 7, 11, 18, 29, 47, and 76. Using these numbers compute the following.

$$1 \cdot L_9 \; = \; \underline{\qquad}$$
$$1 \cdot L_8 \; + \; 1 \cdot L_7 \; = \; \underline{\qquad}$$
$$1 \cdot L_7 \; + \; 2 \cdot L_6 \; + \; 1 \cdot L_5 \; = \; \underline{\qquad}$$
$$1 \cdot L_6 \; + \; 3 \cdot L_5 \; + \; 3 \cdot L_4 \; + \; 1 \cdot L_3 \; = \; \underline{\qquad}$$
$$1 \cdot L_5 \; + \; 4 \cdot L_4 \; + \; 6 \cdot L_3 \; + \; 4 \cdot L_2 \; + \; 1 \cdot L_1 \; = \; \underline{\qquad}$$

Generalizing from the pattern above we have the following formulas, which are the Pascal extensions of Lucas' Rule.

$L_n = 1 \cdot L_n$

$\qquad = 1 \cdot L_{n-1} + 1 \cdot L_{n-2}$

$\qquad = 1 \cdot L_{n-2} + 2 \cdot L_{n-3} + 1 \cdot L_{n-4}$

$\qquad = 1 \cdot L_{n-3} + 3 \cdot L_{n-4} + 3 \cdot L_{n-5} + 1 \cdot L_{n-6}$

$\qquad = 1 \cdot L_{n-4} + 4 \cdot L_{n-5} + 6 \cdot L_{n-6} + 4 \cdot L_{n-7} + 1 \cdot L_{n-8}$

etc.

---

9. Let $n = 10$ and write the first 10 Lucas numbers. Substitute these into the previous formulas and verify that the sums are equal to L_{10}.

10. Compute the following.

$$1 \cdot L_1 \quad = \quad \underline{\qquad}$$
$$1 \cdot L_1 \quad + \quad 1 \cdot L_2 \quad = \quad \underline{\qquad}$$
$$1 \cdot L_1 \quad + \quad 2 \cdot L_2 \quad + \quad 1 \cdot L_3 \quad = \quad \underline{\qquad}$$
$$1 \cdot L_1 \quad + \quad 3 \cdot L_2 \quad + \quad 3 \cdot L_3 \quad + \quad 1 \cdot L_4 \quad = \quad \underline{\qquad}$$
$$1 \cdot L_1 \quad + \quad 4 \cdot L_2 \quad + \quad 6 \cdot L_3 \quad + \quad 4 \cdot L_4 \quad + \quad 1 \cdot L_5 \quad = \quad \underline{\qquad}$$
$$1 \cdot L_1 \quad + \quad 5 \cdot L_2 \quad + \quad 10 \cdot L_3 \quad + \quad 10 \cdot L_4 \quad + \quad 5 \cdot L_5 \quad + \quad 1 \cdot L_6 \quad = \quad \underline{\qquad}$$

Describe the sequence of numbers that result from the previous computations.

11. Compute the following.

$$1 \cdot L_1 \quad = \quad \underline{\qquad}$$
$$1 \cdot L_1 \quad + \quad 2 \cdot L_2 \quad = \quad \underline{\qquad}$$
$$1 \cdot L_1 \quad + \quad 3 \cdot L_2 \quad + \quad 2 \cdot L_3 \quad = \quad \underline{\qquad}$$
$$1 \cdot L_1 \quad + \quad 4 \cdot L_2 \quad + \quad 5 \cdot L_3 \quad + \quad 2 \cdot L_4 \quad = \quad \underline{\qquad}$$
$$1 \cdot L_1 \quad + \quad 5 \cdot L_2 \quad + \quad 9 \cdot L_3 \quad + \quad 7 \cdot L_4 \quad + \quad 2 \cdot L_5 \quad = \quad \underline{\qquad}$$

Describe the sequence of numbers that result from the previous computations.

12. Find the sum of all the numbers enclosed in each Pascal's Triangle shown. What sequence of numbers is formed?

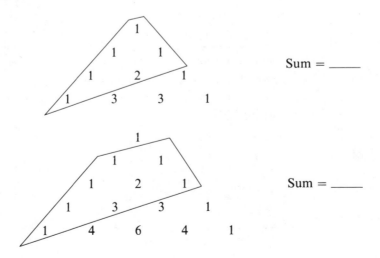

Sum = _____

Sum = _____

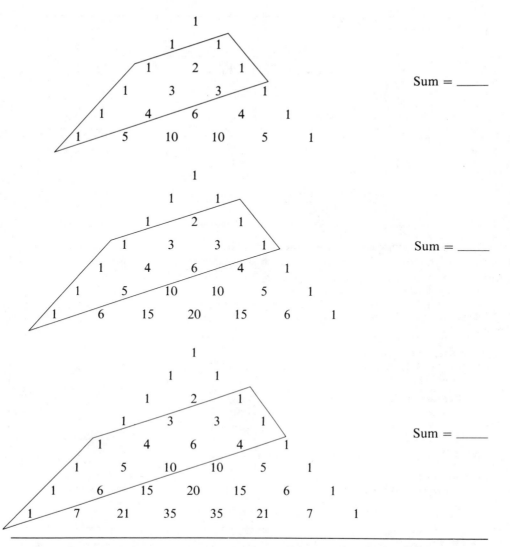

Sum = _____

Sum = _____

Sum = _____

The previous computations involved the addition of all the numbers in four consecutive Fibonacci diagonals in Pascal's Triangle. The results suggest the formula

$$L_n = F_n + F_{n-1} + F_{n-2} + F_{n-3}$$

which in turn is equivalent to

$$L_n = F_{n+1} + F_{n-1}$$

and also

$$L_n = F_n + 2 \cdot F_{n-1}$$

13. Complete this table.

n	L_n	$F_n + F_{n-1} + F_{n-2} + F_{n-3}$	$F_n + 2 \cdot F_{n-1}$
4	$L_4 =$ 7	$3 + 2 + 1 + 1 = 7$	$3 + 2 \cdot 2 = 7$
5	$L_5 =$ 11	$5 + 3 + 2 + 1 = $ _____	$5 + 2 \cdot 3 = $ _____
6	$L_6 = $ _____	$8 + 5 + 3 + 2 = $ _____	$8 + 2 \cdot 5 = $ _____
7	$L_7 = $ _____	$13 + 8 + 5 + 3 = $ _____	$13 + 2 \cdot 8 = $ _____
8	$L_8 = $ _____	___ + ___ + ___ + ___ = ___	___ + 2 · ___ = ___
9	$L_9 = $ _____	___ + ___ + ___ + ___ = ___	___ + 2 · ___ = ___

The following steps illustrate another connection between the Lucas numbers and Pascal's Triangle. We shall demonstrate this relationship for L_6. This is similar to the relationship we illustrated in Section 2.6 for Fibonacci numbers.

Step 1 Write down the 6th row of Pascal's Triangle.	1 6 15 20 15 6 1
Step 2 Separate these numbers into 2 rows.	1 15 15 1 6 20 6
Step 3 Form the string product of the top row with $(5^0, 5^1, 5^2, 5^3)$. (Use as many powers of 5 as needed.)	$1 \cdot 5^0 + 15 \cdot 5^1 + 15 \cdot 5^2 + 1 \cdot 5^3$ 6 20 6
Step 4 Add the numbers in the bottom row and form a fraction.	$\dfrac{1 \cdot 5^0 + 15 \cdot 5^1 + 15 \cdot 5^2 + 1 \cdot 5^3}{6 + 20 + 6}$
Step 5 Evaluate the fraction and verify that it is equal to L_6.	$L_6 = \dfrac{1 \cdot 5^0 + 15 \cdot 5^1 + 15 \cdot 5^2 + 1 \cdot 5^3}{6 + 20 + 6}$ $= \dfrac{1 + 75 + 375 + 125}{32}$ $= \dfrac{576}{32}$ $= 18$

14. Form the fractions for L_4, L_5, and L_7 in the manner demonstrated and verify their values.

The following number triangle was supposed to be a Pascal's Triangle, but the printer lost his glasses and was seeing double. He printed each column of Pascal's Triangle twice.

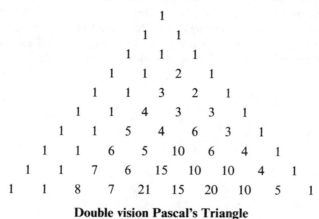

Double vision Pascal's Triangle

---

15. Extend the pattern of the triangle above for two more rows.

16. Find the sum of all the elements in each row of the number triangle above. What sequence of numbers is generated?

17. Form the "Fibonacci diagonals" of this "double vision" triangle and add the numbers in each diagonal. What sequence of numbers is generated?

The number triangle introduced at the beginning of this section is called a Lucas Triangle. If we reverse the order of the elements in each row, the triangle obtained is also a Lucas Triangle.

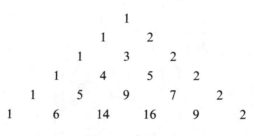

A Lucas Triangle

---

18. Extend the Lucas Triangle above for four more rows.

19. Form a "double vision" version of this Lucas Triangle.

20. Find the sum of all of the elements in each row of the resulting triangle. What sequence of numbers is formed?

The sequence $1, \frac{1}{2}, \frac{1}{3}, \frac{1}{4}, \cdots, \frac{1}{n}, \cdots$ is an example of a harmonic progression. In music, strings whose lengths are proportional to these numbers produce harmonic tones. We will use these numbers to form a Harmonic Triangle. This triangle was first studied by Gottfried Leibniz, a German mathematician, of the 17th and 18th centuries. To form this triangle let's start with Pascal's Triangle and form the reciprocals of all the entries.

$$
\frac{1}{1}
$$

$$
\frac{1}{1} \qquad \frac{1}{1}
$$

$$
\frac{1}{1} \qquad \frac{1}{2} \qquad \frac{1}{1}
$$

$$
\frac{1}{1} \qquad \frac{1}{3} \qquad \frac{1}{3} \qquad \frac{1}{1}
$$

$$
\frac{1}{1} \qquad \frac{1}{4} \qquad \frac{1}{6} \qquad \frac{1}{4} \qquad \frac{1}{1}
$$

Next we multiply each fraction in each row of fractions by successive terms of the harmonic progression $1, \frac{1}{2}, \frac{1}{3}, \frac{1}{4}, \cdots$

$$
\boxed{1} \cdot \frac{1}{1}
$$

$$
\boxed{\frac{1}{2}} \cdot \frac{1}{1} \qquad \boxed{\frac{1}{2}} \cdot \frac{1}{1}
$$

$$
\boxed{\frac{1}{3}} \cdot \frac{1}{1} \qquad \boxed{\frac{1}{3}} \cdot \frac{1}{2} \qquad \boxed{\frac{1}{3}} \cdot \frac{1}{1}
$$

$$
\boxed{\frac{1}{4}} \cdot \frac{1}{1} \qquad \boxed{\frac{1}{4}} \cdot \frac{1}{3} \qquad \boxed{\frac{1}{4}} \cdot \frac{1}{3} \qquad \boxed{\frac{1}{4}} \cdot \frac{1}{1}
$$

$$
\boxed{\frac{1}{5}} \cdot \frac{1}{1} \qquad \boxed{\frac{1}{5}} \cdot \frac{1}{4} \qquad \boxed{\frac{1}{5}} \cdot \frac{1}{6} \qquad \boxed{\frac{1}{5}} \cdot \frac{1}{4} \qquad \boxed{\frac{1}{5}} \cdot \frac{1}{1}
$$

or, equivalently,

$$
\frac{1}{1}
$$

$$
\frac{1}{2} \qquad \frac{1}{2}
$$

$$
\frac{1}{3} \qquad \frac{1}{6} \qquad \frac{1}{3}
$$

$$
\frac{1}{4} \qquad \frac{1}{12} \qquad \frac{1}{12} \qquad \frac{1}{4}
$$

$$
\frac{1}{5} \qquad \frac{1}{20} \qquad \frac{1}{30} \qquad \frac{1}{20} \qquad \frac{1}{5}
$$

Leibniz's Harmonic Triangle

21. Extend Leibniz's Harmonic Triangle to include four more rows.

22. Examine the entries in the rows of the Harmonic Triangle and try to find a rule, similar to Pascal's Rule, that would be valid for this triangle.

2.9 ODD (AND EVEN) NUMBER PATTERNS

There are two kinds of whole numbers: even numbers and odd numbers. The numbers

$0, 2, 4, 6, 8, 10, 12, 14, \ldots$

are even whole numbers and the numbers

$1, 3, 5, 7, 9, 11, 13, 15, \ldots$

are odd whole numbers.

Notice that the sum of two even numbers is an even number. The sum of two odd numbers is also an even number. For example,

$4 + 8 = 12$ $7 + 9 = 16$
even + even = even   odd + odd = even

What is the sum of an even number and an odd number?

If we let E stand for "even" and D stand for "odd," we can summarize the above statements as follows:

Rules for adding odds and evens

$E + E = E$
$D + D = E$
$E + D = D$ There are four possibilities.
$D + E = D$

Determine whether the following sums are odd or even. If the sum is even, write the letter E; if the sum is odd, write the letter D.

1. $28 + 34$ **2.** $56 + 35$

3. $15 + 25$ **4.** $21 + 45$

5. $2001 + 3001$ **6.** $99 + 76$

Suppose we translate the rules for adding odd and even numbers into a geometric pattern. The pattern will be an arrangement of small hexagons. A hexagon with a dark region will represent an odd number and a hexagon with a light region will represent an even number.

⬡ ⟷ Odd   ⬡ ⟷ Even

To form the pattern we do the following: If two "evens" occur in a row, we enter their sum (also even) beneath and centered between the first two.

Two "evens" in a row
Sum (also even)

For two "odds" in a row, we have

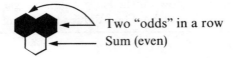

Two "odds" in a row
Sum (even)

and for cases where we have one "even" and one "odd" in a row, we have

Even —→ ← Odd
Sum (odd)

Odd —→ ← Even
Sum (odd)

Study Pascal's Triangle and notice the positions of the even numbers and the odd numbers. Let's write the first few rows of Pascal's Triangle by replacing odd numbers with the letter *D* and replacing even numbers with the letter *E*.

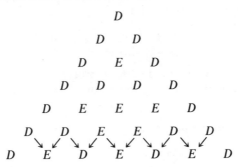

```
              D
            D   D
          D   E   D
        D   D   D   D
      D   E   E   E   D
    D   D   E   E   D   D
  D   E   D   E   D   E   D
```

---

7. Do you see the pattern that is developed using the four rules for adding odds and evens? Fill in the next five rows of the above triangle with the appropriate letters, either *D* or *E*.

If you know the pattern of "odds" and "evens," you don't have to know the numbers in Pascal's Triangle to determine if they are odd or even.

Suppose we reconstruct Pascal's Triangle, replacing each number with a hexagon as shown below.

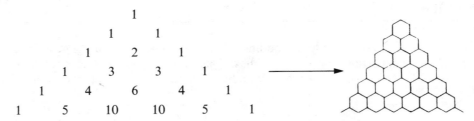

```
              1
           1     1
        1     2     1
     1     3     3     1
   1    4     6     4    1
 1    5    10    10    5    1
```

If the hexagons represent odd numbers, fill them; otherwise leave them blank or use a different color. Notice the odd and even patterns in the diagram that is formed.

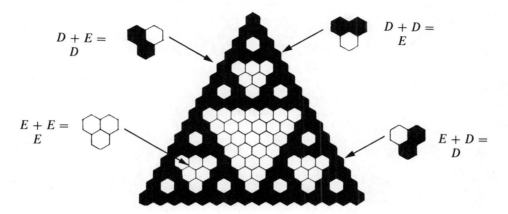

$D + E = \atop D$ $D + D = \atop E$

$E + E = \atop E$ $E + D = \atop D$

Once you know the pattern the rest is easy to complete.

---

8. Complete the pattern on page 98.

You can form different patterns, just as striking, if instead of working with odd and even numbers (sequences of every second number), you work with sequences of every third number. Every whole number is either a multiple of three, or one more than a multiple of three, or one less than a multiple of three. The numbers

0, 3, 6, 9, 12, 15, 18, 21, . . .

are multiples of three. The numbers

1, 4, 7, 10, 13, 16, 19, 22, . . .

are each one more than a multiple of three. The numbers

2, 5, 8, 11, 14, 17, 20, 23, . . .

are each one less than a multiple of three.

In the case of multiples of three you could color all the hexagons that represent multiples of three in Pascal's Triangle and leave all the others blank or a different color. This procedure forms a very interesting pattern. You can follow the same procedure for multiples of other numbers.

---

9. Complete a pattern for multiples of three. Use the chart on page 99.

10. Complete a pattern for multiples of five. Use the chart on page 100.

11. Complete a pattern of your own choice. Using different colors in the chart on page 101.

Use this chart for exercise 8, page 97.

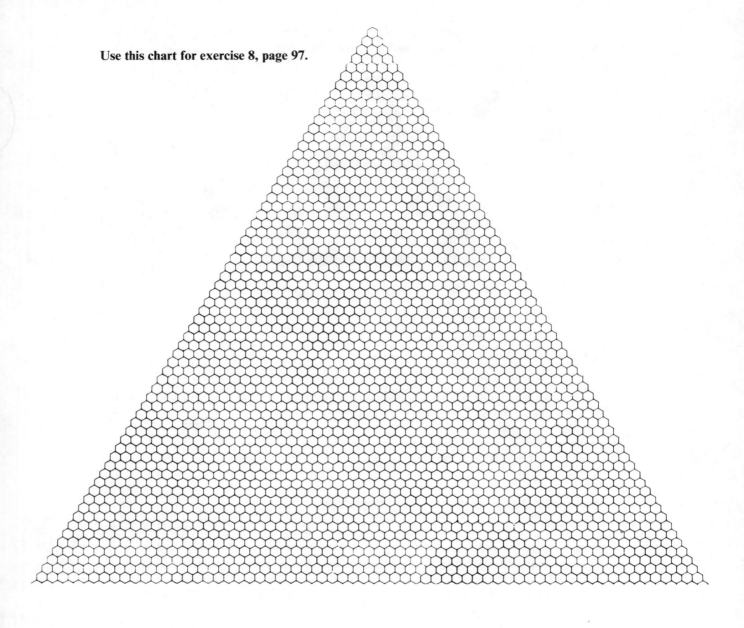

Use this chart for exercise 9, page 97.

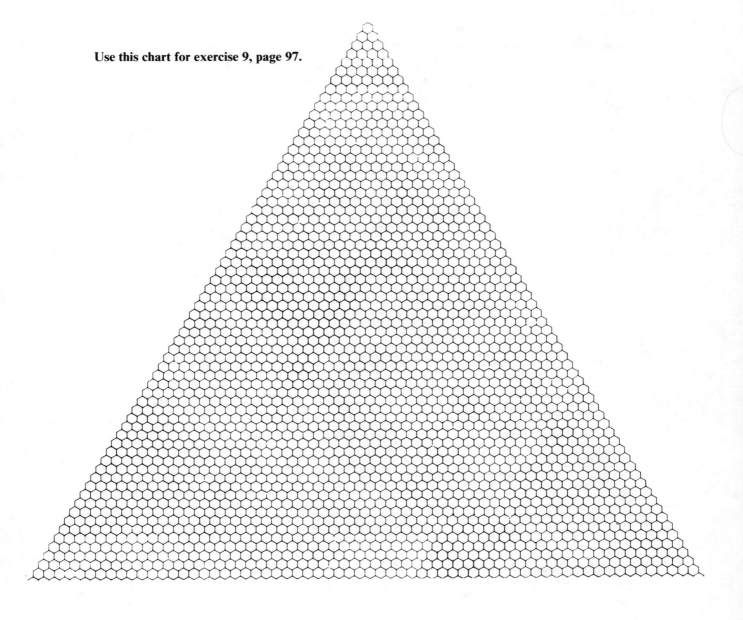

Use this chart for exercise 10, page 97.

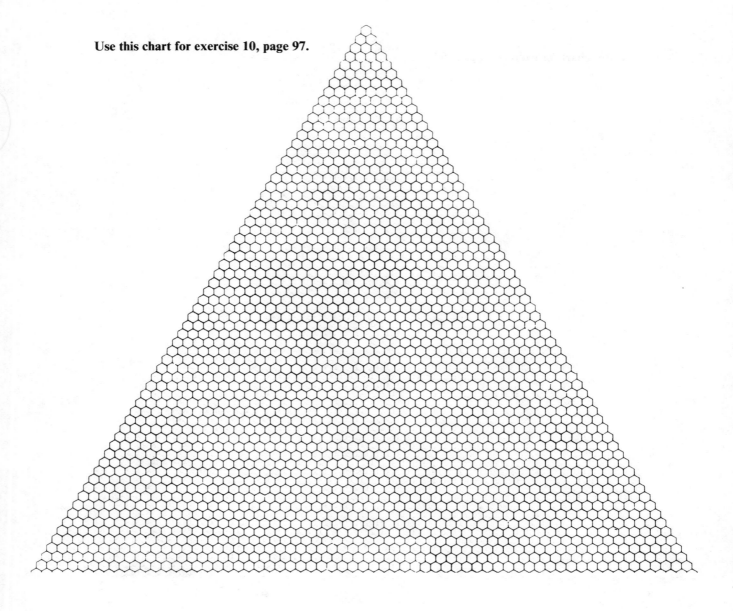

Use this chart for exercise 11, page 97.

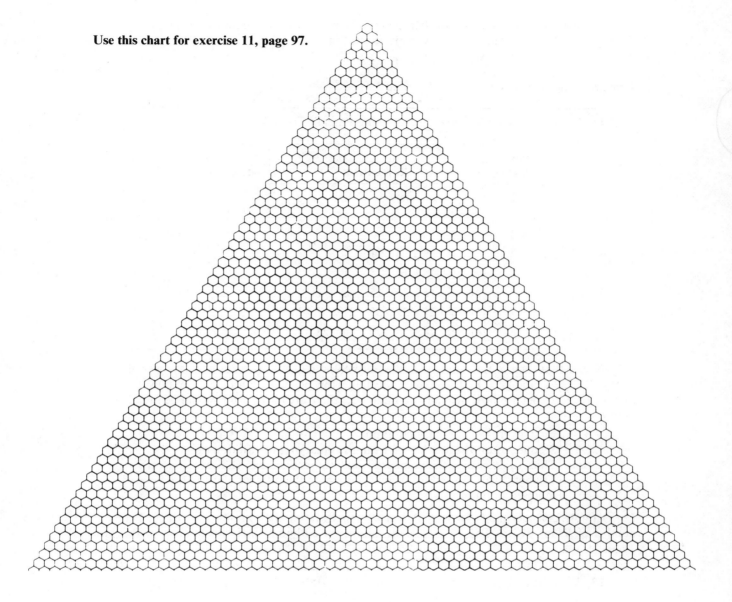

There is an interesting rule for determining the number of odd number entries in any given row of Pascal's Triangle. For example, in the 5th row

| 1 | 5 | 10 | 10 | 5 | 1 |

there are 4 odd numbers, namely, 1, 5, 5, and 1.

---

12. Complete the table below by examining Pascal's Triangle.

Row number	Row entries								Number of odd entries
1	1	1							2
2	1	2	1						2
3	1	3	3	1					4
4	1	4	6	4	1				2
5	1	5	10	10	5	1			4
6	1	6	15	20	15	6	1		4
7	1	7	21	35	35	21	7	1	8
8	1	8	28	56	70	56	28	8	2

Notice that each of the numbers in the third column in the table above is a power of 2: $2^1 = 2$, $2^2 = 4$, and $2^3 = 8$. If we extend this table, this property continues. The power of 2 that is needed to determine how many odd numbers there are in the nth row can be found as follows:

Rule {
First, express n in binary notation.
Second, count the number of 1's in the binary representation of n.
Thus, to determine the number of odd numbers in the nth row of Pascal's Triangle, two is raised to the power equal to the number of 1's in the binary representation of n.
}

For example, consider the 5th row of Pascal's Triangle. In binary notation $5 = 101_{two}$. The number of 1's in 101 is 2. Thus, $2^2 = 4$ is the number of odd numbers in the 5th row of Pascal's Triangle.

---

13. Find the number of odd numbers in the 9th, 10th, and 100th rows of Pascal's Triangle.

14. Complete the following table.

Row number	Binary representation	Number of 1's	Power of 2
1	1	1	$2^1 = 2$
2	10	1	$2^1 =$ ___
3	11	2	$2^2 =$ ___
4	100	1	$2^1 =$ ___
5	101	2	$2^2 =$ ___
6	110	2	$2^2 =$ ___
7	___	___	___ = ___
8	___	___	___ = ___

Compare the results of the last column with the table of exercise 12.

15. **(a)** How many numbers are there in the 5th row of Pascal's Triangle? How many of these are odd? How many are even?

    (b) Answer these questions for the 9th row.

    (c) Answer these questions for the 100th row.

16. What is the total number of odd numbers in the first 8 rows of Pascal's Triangle? What is the total number of even numbers in the first 8 rows?

Are there more odd numbers or more even numbers in Pascal's Triangle? To answer this question let's examine the first 4 rows of Pascal's Triangle. Notice that there is only one even number in the first 4 rows.

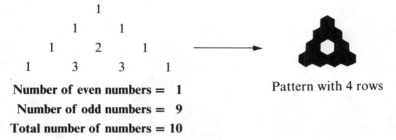

            1
          1   1
        1   2   1
      1   3   3   1

Number of even numbers = 1
Number of odd numbers = 9
Total number of numbers = 10

Pattern with 4 rows

Using the patterns we developed earlier in this section, we can devise a method for counting the odd and even numbers in Pascal's Triangle. The following pattern shows the first 8 rows of Pascal's Triangle. In this pattern there are 9 light regions in a total of 36 regions. Thus, there are 27 dark regions ($27 = 36 - 9$).

Pattern with 8 rows

Number of even numbers = 9
Number of odd numbers = 27
Total number of numbers = 36

The numbers 10 and 36 from the previous diagrams belong to a set of numbers called "triangular numbers." These numbers will be discussed in Chapter 3.

To determine the number of light and dark regions in the pattern consisting of 16 rows, we will make use of the counts for the pattern with 8 rows. The pattern with 16 rows consists of 3 sections that are exactly like the pattern with 8 rows except for an additional center section that is a triangular arrangement of light regions.

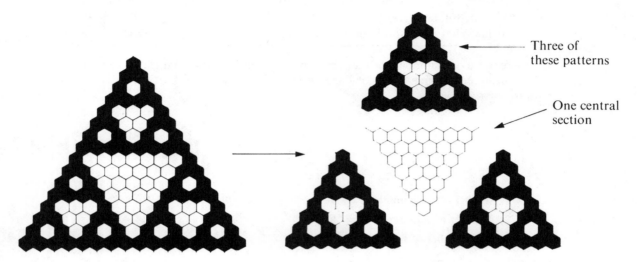

Three of these patterns

One central section

Pattern with 16 rows

To find the number of dark regions in the pattern with 16 rows, multiply the number of dark regions in the previous pattern with 8 rows by 3. This gives us 81 dark regions since $81 = 3 \cdot 27$.

There is a simple formula for finding the total number of regions in a triangular array, that is, for finding the value of a triangular number. The total number of regions is one-half the product of the number of rows and the number that is one more than the number of rows. In the case of 16 rows we have

$$\frac{1}{2} \cdot 16 \cdot 17 = 136$$

Thus, in the pattern with 16 rows there are 55 light regions since $55 = 136 - 81$.

Up through 16 rows the number of odd numbers in Pascal's Triangle exceeds the number of even numbers. In the next pattern let's consider 32 rows. Using the method we devised to count the number of dark and light regions in these patterns we find that the number of dark regions is 243 ($243 = 3 \cdot 81$, 81 is the number of dark regions in the pattern with 16 rows) and the total number of regions is given by $\frac{1}{2} \cdot 32 \cdot 33 = 528$.

17. Find the number of light regions in the pattern with 32 rows. Enter this number in the chart on the next page.

Find the number of dark regions, total number of regions, and number of light regions in the pattern with 64 rows. Do the same for the pattern with 128 rows and the pattern with 256 rows. Enter these numbers on the appropriate charts that follow.

Examine the charts and the numbers and predict whether there are more odd or even numbers in Pascal's Triangle.

18. Examine the charts beginning on page 105 to determine the answers to the following questions.

(a) Which rows consist of odd numbers only? Refer to the top row as the 0th row, the next row as row 1, then row 2 and so on.

(b) Which rows consist of only even numbers except for the first and last entries?

(c) Which rows alternate odd-even?

(d) After a certain point there are more even numbers in Pascal's Triangle than odd numbers. At which row does the number of even numbers exceed the number of odd numbers?

---

4 rows

$$E = 1$$
$$\underline{D = 9}$$
$$T = 10$$

8 rows

$$E = 9$$
$$\underline{D = 27}$$
$$T = 36$$

16 rows

$$E = 55$$
$$\underline{D = 81}$$
$$T = 136$$

32 rows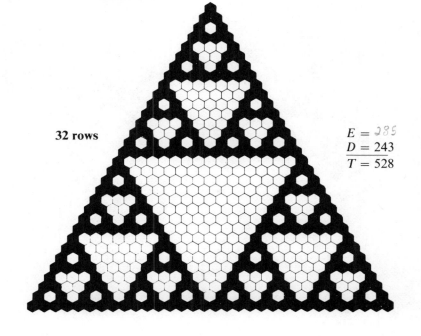

$$E = 285$$
$$\underline{D = 243}$$
$$T = 528$$

64 rows

$E =$

$D =$
$\overline{}$
$T =$

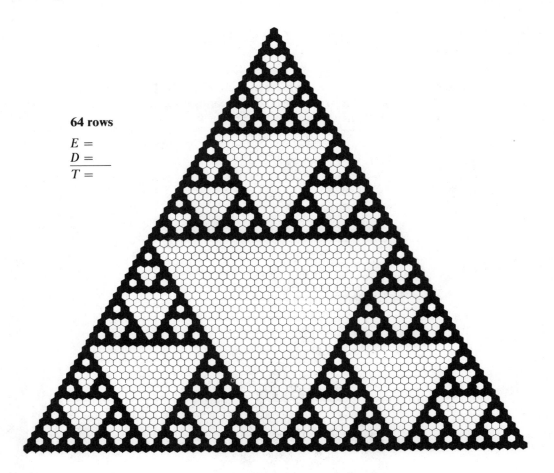

128 rows

$E =$
$D = \overline{}$
$T =$

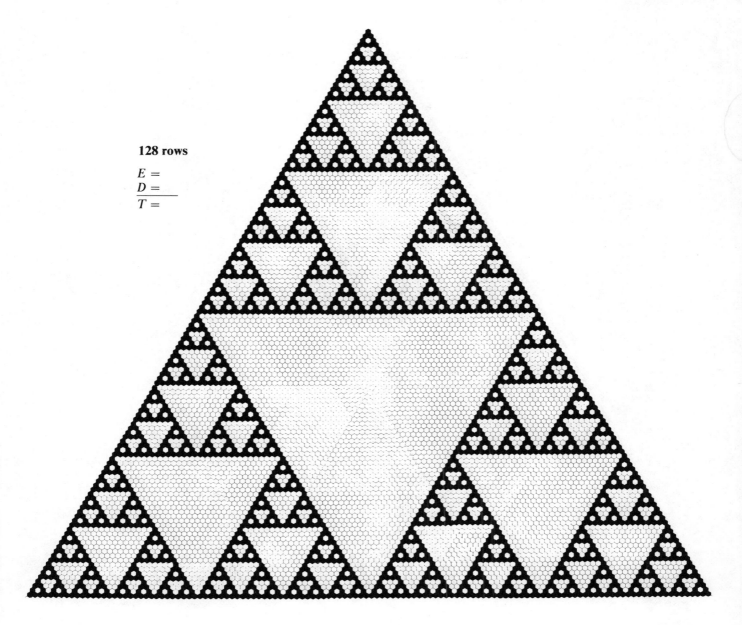

256 rows

$$E =$$
$$D = \overline{}$$
$$T =$$

2.10 A PERFECT/PRIME NUMBER RELATIONSHIP

A whole number greater than one is called a **prime number** if it has no other divisors (without remainders) except itself and the number one, which divides every whole number. If a given whole number has divisors other than itself and one, it is called a **composite** number. The number 7 is a prime number since its only divisors are itself and one. The number 6 is a composite number since it has divisors of 2 and 3 as well as itself and one. The first few prime numbers are

$$2, 3, 5, 7, 11, 13, 17, 19, 23, 29, 31, 37, 41, 43, 47, \ldots$$

The list of prime numbers is infinite and is truly one of the most interesting sets of numbers in mathematics. Much has been written about prime numbers and their relationships with other sets of numbers. Many unanswered questions concerning prime numbers have arisen throughout history. Questions posed by early mathematicians were not answered until centuries later by others taking up the study. Sometimes, earlier results were subsequently proven to be wrong. One of the most fascinating aspects of these numbers is the large number of simply-stated questions that have remained unsolved to this day.

Let's look at one of the interesting relationships involving prime numbers: the connection between prime numbers and Pascal's Triangle. Examine the 5th row of Pascal's Triangle.

$$1 \quad 5 \quad 10 \quad 10 \quad 5 \quad 1$$

Notice that 5 is a prime number and, with the exception of the 1's, the numbers in the fifth row are divisible by 5. This divisibility property is true of every nth row if n is a prime number. This property can be easily verified for the 2nd and 3rd rows.

$$1 \quad 2 \quad 1$$
$$1 \quad 3 \quad 3 \quad 1$$

---

1. Except for the 1's, verify that the numbers of the 7th row are divisible by 7.

2. Verify this divisibility property for the 11th and 13th rows of Pascal's Triangle.

It is a fundamental property of arithmetic that every composite number can be expressed as a product of prime numbers in essentially one unique way. For example,

$$60 = 2 \cdot 2 \cdot 3 \cdot 5 = 2^2 \cdot 3 \cdot 5$$

Some composite numbers are known as **perfect numbers**. A perfect number is a composite number that is equal to the sum of all its divisors, excluding itself. The smallest perfect number is 6. Note that $6 = 1 + 2 + 3$. The next perfect number is 28. Note that $28 = 1 + 2 + 4 + 7 + 14$. The next three perfect numbers are 496, 8128, and 33,550,336. There are only five perfect numbers up to and including 33,550,336. It is not known if there is a largest perfect number or if the list is infinite. Perfect numbers larger than 33,550,336, however, are known to exist. Every known perfect number is even and it is not known if there are any that are odd. In fact, every known perfect number ends in 6 or 28.

The perfect number 496 is equal to the product of 16 and 31. By doubling one factor and halving the other we have

$$496 = 16 \cdot 31$$
$$= 8 \cdot 62$$
$$= 4 \cdot 124$$
$$= 2 \cdot 248$$
$$= 1 \cdot 496$$

Thus, all the divisors of 496, not including 496 itself, are: 1, 2, 4, 8, 16, 31, 62, 124, and 248.

---

3. Show that the sum of all the divisors of 496, not including 496, is equal to 496.

$$1 + 2 + 4 + 8 + 16 + 31 + 62 + 124 + 248 = \underline{\hspace{1.5cm}}$$

A number such as 32, which is a power of 2, is near-perfect, since the sum of its divisors is just one less than itself. The divisors of 32 are 1, 2, 4, 8, and 16, not including 32. The sum is

$$1 + 2 + 4 + 8 + 16 = 31$$

Notice that all the divisors are themselves powers of 2. It is always true that the divisors of a power of 2 are also powers of 2. It is also true that the sum of those divisors is always 1 less than the given power of 2.

---

4. Find all the divisors of 2^6 and show that their sum is $2^6 - 1$.

Perfect numbers appear in Pascal's Triangle in two interesting ways. The perfect number 6 is the sum of the 1st and 2nd rows of Pascal's Triangle.

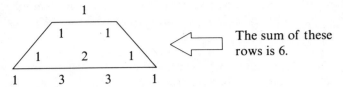

The sum of these rows is 6.

The perfect number 28 is the sum of the 2nd, 3rd, and 4th rows.

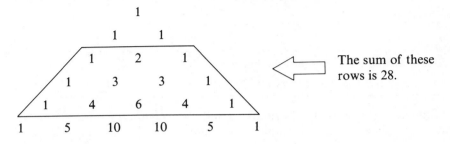

The sum of these rows is 28.

5. Find the next series of consecutive rows of Pascal's Triangle that add up to the 3rd perfect number, 496. (Hint: You do not have to explore beyond the 8th row.)

```
                    1
                  1   1
                1   2   1
              1   3   3   1
            1   4   6   4   1
          1   5  10  10   5   1
        1   6  15  20  15   6   1
      1   7  21  35  35  21   7   1
    1   8  28  56  70  56  28   8   1
```

The sum of the numbers in a row of Pascal's Triangle is always a power of 2. In fact, the sum of the numbers in the nth row is 2^n. Euclid, the Greek geometer of about 2300 years ago, proved that every number of the form $2^{n-1} \cdot (2^n - 1)$ is a perfect number if $(2^n - 1)$ is a prime number. Thus, you can see why there is a close relationship of perfect numbers to Pascal's Triangle. To test Euclid's formula let $n = 3$.

$$2^n - 1 = 2^3 - 1 = 8 - 1 = 7 \text{ (a prime number)}$$

The corresponding perfect number is

$$2^{3-1} \cdot (7) = 2^2 \cdot 7 = 4 \cdot 7 = 28$$

6. Find the other values of n less than 10 for which $2^n - 1$ is prime. Then find their corresponding perfect numbers.

Primes of the form $2^n - 1$ are known as **Mersenne primes**.

7. Verify that $2^{13} - 1$ is a Mersenne prime and show that $2^{13-1} \cdot (2^{13} - 1)$ is equal to 33,550,336, the 5th perfect number. (You will want to use a calculator.)

As a final look at perfect numbers, let's examine the odd-even patterns of the previous section. The "triangles" in the center of this pattern have an interesting number of entries. Look at the triangular patterns in the center of the Pascal's Triangle shown below. The first has 1 entry, the second has 6 entries, the third has 28 entries, and the fourth has 120 entries. Note that 6 and 28 are perfect numbers.

---

8. Verify that the fifth triangular region has 496 entries (the third perfect number).

Pascal's Triangle with the odd number entries filled

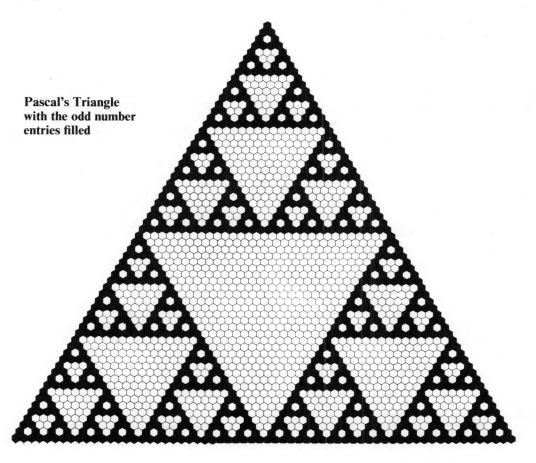

The number 120 is of the form $2^{n-1} \cdot (2^n - 1)$, the same form as all of the known perfect numbers. However, the quantity $(2^n - 1)$ is not prime. The value of n used to get 120 is 4.

$$2^{n-1} \cdot (2^n - 1) = 2^{4-1} \cdot (2^4 - 1)$$
$$= 2^3 \cdot (2^4 - 1)$$
$$= 8 \cdot (16 - 1)$$
$$= 8 \cdot 15$$
$$= 120$$

Since $120 = 8 \cdot 15$, we also have

$$120 = 8 \cdot 15$$
$$= 4 \cdot 30$$
$$= 2 \cdot 60$$
$$= 1 \cdot 120$$

by simply doubling one factor and halving the other. Furthermore, the sum of these factors (divisors) is 120.

$$1 + 2 + 4 + 8 + 15 + 30 + 60 = 120$$

Thus, the number 120 is similar to a perfect number. The difference is that the above list of divisors is not complete. The number 120 also has divisors of 3, 5, and certain multiples of 3 and 5.

---

9. Find all the divisors of 120. Find the sum of all the divisors of 120, not including 120. What relationship does this sum have with 120?

Perfect and quasi-perfect numbers in Pascal's Triangle

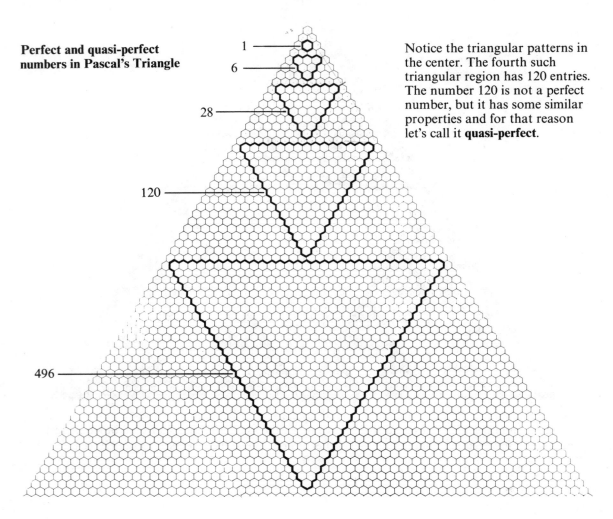

Notice the triangular patterns in the center. The fourth such triangular region has 120 entries. The number 120 is not a perfect number, but it has some similar properties and for that reason let's call it **quasi-perfect**.

The prime factored form of 120 is

$$120 = 2^3 \cdot 3 \cdot 5$$

If 120 were a perfect number, the sum of its divisors would be given by $2^{n-1} \cdot (2^n - 1)$, where $n = 4$. However, it can be shown that the sum of the divisors of 120 is given by

$$\textbf{Sum} = 2^{n-1} \cdot (2^n - 1) + 3 \cdot (2^n - 1) + 5 \cdot (2^n - 1)$$

$$120 = 2^{n-1} \cdot 3 \cdot 5 \qquad (n = 4)$$

where the underlined numbers are the prime factors of 120. The sum of the divisors of 120 is equal to 240 (2 · 120). Therefore, the number 120 is also known as **multiperfect** since the sum of its divisors is a multiple of itself.

---

10. Verify that the sum given in the formula above is 240 when $n = 4$.

Show that the sum is also given by $(2^n - 1) \cdot (2^{n-1} + 3 + 5)$.

In Pascal's Triangle the fifth triangular region in the center has 496 entries, a perfect number. The sixth triangular region in the center has 2016 entries. The number 2016 is **quasi-perfect** since it is of the form $2^{n-1} \cdot (2^n - 1)$ where $n = 6$.

---

11. Verify that $2016 = 2^{n-1} \cdot (2^n - 1)$ where $n = 6$. Also, verify that $2^n - 1$ is not a prime number.

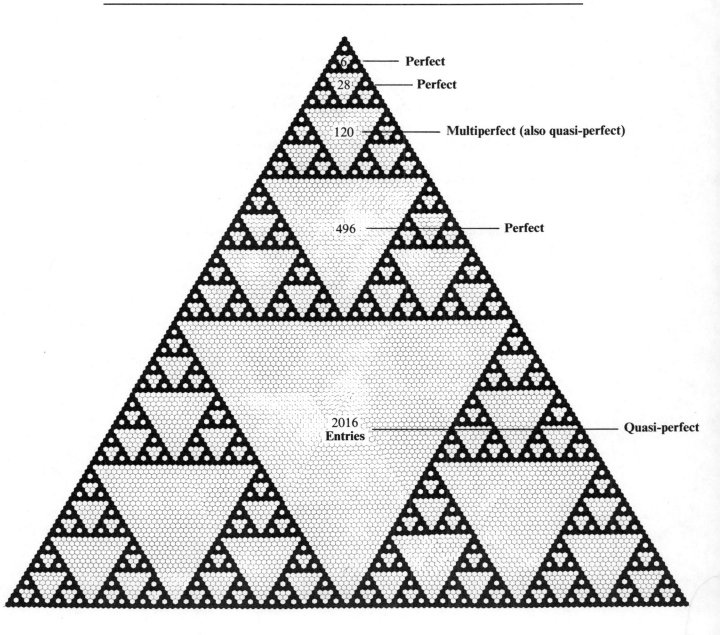

6 —— **Perfect**

28 —— **Perfect**

120 —— **Multiperfect (also quasi-perfect)**

496 —— **Perfect**

2016 Entries —— **Quasi-perfect**

Since $2016 = 32 \cdot 63$, we also have

$$
\begin{aligned}
2016 &= 32 \cdot \quad 63 \\
&= 16 \cdot \quad 126 \\
&= 8 \cdot \quad 252 \\
&= 4 \cdot \quad 504 \\
&= 2 \cdot 1008 \\
&= 1 \cdot 2016
\end{aligned}
$$

---

12. Find the sum of the divisors shown above:

$\quad 1 + 2 + 4 + 8 + 16 + 32 + 63 + 126 + 252 + 504 + 1008 = \underline{\quad\quad\quad}$

The prime factored form of 2016 is

$2016 = 2^5 \cdot 3^2 \cdot 7$

In this case, it can be shown that the sum of all the divisors of 2016 is given by

$$
\begin{aligned}
\textbf{Sum} &= 2^{n-1} \cdot (2^n - 1) + 3 \cdot (2^n - 1) + 3^2 \cdot (2^n - 1) + 7 \cdot (2^n - 1) + 3 \cdot 7 \cdot (2^n - 1) \\
&= (2^n - 1) \cdot (2^{n-1} + 3 + 3^2 + 7 + 3 \cdot 7) \qquad \text{(where } n = 6)
\end{aligned}
$$

Note: $2^n - 1$ is a common factor in the expression for **Sum**.

---

13. (a) Find the value of the sum given in the above formula.

  (b) Find all the divisors of 2016. What is their sum, excluding the number 2016 itself? Does this check with the first sum?

  (c) Is the sum a multiple of 2016?

Since the sum of all the divisors of 2016, not including 2016, is not a multiple of 2016, the number 2016 is not multiperfect, only quasi-perfect.

3 Figurate Numbers and Pascal's Triangle

3.1 TRIANGULAR NUMBERS

How many pins must a bowler knock down to get a strike? For those of you who are not bowlers the answer is ten. These ten pins are arranged in a triangular pattern as shown.

The number 10 is one of a group of numbers called "triangular numbers." Other triangular numbers are 1, 3, and 6.

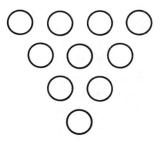

**1st Triangular
number = 1**

**2nd Triangular
number = 3**

**3rd Triangular
number = 6**

---

1. What is the next number in the sequence: 1, 3, 6, 10, _____?

If you answered fifteen to the preceding question, you are correct. Fifteen is the 5th triangular number. It is 5 more than the 4th triangular number.

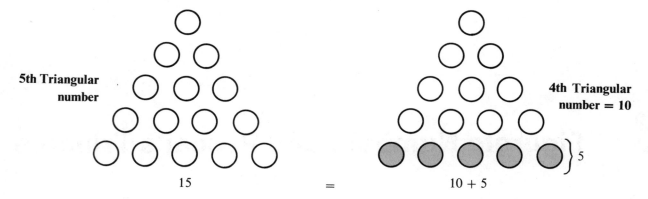

5th Triangular number

4th Triangular number = 10

15   =   10 + 5

In the previous diagram notice that

The 5th triangular number = The 4th triangular number + 5

---

2. Verify the following equations from the preceding diagrams.

The 2nd triangular number = The 1st triangular number + 2

The 3rd triangular number = The 2nd triangular number + 3

The 4th triangular number = The 3rd triangular number + 4

Complete the following equations.

The 6th triangular number   = The 5th triangular number   + _____

The 7th triangular number   = _____   + _____

The _____ triangular number = The 7th triangular number   + _____

The _____ triangular number = The _____ triangular number   + 10

The nth triangular number   = The $(n-1)$th triangular number + _____

Suppose T_1 represents the 1st triangular number, T_2 represents the 2nd triangular number, T_3 represents the 3rd triangular number, and so on to T_n, which represents the nth triangular number. The previous equations can be written as

$T_2 = T_1 + 2$

$T_3 = T_2 + 3$

$T_4 = T_3 + 4$

and so on.

The general statement would be

$T_n = T_{n-1} + n$ (for $n \geq 2$)

Note: If $n = 10$, then T_n represents the 10th triangular number and T_{n-1} represents the 9th triangular number.

3. Complete the following table.

$$T_1 = 1 = 1$$
$$T_2 = 1 + 2 = 3$$
$$T_3 = 3 + 3 = 6$$
$$T_4 = 6 + 4 = 10$$
$$T_5 = 10 + 5 = \underline{\quad}$$
$$T_6 = \underline{\quad} + 6 = \underline{\quad}$$
$$T_7 = \underline{\quad} + \underline{\quad} = \underline{\quad}$$
$$T_8 = \underline{\quad} + \underline{\quad} = \underline{\quad}$$
$$T_9 = \underline{\quad} + \underline{\quad} = \underline{\quad}$$
$$T_{10} = \underline{\quad} + \underline{\quad} = \underline{\quad}$$

4. Draw the triangular arrays for T_6, T_7, T_8, T_9, and T_{10}.

5. Examine Pascal's Triangle and try to find the triangular numbers. Circle the triangular numbers you find that line up in a row or column.

```
                        1
                     1     1
                  1     2     1
               1     3     3     1
            1     4     6     4     1
         1     5    10    10     5     1
      1     6    15    20    15     6     1
   1     7    21    35    35    21     7     1
1     8    28    56    70    56    28     8     1
1  9   36   84   126   126   84   36    9    1
```

6. If the 17th triangular number is 153, what is the 18th triangular number?

7. How many numbers are there in the first 2 rows of Pascal's Triangle? The first 3 rows? The first 4 rows? The first 5 rows? The first 18 rows?

The formula $T_n = T_{n-1} + n$ permits us to find the nth triangular number only if we know the $(n-1)$th triangular number, that is, the one just before the nth one. To find the 100th triangular number we would need to know the 99th triangular number. To find the 99th triangular number we would need to know the 98th triangular number, and so on until we found a triangular number whose value we know. Fortunately, there is another way to find the value of the nth triangular number that does not depend upon knowing the $(n-1)$th triangular number.

The 4th triangular number, 10, is equal to $1 + 2 + 3 + 4$. The 5th triangular number, 15, is equal to $1 + 2 + 3 + 4 + 5$. This can be easily seen in the following diagrams.

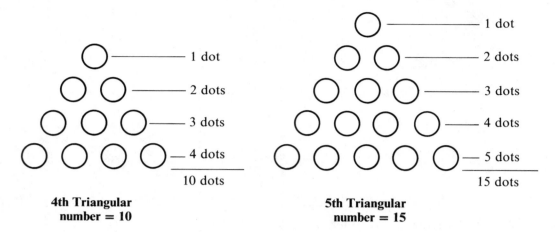

4th Triangular number = 10   **5th Triangular number = 15**

8. Complete the following table.

$$T_1 = 1 = 1$$
$$T_2 = 1 + 2 = 3$$
$$T_3 = 1 + 2 + 3 = 6$$
$$T_4 = 1 + 2 + 3 + 4 = \underline{\hspace{1cm}}$$
$$T_5 = 1 + 2 + 3 + 4 + 5 = \underline{\hspace{1cm}}$$
$$T_6 = 1 + 2 + 3 + 4 + 5 + 6 = \underline{\hspace{1cm}}$$
$$T_7 = \underline{\ } + \underline{\ } + \underline{\ } + \underline{\ } + \underline{\ } + \underline{\ } + \underline{\ } = \underline{\hspace{1cm}}$$
$$T_n = 1 + 2 + 3 + \cdots + \underline{\hspace{1cm}}$$

Recall from Chapter 2 the "hockey stick" property inherent in Pascal's Triangle. The numbers in the handle of the hockey stick add up to the number in the head of the stick.

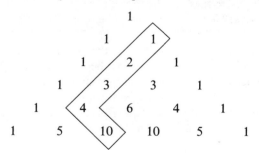

This illustrates the property that $T_n = 1 + 2 + 3 + \cdots + n$.

9. Draw the hockey stick that illustrates that the sum of the first 5 counting numbers is equal to the fifth triangular number.

$$
\begin{array}{ccccccccc}
 & & & & 1 & & & & \\
 & & & 1 & & 1 & & & \\
 & & 1 & & 2 & & 1 & & \\
 & 1 & & 3 & & 3 & & 1 & \\
1 & & 4 & & 6 & & 4 & & 1 \\
\end{array}
$$

$$
\begin{array}{ccccccccccc}
1 & & 5 & & 10 & & 10 & & 5 & & 1 \\
1 & & 6 & & 15 & & 20 & & 15 & & 6 & & 1 \\
\end{array}
$$

$1 + 2 + 3 + 4 + 5 = \underline{\hspace{2cm}}$

To develop a formula for T_n, let's begin with the 3rd triangular number and arrange the triangular array of dots into a new triangular form.

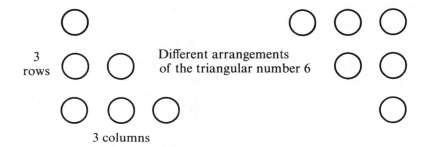

3 rows

Different arrangements of the triangular number 6

3 columns

Now put the two triangular forms together and form the rectangular array below.

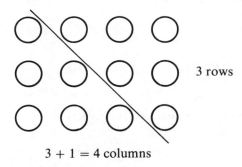

3 rows

$3 + 1 = 4$ columns

The rectangular array has $3 \cdot 4$ dots. Half of this total yields the value of the 3rd triangular number. Thus,

$$
T_3 = \frac{3 \cdot (3 + 1)}{2} = \frac{3 \cdot 4}{2} = \frac{12}{2} = 6
$$

---

10. Using a drawing similar to the one above verify that

$$T_4 = \frac{4 \cdot (4 + 1)}{2}$$

If two triangular arrays representing the triangular number T_n are put together to form a rectangular array, it will have n rows and $(n + 1)$ columns, for a total of $n(n + 1)$ dots. Half of this total yields the value of T_n. Thus,

$$T_n = \frac{n(n + 1)}{2}$$

This formula can be used to find any triangular number without knowing the previous triangular numbers. For instance, the 5th triangular number is given by

$$T_5 = \frac{5(5 + 1)}{2} = \frac{5 \cdot 6}{2} = \frac{30}{2} = 15$$

Furthermore, since $1 + 2 + 3 + \cdots + n = T_n$, it follows that

$$1 + 2 + 3 + \cdots + n = \frac{n(n + 1)}{2}$$

For example, $1 + 2 + 3 + 4 + 5 = \dfrac{5(5 + 1)}{2}$

$$= \frac{5 \cdot 6}{2}$$

$$= 15$$

---

11. Use the formula $T_n = \dfrac{n(n + 1)}{2}$ to find

$$T_{10} = \underline{\hspace{1cm}}$$
$$T_{100} = \underline{\hspace{1cm}}$$

Find the sum of the numbers 1 through 10.

$$1 + 2 + 3 + 4 + 5 + 6 + 7 + 8 + 9 + 10 = \underline{\hspace{1cm}}$$

Find the sum of the numbers 1 through 100.

$$1 + 2 + 3 + \cdots + 100 = \underline{\hspace{1cm}}$$

The problem of finding the sum of the numbers from one to 100 was solved by the great mathematician Karl F. Gauss while he was still a schoolboy. It is thought that Gauss deductively arrived at his answer in a matter of minutes by pairing the numbers in the following way.

$$1 + 2 + 3 + \cdots + 98 + 99 + 100$$

```
1 + 2 + 3 + ... + 98 + 99 + 100
↑   ↑   ↑           ↑    ↑    ↑
│   │   └─ 101 ─────┘    │    │
│   └───── 101 ──────────┘    │
└───────── 101 ───────────────┘
```

Each pair gives a sum of 101. Probably Gauss reasoned there would be exactly 50 such pairs. Consequently, he multiplied 101 by 50. Since 50 is half of 100, the formula $\dfrac{100(100 + 1)}{2}$ is equivalent to $50 \cdot 101$.

12. Devise a method to find the sum of all the whole numbers from 51 to 100.

13. In each of the diagrams below, the number of unit squares is equal to a triangular number.

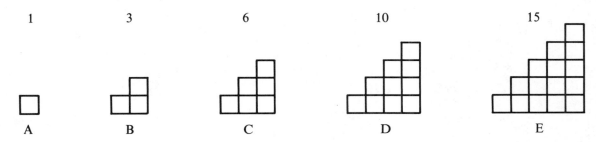

If we put two of each of the above diagrams together a rectangle is formed. Make a sketch of rectangle E and give its dimensions.

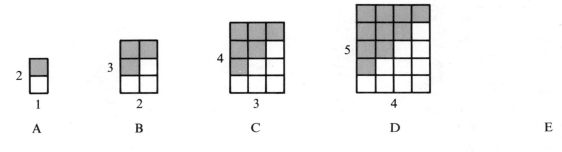

Complete the following table.

Rectangle	Base	Width	Area of rectangle	Number of unshaded squares	Number of unshaded squares by level	Formula
A	1	2	$1 \cdot 2$	$\dfrac{1 \cdot 2}{2}$	1	$\dfrac{1 \cdot 2}{2} = 1$
B	2	3	$2 \cdot 3$	$\dfrac{2 \cdot 3}{2}$	$1 + 2$	$\dfrac{2 \cdot 3}{2} = 1 + 2 = 3$
C	3	4	$3 \cdot 4$	$\dfrac{3 \cdot 4}{2}$	$1 + 2 + 3$	$\dfrac{3 \cdot 4}{2} = 1 + 2 + 3 = 6$
D						
E						

The famous French mathematician Pierre de Fermat (1601–65) stated that every positive whole number is either a triangular number or a sum of two or three triangular numbers. Thus, $9 = 6 + 3$, $17 = 10 + 6 + 1$ and so on.

14. Express each of these numbers as a sum of one, two, or three triangular numbers.

1 =	21 =
2 =	22 =
3 =	23 =
4 =	24 =
5 =	25 =
6 =	26 =
7 =	27 =
8 =	28 =
9 =	29 =
10 =	30 =
11 =	31 =
12 =	32 =
13 =	33 =
14 =	34 =
15 =	35 =
16 =	36 =
17 =	37 =
18 =	38 =
19 =	39 =
20 =	40 =

15. (a) Add the numbers encircled in Pascal's Triangle below. What sequence of numbers is generated?

```
                    1
              (1)      1
           (1    2)      1
         1   (3    3)      1
       1    4   (6    4)      1
     1    5   10  (10    5)      1
   1    6   15   20  (15    6)    1
```

(b) Multiply the numbers encircled in Pascal's Triangle below. What sequence of numbers is generated? Divide each product by two; what sequence is generated?

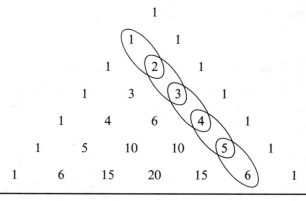

Select any odd number. For example, suppose you select 7. Now, express this number as the sum of two whole numbers that differ only by 1. Note that $7 = 3 + 4$. The product of each smaller number and 7 is a triangular number.

$7 \cdot 3 = 21 = T_6$
$7 \cdot 4 = 28 = T_7$

In general, there are always two consecutive triangular numbers that are multiples of some odd number.

---

16. (a) In the chart below, each row of numbers consists of the multiples of the odd numbers found at the beginning of each row. Circle all the triangular numbers in the chart. T_6 and T_7 have already been circled.

1	2	3	4	5	6	7	8	$\cdots$
3	6	9	12	15	18	21	24	$\cdots$
5	10	15	20	25	30	35	40	$\cdots$
7	14	(21)	(28)	35	42	49	56	$\cdots$
9	18	27	36	45	54	63	72	$\cdots$
11	22	33	44	55	66	77	88	$\cdots$
13	26	39	52	65	78	91	104	$\cdots$
15	30	45	60	75	90	105	120	$\cdots$
$\vdots$	$\vdots$	$\vdots$	$\vdots$	$\vdots$	$\vdots$	$\vdots$	$\vdots$	

(b) Express the odd number 17 as the sum of two numbers that differ by only 1. Multiply each of these numbers by 17 and verify that they are T_{16} and T_{17}.

(c) Add T_6 and T_7 and verify that their sum is equal to 7^2. Add T_{16} and T_{17} and verify that their sum is equal to 17^2. Pick any two consecutive triangular numbers and show that their sum is equal to a square.

Every whole number can be expressed as the difference of two triangular numbers. For example, the number 5 is the difference between the triangular numbers 10 and 15 or 1 and 6.

---

17. (a) Subtract the smaller number from the larger number in each of the circled groups below. What sequence of numbers is generated?

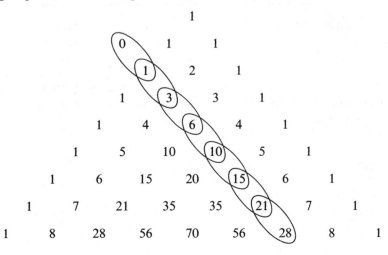

(b) Subtract the smaller number from the larger number in each of the circled groups below. What sequence of numbers is generated?

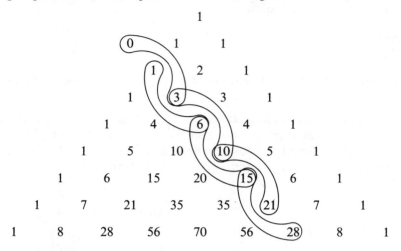

18. Subtract the smaller number from the larger number in each of the circled groups below. What sequence of numbers is generated?

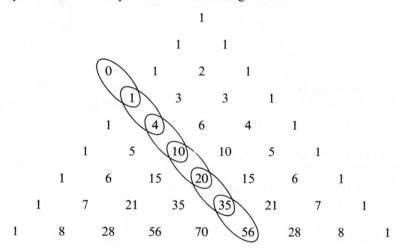

Every known perfect number (see Section 2.10) is a triangular number. However, not every triangular number is a perfect number. Perfect numbers are given by the formula

$$2^{n-1}(2^n - 1)$$

if the quantity $2^n - 1$ is prime. If we multiply this formula by 2 and then divide by 2 (not changing the overall value of the formula), we find the form for a triangular number.

$$\frac{2 \cdot 2^{n-1}(2^n - 1)}{2} = \frac{2^n(2^n - 1)}{2}$$

This is the triangular number given by $T_{2^n - 1}$.

19. Complete the chart below.

n	$2^n - 1$	Is $2^n - 1$ prime?	$T_{2^n - 1}$	Is $T_{2^n - 1}$ perfect?
1	$2^1 - 1 = 1$	No	$\dfrac{1(1+1)}{2} = 1$	No
2	$2^2 - 1 = 3$	Yes	$\dfrac{3(3+1)}{2} = 6$	Yes
3	$2^3 - 1 = $ _____	Yes	$\dfrac{7(7+1)}{2} = $ _____	Yes
4	$2^4 - 1 = $ _____			
5				

In arithmetic you learned that two fractions are equal if: The product of the numerator of the first fraction and the denominator of the second fraction is equal to the product of the denominator of the first fraction and the numerator of the second fraction. For example,

$$\frac{3}{8} = \frac{9}{24} \quad \text{because} \quad 3 \cdot 24 = 8 \cdot 9$$

Both products are equal to 72. Another way to express the same information is to say the difference of the two products is equal to zero. That is,

$$(3 \cdot 24) - (8 \cdot 9) = 0$$

This particular expression is called the **value of the determinant** of the numbers 3, 24, 8, and 9. The **determinant** of these numbers is written in the form of a square array as shown.

$$\begin{vmatrix} 3 & 9 \\ 8 & 24 \end{vmatrix}$$

The value of the 2 by 2 determinant above is given by the difference in the products of the numbers across each diagonal.

$$\begin{vmatrix} 3 & 9 \\ 8 & 24 \end{vmatrix} = (3 \cdot 24) - (8 \cdot 9) = 0$$

In general, the value of any 2 by 2 determinant is found in this way.

$$\begin{vmatrix} a & b \\ c & d \end{vmatrix} = ad - cb$$

Determinants are studied in algebra classes in both high school and college because they are useful in several applications including methods for solving systems of equations.

In this next exercise, we generate the triangular numbers by considering 2 by 2 determinants of certain groups of numbers in Pascal's Triangle.

The determinant of the group of numbers circled above is

$$\begin{vmatrix} 2 & 1 \\ 3 & 3 \end{vmatrix} = (2 \cdot 3) - (3 \cdot 1) = 3 = T_2$$

---

20. For each encircled group of numbers find the value of the determinant.

(a)

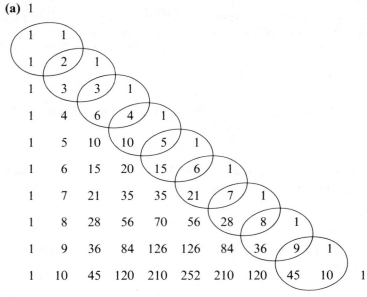

(b)

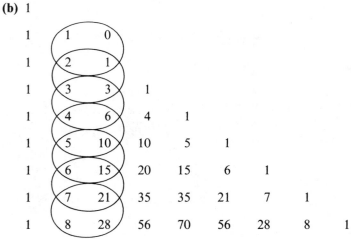

(c)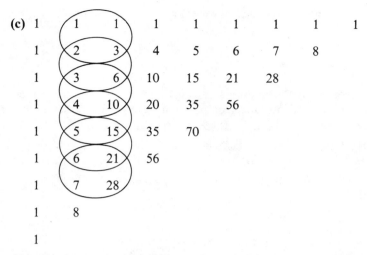

(d) In each of the three cases above what sequence of numbers was generated?

(e) The last case suggests that $nT_{n+1} - (n+1)T_n = T_n$. Verify this formula for $n = 1$, $n = 2$, and $n = 3$. This formula also suggests that $nT_{n+1} = (n+2)T_n$. Verify this formula for $n = 1$, $n = 2$, and $n = 3$.

21. Each of the determinants in the first of the foregoing exercises is of the form:

$$\begin{vmatrix} n & 1 \\ \dfrac{n(n+1)}{2} & n+1 \end{vmatrix}$$

Show that this determinant is equal to T_n.

In conclusion, we give a summary of properties and formulas involving triangular numbers. Some of these may seem complex but you will be asked to verify the formula only for a specific value. For example, an expression like T_{n^2} means to find the value of the triangular number whose subscript is equal to n^2. Thus, if $n = 3$, then $n^2 = 3^2 = 3 \cdot 3 = 9$ and $T_{n^2} = T_9$.

Then T_9 is evaluated by using the formula for any triangular number, $T_n = \dfrac{n(n+1)}{2}$. Thus,

$T_9 = \dfrac{9(9+1)}{2} = \dfrac{9(10)}{2} = 45$. Thus, $T_{n^2} = 45$ when $n = 3$.

To verify a formula means to find a value for each member of the formula and then check to see whether the members have the same value. For example, to verify the formula

$$T_{n^2}^2 - T_{n^2-1}^2 = n^6$$

for $n = 3$ means to find the value of $T_{n^2}^2 - T_{n^2-1}^2$ when $n = 3$ and the value of n^6 when $n = 3$ and see whether the two values are equal. In this case we have

$$
\begin{aligned}
T_{n^2}^2 - T_{n^2-1}^2 &= T_9^2 - T_8^2 & n^6 &= 3^6 \\
&= 45^2 - 36^2 & &= 3 \cdot 3 \cdot 3 \cdot 3 \cdot 3 \cdot 3 \\
&= 2025 - 1296 & &= 729 \quad \textbf{Right member}
\end{aligned}
$$

Left member $= 729$

Since both members of the formula equal 729, the formula is verified for $n = 3$.

---

22. (a) Find a pair of triangular numbers whose sum and difference are themselves triangular numbers. (Hint: One such pair can be found in the set of the first ten triangular numbers.)

(b) Find the values of T_{14} and T_{18}. Show that

$$T_{18} - T_{14} = T_{11}$$

and

$$T_{18} + T_{14} = T_{23}$$

(c) Find a pair of triangular numbers, each greater than 1, whose product is a triangular number. (Hint: One such pair can be found in the set of the first ten triangular numbers.)

(d) Verify that $T_3 + T_4 + 3 \cdot 4 = T_{3+4} = T_7$ and $T_3 + T_5 + 3 \cdot 5 = T_{3+5} = T_8$.

Pick your own two numbers, one for n and one for m, and verify the following formula.

$$T_n + T_m + m \cdot n = T_{n+m}$$

(e) After verifying the first three of the following formulas complete the next two formulas and verify each; then write a general formula based on this pattern.

$$
\begin{aligned}
T_3 &= 3 \cdot 2 \cdot T_1 \\
T_3 + T_6 &= 3 \cdot 3 \cdot T_2 \\
T_3 + T_6 + T_9 &= 3 \cdot 4 \cdot T_3 \\
T_3 + T_6 + T_9 + T_{12} &= \underline{\hspace{2cm}} \\
T_3 + T_6 + T_9 + T_{12} + T_{15} &= \underline{\hspace{2cm}} \\
&\;\;\vdots \\
T_3 + T_6 + T_9 + \cdots + T_{3n} &= \underline{\hspace{2cm}}
\end{aligned}
$$

(f) Verify that
$$
\begin{aligned}
T_6 &= 21 \\
T_{66} &= 2211 \\
T_{666} &= 222111
\end{aligned}
$$

Find T_{6666}.

(g) Every nth power of any number is a sum of n triangular numbers. For example,

$$
\begin{aligned}
3^4 &= 55 + 15 + 10 + 1 = 81 \\
2^5 &= 15 + 10 + 3 + 3 + 1 = 32
\end{aligned}
$$

Find 4 triangular numbers whose sum is 4^4.
Find 5 triangular numbers whose sum is 3^5.
Find 6 triangular numbers whose sum is 2^6.

(h) Verify the first three formulas below, complete the next two formulas and verify each; then write a general formula based on this pattern.

$$
\begin{aligned}
1^3 &= T_1^2 = 1^2 = 1 \\
1^3 + 2^3 &= T_2^2 = 3^2 = 9 \\
1^3 + 2^3 + 3^3 &= T_3^2 = 6^2 = 36 \\
1^3 + 2^3 + 3^3 + 4^3 &= T_4^2 = 10^2 = \underline{\hspace{1cm}} \\
1^3 + 2^3 + 3^3 + 4^3 + 5^3 &= \underline{\hspace{1cm}} = \underline{\hspace{1cm}} = \underline{\hspace{1cm}} \\
&\;\;\vdots \\
1^3 + 2^3 + 3^3 + \cdots + n^3 &= \underline{\hspace{1cm}}
\end{aligned}
$$

(i) Verify the following formulas.

n odd

$$1 = 1^2$$
$$1 + 3 + 6 = 1^2 + 3^2$$
$$1 + 3 + 6 + 10 + 15 = 1^2 + 3^2 + 5^2$$

n even

$$1 + 3 = 2^2$$
$$1 + 3 + 6 + 10 = 2^2 + 4^2$$
$$1 + 3 + 6 + 10 + 15 + 21 = 2^2 + 4^2 + 6^2$$

(j) Determine if $2T_n - 1$ is prime for $n \leq 9$.

(k) Verify that

$$(2 + 1)^3 + (2 + 2)^3 + (2 + 3)^3 + (2 + 4)^3 = (T_{2+4})^2 - T_2^2$$

Choose your own values for m and n and verify the following formula.

$$(n + 1)^3 + (n + 2)^3 + (n + 3)^3 + \cdots + (n + m)^3 = (T_{m+n})^2 - T_n^2$$

(l) Verify that

$$T_{T_5} - T_{T_4} = 4T_5 + 5$$

Note: $T_5 = 15$ and therefore, $T_{T_5} = T_{15} = \dfrac{15(15 + 1)}{2} = 120$

Choose your own value for n and verify the following formula.

$$T_{T_n} - T_{T_{n-1}} = (n - 1)T_n + n$$

(m) The sum of the averages of a number and its cube from 1 to n is the T_nth triangular number.

$$\frac{1 + 1^3}{2} + \frac{2 + 2^3}{2} + \frac{3 + 3^3}{2} + \frac{4 + 4^3}{2} = T_{T_4} = T_{10}$$

Verify the above formula. Choose your own value for n and verify the following.

$$\frac{1 + 1^3}{2} + \frac{2 + 2^3}{2} + \frac{3 + 3^3}{2} + \cdots + \frac{n + n^3}{2} = T_{T_n}$$

(n) Verify that

$$3T_4 + T_5 = T_9 \quad \text{and} \quad 3T_6 + T_7 = T_{13}$$

Choose your own value for n and verify the following formula.

$$3T_n + T_{n+1} = T_{2n+1}$$

The following diagram shows that

$$3T_n + T_{n-1} = T_{2n}$$

for $n = 4$. Draw a similar diagram for $n = 5$.

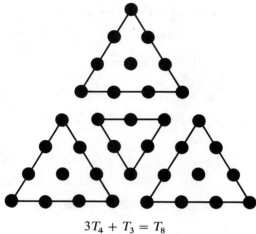

$$3T_4 + T_3 = T_8$$

(o) Verify that

$$T_4 + T_5 = 5^2 \quad \text{and} \quad T_6 + T_7 = 7^2$$

Choose your own value for n and verify the following formula.

$$T_{n-1} + T_n = n^2$$

(p) Verify that

$$T_{4^2} + T_{4^2-1} = 4^4$$

Choose your own value for n and verify the following formula.

$$T_{n^2} + T_{n^2-1} = n^4$$

(q) Verify that

$$T_n^2 + T_{n-1}^2 = T_{n^2}$$

for $n = 2$, $n = 3$, and $n = 4$. Choose your own value for n and verify the same formula.

(r) Verify that

$$T_n - T_{n-1} = n$$

for $n = 2$, $n = 3$, and $n = 4$. Choose your own value for n and verify the same formula.

(s) Verify that

$$T_n^2 - T_{n-1}^2 = n^3$$

for $n = 2$, $n = 3$, and $n = 4$. Choose your own value for n and verify the same formula.

(t) Verify that

$$T_{n^2} - T_{n^2-1} = n^2$$

for $n = 2$, $n = 3$, and $n = 4$. Choose your own value for n and verify the same formula.

(u) Verify that

$$T_4 \cdot T_3 = \frac{1}{2} T_{4^2-1}$$

Choose your own value for n and verify the following formula.

$$T_n \cdot T_{n-1} = \frac{1}{2} T_{n^2-1}$$

(v) Verify that

$$T_3 \cdot T_5 = 2T_{(T_4-1)} \qquad \text{Note: } T_{(T_4-1)} = T_{(10-1)} = T_9$$

Choose your own value for n and verify the following formula.

$$T_{n-1} \cdot T_{n+1} = 2 \cdot T_{(T_n-1)}$$

(w) Verify that

$$(T_{3^2}) \cdot (T_{3^2-1}) = \frac{1}{2} \cdot T_{3^4-1}$$

Choose your own value for n and verify the following formula.

$$(T_{n^2}) \cdot (T_{n^2-1}) = \frac{1}{2} \cdot T_{n^4-1}$$

(x) Verify that

$$T_{3^3}^2 - T_{3^3-1}^2 = 3^9$$

Choose your own value for n and verify the following formula.

$$T_{n^3}^2 - T_{n^3-1}^2 = n^9$$

(y) Verify that

$$T_{3^3}^2 + T_{3^3-1}^2 = T_{3^6}$$

Choose your own value for n and verify the following formula.

$$T_{n^3}^2 + T_{n^3-1}^2 = T_{n^6}$$

(z) Verify that

$$2(T_n + T_n^2) = n + n^2 + n^3 + T_{n^2}$$

for $n = 1$, $n = 2$, $n = 3$, and $n = 4$.

3.2 SQUARE NUMBERS

Any whole number multiplied by itself is a square number. For example, $3 \cdot 3 = 3^2 = 9$. The number 9 is the 3rd square number.

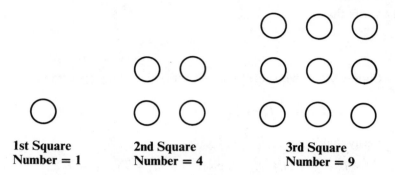

**1st Square
Number = 1**   **2nd Square
Number = 4**   **3rd Square
Number = 9**

Instead of using the dot diagrams, let's represent the square numbers as follows.

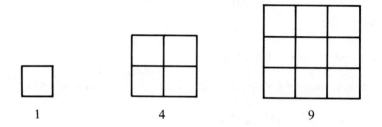

1   4   9

Notice that each square number can be represented as the sum of two consecutive triangular numbers. The next diagram shows how 4^2 is equal to $T_3 + T_4$.

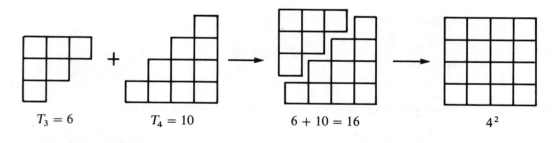

$T_3 = 6$ $T_4 = 10$ $6 + 10 = 16$ 4^2

1. Draw the diagram for 5^2. What pair of consecutive triangular numbers is used?

2. Add the pair of numbers in each encircled group in Pascal's Triangle below. What sequence of numbers results? What numbers have been circled?

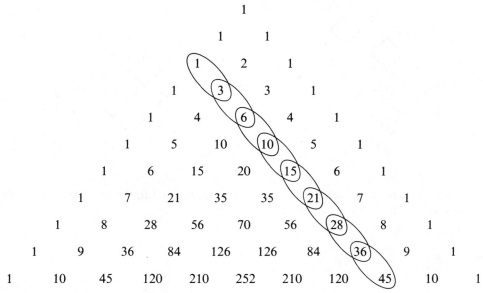

3. Complete the table below.

n	n^2	T_n	T_{n-1}	$n^2 = T_n + T_{n-1}$
1	$1^2 = 1$	$T_1 = 1$	$T_0 = 0$	$1 = 1 + 0$
2	$2^2 = 4$	$T_2 = 3$	$T_1 = 1$	$4 = 3 + 1$
3	$3^2 = 9$	$T_3 = 6$	$T_2 = 3$	$9 = 6 + 3$
4	$4^2 = $ _____	$T_4 = $ _____	$T_3 = $ _____	_____ $=$ _____
5				
6				
7				

4. Add the numbers in each group indicated in Pascal's Triangle below.

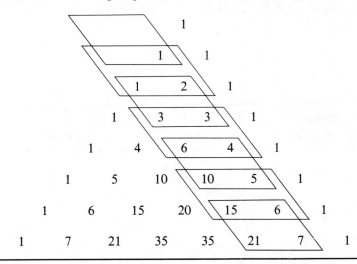

Another way of looking at the square number 4^2 is to keep the main diagonal and break away two equal triangular numbers.

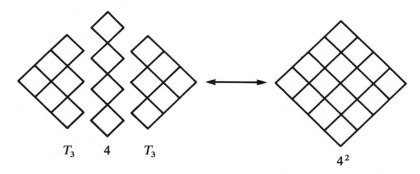

$$T_3 \qquad 4 \qquad T_3 \qquad\qquad\qquad 4^2$$

Notice that the number of square units on the diagonal is equal to the number of units on the side of the square. Thus, in the diagram above we have

$$2 \cdot T_3 + 4 = 4^2$$

In general, we have

$$2 \cdot T_{n-1} + n = n^2$$

In a slightly different way we can also discover a formula for the triangular number T_4. If we take one diagonal away from the sum $T_4 + T_4$, we get 4^2. See the following diagram.

$$T_4 \qquad T_4 \qquad\qquad T_3 \quad 4 \quad T_4 \qquad\qquad 4 \qquad 4^2$$

The diagram above shows that $2 \cdot T_4 = 4 + 4^2$, or equivalently,

$$2 \cdot T_4 - 4 = 4^2$$

In general,

$$2 \cdot T_n - n = n^2$$

---

5. Verify the formula $2T_n - n = n^2$ for $n = 1$, $n = 2$, and $n = 3$.
6. Verify the formula $2 \cdot T_{n-1} + n = n^2$ for $n = 2$, $n = 3$, and $n = 4$.

Another way of looking at 4^2 involves counting the number of unit squares along parallel vertical diagonals.

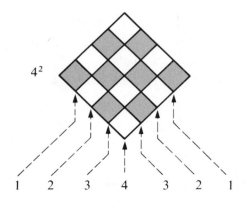

$$4^2$$

$$1 \quad 2 \quad 3 \quad 4 \quad 3 \quad 2 \quad 1$$

In the figure above notice that the total number of unit squares in the entire figure is equal to the sum of the number of unit squares in each of the parallel diagonals. That is

$$4^2 = 1 + 2 + 3 + 4 + 3 + 2 + 1$$

Also, $1 + 2 + 3 + 4 = T_4$ and $1 + 2 + 3 = 3 + 2 + 1 = T_3$ and therefore,

$$4^2 = (1 + 2 + 3 + 4) + (3 + 2 + 1)$$
$$= \qquad T_4 \qquad + \qquad T_3$$

This is the same formula we examined at the beginning of this section.

---

7. In the diagram below find the number of unit squares in each of the parallel diagonals. Then, complete the equation.

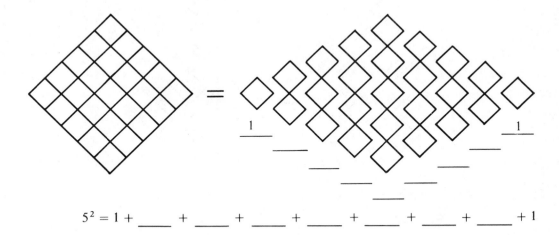

$$5^2 = 1 + \underline{\quad} + \underline{\quad} + \underline{\quad} + \underline{\quad} + \underline{\quad} + \underline{\quad} + \underline{\quad} + 1$$

8. Complete the following equations.

$$1 = 1^2$$
$$1 + 2 + 1 = 2^2$$
$$1 + 2 + 3 + 2 + 1 = 3^2$$
$$1 + 2 + 3 + 4 + 3 + 2 + 1 = \underline{\quad}$$
$$1 + 2 + 3 + 4 + 5 + 4 + 3 + 2 + 1 = \underline{\quad}$$
$$1 + 2 + 3 + 4 + 5 + 6 + 5 + 4 + 3 + 2 + 1 = \underline{\quad}$$

$$1 + 2 + 3 + \cdots + 7 + \cdots + 3 + 2 + 1 = \underline{\quad}$$
$$1 + 2 + 3 + \cdots + 10 + \cdots + 3 + 2 + 1 = \underline{\quad}$$
$$1 + 2 + 3 + \cdots + n + \cdots + 3 + 2 + 1 = \underline{\quad}$$

An interesting relationship between the square numbers and the odd numbers can also be explored with diagrams. The diagrams for the first four odd numbers are shown below.

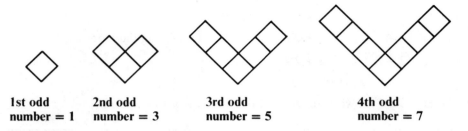

1st odd number = 1 **2nd odd number = 3** **3rd odd number = 5** **4th odd number = 7**

When these odd numbers are put together, a square is formed.

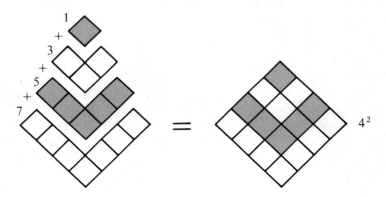

Thus, $1 + 3 + 5 + 7 = 4^2$.

9. Find the square number equal to each of the following sums.

$$
\begin{aligned}
1 &= 1 = 1^2 \\
1 + 3 &= \underline{} = 2^2 \\
1 + 3 + 5 &= \underline{} = 3^2 \\
1 + 3 + 5 + 7 &= \underline{} = \underline{} \\
1 + 3 + 5 + 7 + 9 &= \underline{} = \underline{} \\
1 + 3 + 5 + 7 + 9 + 11 &= \underline{} = \underline{} \\
1 + 3 + 5 + 7 + 9 + 11 + 13 &= \underline{} = \underline{} \\
1 + 3 + 5 + 7 + 9 + 11 + 13 + 15 &= \underline{} = \underline{}
\end{aligned}
$$

Extend the patterns above and find the sum of the first 10 odd numbers. What is the 10th odd number?

To form a sum equal to 10^2, we need to add the first 10 odd numbers. To form a sum equal to 11^2, we need to add the first 11 odd numbers, and so on. What is the 10th odd number? What is the 11th odd number? What is the 50th odd number? To answer these questions we can establish a correspondence between the counting numbers and the odd numbers.

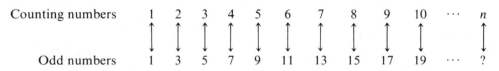

Counting numbers   1   2   3   4   5   6   7   8   9   10 $\cdots$ n

Odd numbers   1   3   5   7   9   11   13   15   17   19 $\cdots$?

Notice that the 10th odd number is 19 and 19 is 1 less than 20, which is twice 10. Similarly, the 7th odd number is 13 and 13 is 1 less than 14, which is twice 7. This pattern can be observed in each of the above circumstances. According to this rule, the 50th odd number is 1 less than twice 50 or $2 \cdot 50 - 1 = 100 - 1 = 99$. In general, the nth odd number is one less than twice n.

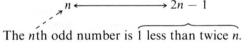

The nth odd number is 1 less than twice n.

10. (a) What is the 100th odd number?

    (b) What is the 75th odd number?

    (c) What is the nth odd number?

Note that the sum of the first n odd numbers is n^2. The nth odd number, the last one in the sum, is $2n - 1$. Thus, our general rule for the sum of the first n odd numbers is

$$1 + 3 + 5 + \cdots + (2n - 1) = n^2$$

The sum of the first 50 odd numbers is $50^2 = 2500$. The 50th odd number is $2 \cdot 50 - 1 = 100 - 1 = 99$. Thus, we can write

$$1 + 3 + 5 + \cdots + 99 = 2500$$

Suppose we want to compute the sum $1 + 3 + 5 + \cdots + 39$. To find this sum we need to know the position of 39 in the sequence of odd numbers. Thus, 39 is 1 less than 40, which is twice 20. Therefore, 39 is the 20th odd number. The sum of the odd numbers from 1 to 39 is $20^2 = 400$.

$$1 + 3 + 5 + \cdots + 39 = 20^2 = 400$$

11. Complete each of the following.

$$1 + 3 + 5 + 7 + 9 + 11 = \underline{\hspace{1cm}}$$
$$1 + 3 + 5 + 7 + 9 + 11 + \underline{\hspace{1cm}} = 7^2$$
$$1 + 3 + 5 + \cdots + 19 = \underline{\hspace{1cm}}$$
$$1 + 3 + 5 + \cdots + \underline{\hspace{1cm}} = 12^2$$
$$1 + 3 + 5 + \cdots + \underline{\hspace{1cm}} = 100^2$$
$$1 + 3 + 5 + \cdots + \underline{\hspace{1cm}} = 100$$

12. Find the differences between the consecutive squares.

$$2^2 - 1^2 =$$
$$3^2 - 2^2 =$$
$$4^2 - 3^2 =$$
$$5^2 - 4^2 =$$
$$6^2 - 5^2 =$$
$$7^2 - 6^2 =$$
$$8^2 - 7^2 =$$
$$9^2 - 8^2 =$$
$$10^2 - 9^2 =$$

13. Verify the formula

$$n^2 - (n - 1)^2 = 2n - 1$$

for $n = 2$, $n = 3$, $n = 4$, and $n = 5$.

14. Verify the formulas

$$(T_n + T_{n-1}) - (T_{n-1} + T_{n-2}) = 2n - 1$$

and

$$T_n - T_{n-2} = 2n - 1$$

for $n = 3$, $n = 4$, and $n = 5$, where T_n represents the nth triangular number.

In the previous section on triangular numbers we learned Fermat's statement that every positive whole number is either a triangular number or a sum of two or three triangular numbers. Fermat also stated that every positive whole number is either a square number or a sum of two, three, or four square numbers. Thus, $15 = 9 + 4 + 1 + 1$, $20 = 16 + 4$, and so on.

15. Express each of the following numbers as a sum of one, two, three, or four square numbers.

$1 =$	$11 =$
$2 =$	$12 =$
$3 =$	$13 =$
$4 =$	$14 =$
$5 =$	$15 =$
$6 =$	$16 =$
$7 =$	$17 =$
$8 =$	$18 =$
$9 =$	$19 =$
$10 =$	$20 =$

21 =	31 =
22 =	32 =
23 =	33 =
24 =	34 =
25 =	35 =
26 =	36 =
27 =	37 =
28 =	38 =
29 =	39 =
30 =	40 =

48 =

80 =

99 =

999 =

Suppose we divide a rectangle into two parts with a vertical line and then we divide those parts again with a horizontal line. Notice that the product of the areas of the parts corresponding to one pair of opposite corners is equal to the product of the parts corresponding to the other pair of opposite corners. Refer to the figure below.

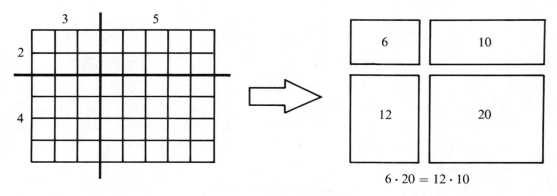

$$6 \cdot 20 = 12 \cdot 10$$

If the area of the original rectangle is an odd square, we find an interesting formula. Study the drawing of the odd square 25. It is divided by a vertical line and a horizontal line to form two consecutive square numbers in one pair of opposite corners. In the other pair of opposite corners, a set of four triangular numbers is formed.

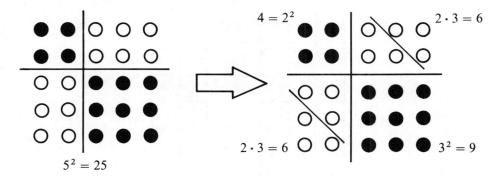

Furthermore, $4 \cdot 9 = 6 \cdot 6$, or, equivalently, $2^2 \cdot 3^2 = 2T_2 \cdot 2T_2$. More generally, if S_n represents the nth square number, that is, n^2, we have the formula

$$S_n \cdot S_{n+1} = 4 \cdot T_n^2$$

Note: If $n = 7$, then S_n represents the 7th square number, S_{n+1} represents the 8th square number, and T_n represents the 7th triangular number.

---

16. Draw the next odd square, 49, and verify the formula above for $n = 3$.
    Do the same for $n = 4$.

17. Complete the following table.

n	T_n	$8T_n + 1$	$(2n + 1)^2$
1	1	$8 \cdot 1 + 1 = 9$	$3^2 = 9$
2	3	$8 \cdot 3 + 1 = 25$	$5^2 = 25$
3	6	$8 \cdot 6 + 1 = 49$	$7^2 = 49$
4	10	$8 \cdot 10 + 1 = 81$	$9^2 = 81$
5	___	$8 \cdot$ ___ $+ 1 =$ ___	___$^2 =$ ___
6	___	___ $\cdot$ ___ $+$ ___ $=$ ___	___ $=$ ___
7			
8			
9			
10			

18. Verify the formula

$$8T_n + 1 = (2n + 1)^2$$

for $n = 11$.

19. In the following diagram, a certain square number is partitioned into 8 triangular numbers plus 1. What is the square number? What is the value of each of the triangular numbers? Write an equation showing the value of the square number.

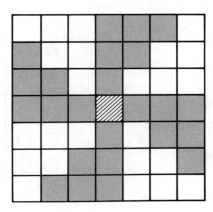

20. Verify the following formulas. Based on the pattern you observe, predict the next two formulas in the sequence.

$$9 + 1 = T_{3+1}$$
$$25 + 3 = T_{5+2}$$
$$49 + 6 = T_{7+3}$$
$$81 + 10 = T_{9+4}$$

Choose your own value for n (greater than 6) and verify the formula

$$(2n + 1)^2 + T_n = T_{2n+1+n}$$

21. Verify the following set of formulas for $n = 1$, $n = 2$, and $n = 3$. Extend the set of formulas to include a fifth formula.

$$9 \cdot T_n + 1 = T_{3n+1}$$
$$25 \cdot T_n + 3 = T_{5n+2}$$
$$49 \cdot T_n + 6 = T_{7n+3}$$
$$81 \cdot T_n + 10 = T_{9n+4}$$

22. Choose your own triangular number, T_x, and verify the following formula for $n = 1$, $n = 2$, and $n = 3$.

$$(2n + 1)^2 T_x + T_n = T_{(2n+1)x+n}$$

23. Add these two sequences together term by term. What sequence of numbers is generated?

	1	3	6	10	15	21	28	36	45	$\cdots$
+	1	3	6	10	15	21	28	36	45	55	$\cdots$

24. Subtract the smaller number from the larger number in each of the circled groups below. What sequence of numbers is generated?

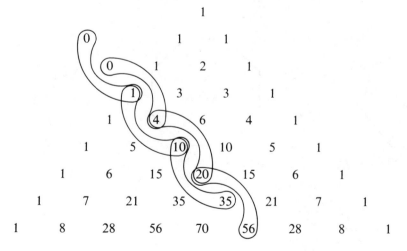

25. Verify the formula

$$T_{T_n} + T_{T_{n-1}} = \frac{1}{2}\left[T_{S_n} + S_n\right]$$

for $n = 2$, $n = 3$, and $n = 4$.

Note: If $n = 3$, then $T_{T_n} = T_{T_3} = T_6 = \frac{6 \cdot 7}{2} = 21$ and

$$T_{S_n} = T_{S_3} = T_9 = \frac{9 \cdot 10}{2} = 45.$$

3.3 PENTAGONAL NUMBERS, HEXAGONAL NUMBERS, AND OTHERS

In this section we take a brief look at some other polygonal numbers, such as the pentagonal, hexagonal, heptagonal, and octagonal numbers. These number forms were studied by the ancient Greeks. Diophantus of Alexandria wrote about many of their properties probably during the first century of our era. Pascal also wrote "Treatise of Figurate Numbers" published in 1665.

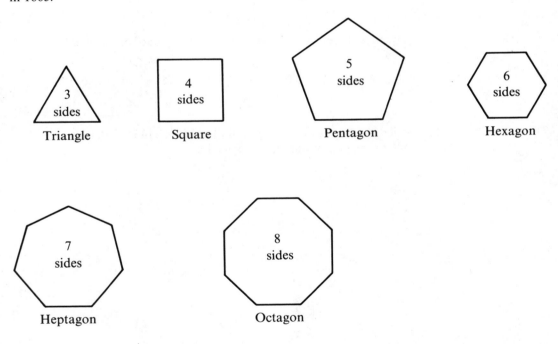

In the table below are the first four polygonal numbers of each kind.

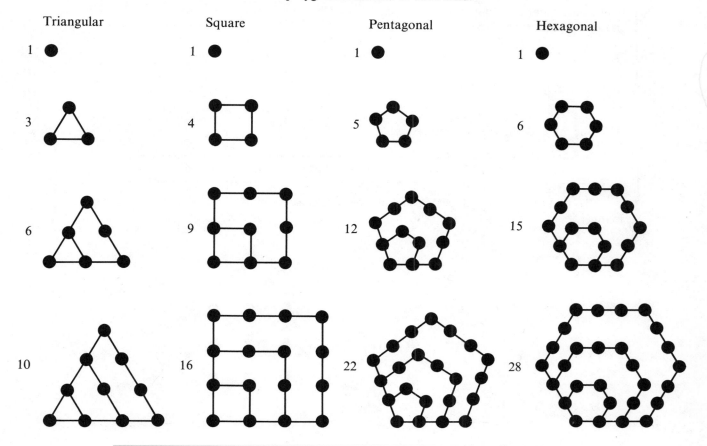

Triangular   Square   Pentagonal   Hexagonal

---

1. Study the chart for the first 4 pentagonal and hexagonal numbers. Try to predict the 5th pentagonal and the 5th hexagonal number. Draw a diagram of these numbers.

Examine the following chart showing the polygonal numbers.

n	Triangle	Square	Pentagon	Hexagon	Heptagon
1	1	1	1	1	____
2	3	4	5	6	____
3	6	9	12	15	____
4	10	16	22	28	____
5	____	____	____	____	____
6	____	____	____	____	____

Notice that the 1st row of numbers consists of 1's. The 2nd row consists of the counting numbers; each one is 1 more than the former. The 3rd row consists of the multiples of 3; each entry is 3 more than the former entry moving from left to right in that row.

---

2. Using the previous observations, enter the first 3 heptagonal numbers into the table.

In the 4th row of the table each entry is 6 more than the former entry. Therefore, the 4th heptagonal number is equal to 34. What about the 5th and 6th rows? We know the 5th and 6th triangular numbers are 15 and 21.

$$T_5 = \frac{5(5+1)}{2} = 15$$

$$T_6 = \frac{6(6+1)}{2} = 21$$

Also, the 5th and 6th square numbers are $5^2 = 25$ and $6^2 = 36$.

---

3. Enter the 5th and 6th triangular and square numbers into the preceding table.

To find the 5th and 6th pentagonal numbers suppose we build "houses" in the following manner.

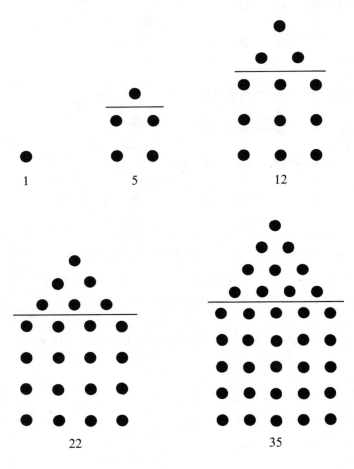

---

4. Draw the sixth "house."

Notice that each "house" is formed from a square and a triangle.

n	Pentagonal number	= Square	+	Triangle
1	1	= 1	+	0
2	5	= 4	+	1
3	12	= 9	+	3
4	22	= 16	+	6
5	35	= 25	+	10
6	51	= 36	+	15

In general, the nth pentagonal number, or P_n, can be found by using the formula

$$P_n = n^2 + T_{n-1}$$

or, equivalently,

$$P_n = S_n + T_{n-1}$$

Note: P_n represents the nth pentagonal number, S_n represents the nth square number, and T_{n-1} represents the $(n-1)$th triangular number.

---

5. Verify the formula

$$P_n = n^2 + T_{n-1}$$

for $n = 2$, $n = 3$, and $n = 4$.

Using this formula find P_7, P_8, P_9, and P_{10}.

In the previous section, we demonstrated that each square number can be represented as the sum of 2 consecutive triangular numbers.

$$n^2 = T_n + T_{n-1}$$

Substituting this in the formula for pentagonal numbers, we have

$$P_n = T_n + T_{n-1} + T_{n-1}$$
$$= T_n + 2 \cdot T_{n-1}$$

The fact that a pentagonal number can be represented in terms of triangular numbers can be seen geometrically.

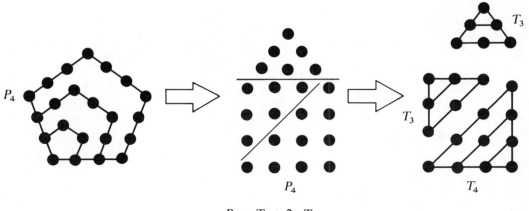

$$P_4 = T_4 + 2 \cdot T_3$$

6. Verify the following equations. Then write the next two equations in the sequence.

n	P_n	$=$	T_n	$+ 2 \cdot T_{n-1}$
1	1	=	1	+ 2· 0
2	5	=	3	+ 2· 1
3	12	=	6	+ 2· 3
4	22	=	10	+ 2· 6
5	35	=	15	+ 2·10
6	___	=	___	+ 2·___
7	___	=	___	+ 2·___

Let's return to the chart showing the polygonal numbers.

n	Triangle	Square	Pentagon	Hexagon	Heptagon	Octagon
1	1	1	1	1	1	____
2	3	4	5	6	7	____
3	6	9	12	15	18	____
4	10	16	22	28	34	____
5	15	25	35	____	____	____
6	21	36	51	____	____	____

Each row of numbers consists of entries that differ by a constant amount. In each case the difference is the triangular number of the previous row. Thus, in the 5th row the constant difference is 10, the triangular number in the 4th row. Thus, the 5th hexagonal number is equal to $P_5 + T_4 = 35 + 10 = 45$. If H_n represents the nth hexagonal number, then we have

$$H_n = P_n + T_{n-1}$$

7. Fill out the missing entries in the table above. Use the fact that the constant difference in consecutive entries in each row is the triangular number of the previous row.

8. Complete the following table.

n	Triangle	Square	Pentagon	Hexagon
1	$1 = 1$	$1 = 1$	$1 = 1$	$1 = 1$
2	$3 = 2 + 1$	$4 = 2 + 2 \cdot 1$	$5 = 2 + 3 \cdot 1$	$6 = 2 + 4 \cdot 1$
3	$6 = 3 + 3$	$9 = 3 + 2 \cdot 3$	$12 = 3 + 3 \cdot 3$	$15 = 3 + 4 \cdot 3$
4	$10 = 4 + 6$	$16 = 4 + 2 \cdot 6$	$22 = 4 + 3 \cdot 6$	$28 = 4 + 4 \cdot 6$
5	$15 = 5 + 10$	$25 = 5 + 2 \cdot 10$	$35 = 5 + 3 \cdot 10$	$45 = 5 + 4 \cdot 10$
6	$21 = \underline{\quad} + \underline{\quad}$	$36 = \underline{\quad} + 2 \cdot \underline{\quad}$	$51 = \underline{\quad} + 3 \cdot \underline{\quad}$	$66 = \underline{\quad} + 4 \cdot \underline{\quad}$
7	$\underline{\quad} = \underline{\quad} + \underline{\quad}$	$\underline{\quad} = \underline{\quad} + 2 \cdot \underline{\quad}$	$\underline{\quad} = \underline{\quad} + 3 \cdot \underline{\quad}$	$\underline{\quad} = \underline{\quad} + 4 \cdot \underline{\quad}$
8				
9				
10				
$\vdots$				
n	$T_n = n + T_{n-1}$	$S_n = n + 2 \cdot T_{n-1}$	$P_n = n + \underline{\quad} \cdot T_{n-1}$	$H_n = \underline{\quad} + \underline{\quad} \cdot \underline{\quad}$

9. Verify the equations indicated in the following table.

n	Triangle	Square	Pentagon	Hexagon
1	1	1	1	1
2	3	4 $=$	5	6
3	6	9 $=$	12	15
4	10	16 $=$	22	28
5	15	25 $=$	35	45
6	21	36 $=$	51	66

The formulas listed below are derived from the observations in the table of polygonal numbers above.

nth triangular number $= n + T_{n-1}$

nth square number $= n$th triangular number $+ T_{n-1}$

nth pentagonal number $= n$th square number $+ T_{n-1}$

nth hexagonal number $= n$th pentagonal number $+ T_{n-1}$

nth heptagonal number $= n$th hexagonal number $+ T_{n-1}$

nth octagonal number $= n$th heptagonal number $+ T_{n-1}$

$$\vdots \qquad\qquad \vdots$$

From these formulas we can conclude the new formulas listed as follows, which show that every polygonal number can be expressed in terms of triangular numbers.

nth triangular number $= n + T_{n-1}$

nth square number $= T_n + T_{n-1}$

nth pentagonal number $= T_n + 2T_{n-1}$

nth hexagonal number $= T_n + 3T_{n-1}$
nth heptagonal number $= T_n + 4T_{n-1}$
nth octagonal number $= T_n + 5T_{n-1}$

---

10. Using the formulas given above find the

> 10th pentagonal number
> 10th hexagonal number
> 10th heptagonal number
> 10th octagonal number

Predict the formula for the nth nonagonal number (a nonagon is a nine-sided polygon).

Predict the formula for the nth decagonal number (a decagon is a ten-sided polygon).

11. Show that $T_{20} = P_{12}$.

12. Let H_n represent the nth hexagonal number. Show that

$$H_1 = T_1$$
$$H_2 = T_3$$
$$H_3 = T_5$$
$$H_4 = T_7$$

Verify the formula $H_n = T_{2n-1}$ for $n = 5$, $n = 6$, and $n = 7$.

Circle the hexagonal numbers in Pascal's Triangle below.

```
                        1
                     1     1
                  1     2     1
               1     3     3     1
            1     4     6     4     1
         1     5     10    10    5     1
      1     6     15    20    15    6     1
   1     7     21    35    35    21    7     1
1     8     28    56    70    56    28    8     1
```

13. Verify each of the following formulas for $n = 1$, $n = 2$, and $n = 3$.

$$n \cdot T_{n+1} = (n + 2)T_n$$
$$n \cdot S_{n+1} = (n + 2)S_n + n$$
$$n \cdot P_{n+1} = (n + 2)P_n + 2n$$
$$n \cdot H_{n+1} = (n + 2)H_n + 3n$$

14. Verify each of the following formulas for $n = 2$, $n = 3$, and $n = 4$.

$$T_n^2 - T_{n-1} \cdot T_{n+1} = 1 \cdot T_n - 0$$
$$S_n^2 - S_{n-1} \cdot S_{n+1} = 2 \cdot S_n - 1$$
$$P_n^2 - P_{n-1} \cdot P_{n+1} = 3 \cdot P_n - 2$$
$$H_n^2 - H_{n-1} \cdot H_{n+1} = 4 \cdot H_n - 3$$

15. Verify each of the following formulas for $n = 1$, $n = 2$, $n = 3$, and $n = 4$.

$$T_n = \frac{1}{2}n(n + 1)$$

$$S_n = \frac{1}{2}n(2n + 0)$$

$$P_n = \frac{1}{2}n(3n - 1)$$

$$H_n = \frac{1}{2}n(4n - 2)$$

16. Verify the following formulas

$$P_1 = T_1$$
$$P_1 + P_2 = 2 \cdot T_2$$
$$P_1 + P_2 + P_3 = 3 \cdot T_3$$
$$P_1 + P_2 + P_3 + P_4 = 4 \cdot T_4$$
$$P_1 + P_2 + P_3 + P_4 + P_5 = 5 \cdot T_5$$

Choose your own value for n (greater than 5) and verify the formula

$$P_1 + P_2 + P_3 + \cdots + P_n = n \cdot T_n$$

In the section on triangular numbers we found the formula

$$T_{n+m} = T_n + T_m + n \cdot m(1)$$

A similar formula exists for every polygonal number. For example, if S_n represents the nth square number, then

$$S_{n+m} = S_n + S_m + n \cdot m \cdot (2)$$

Thus, if $n = 3$ and $m = 4$, then

$$S_{3+4} = S_3 + S_4 + 3 \cdot 4 \cdot (2)$$
$$= 3^2 + 4^2 + 24$$
$$= 9 + 16 + 24$$
$$= 49$$
$$= 7^2$$
$$= S_n$$

Furthermore, $S_{3+4} = (3 + 4)^2$ and $S_3 + S_4 + 3 \cdot 4 \cdot (2) = 3^2 + 4^2 + 2 \cdot 3 \cdot 4$. Therefore, S_{3+4} is equal to the binomial expansion

$$(3 + 4)^2 = 3^2 + 4^2 + 2 \cdot 3 \cdot 4$$

In general, $S_{m+n} = S_m + S_n + 2mn$ is equivalent to

$$(m + n)^2 = m^2 + n^2 + 2mn$$

This expression is the expansion of the binomial $(m + n)$ to the second power.

17. Find the expansion of $(3 + 5)^2$.
18. Find the expansion of $(x + y)^2$.
19. Verify that $S_8 = S_{3+5} = S_3 + S_5 + 2 \cdot 3 \cdot 5$.
20. Pick your own two numbers, one for n and one for m, and verify the following formula.

$$S_{m+n} = S_m + S_n + m \cdot n \cdot (2)$$

Listed below are the other formulas for the polygonal numbers similar to the formula above.

$T_{n+m} = T_n + T_m + m \cdot n \cdot 1$	(Triangular)
$S_{n+m} = S_n + S_m + m \cdot n \cdot 2$	(Square)
$P_{n+m} = P_n + P_m + m \cdot n \cdot 3$	(Pentagonal)
$H_{n+m} = H_n + H_m + m \cdot n \cdot 4$	(Hexagonal)

21. Verify each of the above formulas for $n = 2$ and $m = 4$.
22. Devise a formula similar to the above for heptagonal numbers and one for octagonal numbers.
23. Let $m = 1$ in each of the formulas above and write down the results. Remember that T_1, S_1, P_1, and H_1 are all equal to 1.

In Section 3.1, we studied the following 2 by 2 determinants.

$$\begin{vmatrix} 1 & 1 \\ 2 & 3 \end{vmatrix} = 1$$

$$\begin{vmatrix} 2 & 3 \\ 3 & 6 \end{vmatrix} = 3$$

$$\begin{vmatrix} 3 & 6 \\ 4 & 10 \end{vmatrix} = 6$$

$$\vdots \qquad \vdots$$

24. Write the next three determinants and evaluate them.
25. Evaluate the following determinants. What sequence of numbers is generated?

$$\begin{vmatrix} 1 & 1 \\ 3 & 4 \end{vmatrix} =$$

$$\begin{vmatrix} 3 & 4 \\ 6 & 9 \end{vmatrix} =$$

$$\begin{vmatrix} 6 & 9 \\ 10 & 16 \end{vmatrix} =$$

$$\vdots$$

Write the next three determinants in this sequence and evaluate them. These determinants suggest that $T_n \cdot S_{n+1} - T_{n+1} \cdot S_n = T_n$, where T_n is the nth triangular number and S_n is the nth square number. Verify this formula for $n = 1$, $n = 2$, $n = 3$, and $n = 4$.

26. Complete the tables below. Notice the patterns with triangular numbers.

n	Triangular numbers T_n	Square numbers S_n	Pentagonal numbers P_n	Hexagonal numbers H_n
1	$\begin{vmatrix} 1 & 1 \\ 2 & 3 \end{vmatrix} = 1$	$\begin{vmatrix} 1 & 1 \\ 2 & 4 \end{vmatrix} = 2 = 2\cdot 1$	$\begin{vmatrix} 1 & 1 \\ 2 & 5 \end{vmatrix} = 3 = 3\cdot 1$	$\begin{vmatrix} 1 & 1 \\ 2 & 6 \end{vmatrix} = 4 = 4\cdot 1$
2	$\begin{vmatrix} 2 & 3 \\ 3 & 6 \end{vmatrix} = 3$	$\begin{vmatrix} 2 & 4 \\ 3 & 9 \end{vmatrix} = 6 = 2\cdot 3$	$\begin{vmatrix} 2 & 5 \\ 3 & 12 \end{vmatrix} = 9 = 3\cdot 3$	$\begin{vmatrix} 2 & 6 \\ 3 & 15 \end{vmatrix} = 12 = 4\cdot 3$
3	$\begin{vmatrix} 3 & 6 \\ 4 & 10 \end{vmatrix} = 6$	$\begin{vmatrix} 3 & 9 \\ 4 & 16 \end{vmatrix} = 12 = 2\cdot 6$	$\begin{vmatrix} 3 & 12 \\ 4 & 22 \end{vmatrix} = 18 = 3\cdot 6$	$\begin{vmatrix} 3 & 15 \\ 4 & 28 \end{vmatrix} = 24 = 4\cdot 6$
4	$\begin{vmatrix} 4 & 10 \\ 5 & 15 \end{vmatrix} =$	$\begin{vmatrix} 4 & 16 \\ 5 & 25 \end{vmatrix} =$	$\begin{vmatrix} 4 & 22 \\ 5 & 35 \end{vmatrix} =$	$\begin{vmatrix} 4 & 28 \\ 5 & 45 \end{vmatrix} =$
5	$=$	$=$	$=$	$=$
6	$=$	$=$	$=$	$=$
⋮				
n	$\begin{vmatrix} n & T_n \\ n+1 & T_{n+1} \end{vmatrix} = T_n$	$\begin{vmatrix} n & S_n \\ n+1 & S_{n+1} \end{vmatrix} = 2\cdot T_n$	$\begin{vmatrix} n & P_n \\ n+1 & P_{n+1} \end{vmatrix} = \underline{\hspace{1cm}}$	$\begin{vmatrix} n & H_n \\ n+1 & H_{n+1} \end{vmatrix} = \underline{\hspace{1cm}}$

27. The foregoing determinants suggest the following formulas

$$n \cdot T_{n+1} - (n+1)T_n = T_n$$
$$n \cdot S_{n+1} - (n+1)S_n = 2 \cdot T_n$$
$$n \cdot P_{n+1} - (n+1)P_n = 3 \cdot T_n$$
$$n \cdot H_{n+1} - (n+1)H_n = 4 \cdot T_n$$

Complete the tables below by verifying these formulas for $n = 1$, $n = 2$, $n = 3$, and $n = 4$.

n	T_n	T_{n+1}	$n \cdot T_{n+1}$	$(n+1)T_n$
1				
2				
3				
4				

n	S_n	S_{n+1}	$n \cdot S_{n+1}$	$(n+1)S_n$
1				
2				
3				
4				

n	P_n	P_{n+1}	$n \cdot P_{n+1}$	$(n+1)P_n$
1				
2				
3				
4				

n	H_n	H_{n+1}	$n \cdot H_{n+1}$	$(n+1)H_n$
1				
2				
3				
4				

28. (a) Evaluate the following determinants and predict the next three entries in each column. What sequence of numbers is generated?

$$\begin{vmatrix} 1 & 1 \\ 4 & 5 \end{vmatrix} = \qquad\qquad \begin{vmatrix} 1 & 1 \\ 5 & 6 \end{vmatrix} =$$

$$\begin{vmatrix} 4 & 5 \\ 9 & 12 \end{vmatrix} = \qquad\qquad \begin{vmatrix} 5 & 6 \\ 12 & 15 \end{vmatrix} =$$

$$\begin{vmatrix} 9 & 12 \\ 16 & 22 \end{vmatrix} = \qquad\qquad \begin{vmatrix} 12 & 15 \\ 22 & 28 \end{vmatrix} =$$

$$\vdots \qquad\qquad\qquad \vdots$$

(b) Evaluate the following determinants. What sequence of numbers is generated?

$$\begin{vmatrix} 1 & 1 \\ 3 & 5 \end{vmatrix} = \qquad \begin{vmatrix} 1 & 1 \\ 3 & 6 \end{vmatrix} = \qquad \begin{vmatrix} 1 & 1 \\ 4 & 6 \end{vmatrix} =$$

$$\begin{vmatrix} 3 & 5 \\ 6 & 12 \end{vmatrix} = \qquad \begin{vmatrix} 3 & 6 \\ 6 & 15 \end{vmatrix} = \qquad \begin{vmatrix} 4 & 6 \\ 9 & 15 \end{vmatrix} =$$

$$\begin{vmatrix} 6 & 12 \\ 10 & 22 \end{vmatrix} = \qquad \begin{vmatrix} 6 & 15 \\ 10 & 28 \end{vmatrix} = \qquad \begin{vmatrix} 9 & 15 \\ 16 & 28 \end{vmatrix} =$$

$$\begin{vmatrix} 10 & 22 \\ 15 & 35 \end{vmatrix} = \qquad \begin{vmatrix} 10 & 28 \\ 15 & 45 \end{vmatrix} = \qquad \begin{vmatrix} 16 & 28 \\ 25 & 45 \end{vmatrix} =$$

$$\vdots \qquad\qquad \vdots \qquad\qquad \vdots$$

29. The foregoing determinants suggest the following formulas.

$$S_n P_{n+1} - S_{n+1} P_n = T_n$$
$$P_n H_{n+1} - P_{n+1} H_n = T_n$$

and

$$T_n P_{n+1} - T_{n+1} P_n = 2T_n$$
$$T_n H_{n+1} - T_{n+1} H_n = 3T_n$$
$$S_n H_{n+1} - S_{n+1} H_n = 2T_n$$

Verify these formulas for $n = 1$, $n = 2$, and $n = 3$.

3.4 PYTHAGOREAN TRIPLES

The followers of Pythagoras (circa 500 BC) probably originated the idea of figurate numbers, which are arrangements of points into certain geometrical configurations. This school of ancient Greek scholars also classified numbers as being odd or even and observed that the sums of successive sequences of odd numbers were corresponding squares.

$$
\begin{aligned}
1 &= 1 = 1^2 \\
1 + 3 &= 4 = 2^2 \\
1 + 3 + 5 &= 9 = 3^2 \\
1 + 3 + 5 + 7 &= 16 = 4^2 \\
1 + 3 + 5 + 7 + 9 &= 25 = 5^2 \\
\vdots \;\; &= \;\; \vdots \qquad \vdots \\
1 + 3 + 5 + \cdots + (2n - 1) &= n^2
\end{aligned}
$$

The Pythagoreans also observed a pattern in the sums of successive sequences of even numbers as shown below.

$$
\begin{aligned}
2 &= 2 = 2 \cdot 1 \\
2 + 4 &= 6 = 2 \cdot 3 \\
2 + 4 + 6 &= 12 = 2 \cdot 6 \\
2 + 4 + 6 + 8 &= 20 = 2 \cdot 10 \\
2 + 4 + 6 + 8 + 10 &= 30 = 2 \cdot 15
\end{aligned}
$$

---

1. Extend the above pattern to write and verify the next three equations in the sequence.

The above equations suggest the following general rule:

$$2 + 4 + 6 + \cdots + 2n = 2 \cdot T_n$$

---

2. Verify this formula for $n = 1$, $n = 2$, $n = 3$, and $n = 4$.

3. Find the sum of the first 100 even numbers.

We might also analyze the sum of a sequence of even numbers using our prior knowledge of the sum of a sequence of odd numbers. Thus, we might reason this way:

The odd number sum is a square, and the even number sum is, for each term, one more than the odd case. Therefore, the sum of the even numbers must equal the sum of the odd numbers plus one more for every term. In conclusion, if there are n terms and the sum of n odd numbers is n^2, then the sum of n even terms is $n^2 + n$.

The above argument is illustrated as follows:

$$
\begin{aligned}
1 + 3 + 5 + \cdots + (2n - 1) &= n^2 \\
\underline{1 + 1 + 1 + \cdots + \qquad 1 \quad} &= n \\
2 + 4 + 6 + \cdots + \qquad 2n \quad &= n^2 + n
\end{aligned}
$$

---

4. Verify the formula above for $n = 1$, $n = 2$, $n = 3$, and $n = 4$.

The Pythagoreans were more geometric in their thinking than algebraic. For example, the most famous Pythagorean Theorem states algebraically that for any right triangle

$$a^2 + b^2 = c^2$$

where a and b are the triangle's legs and c is the hypotenuse, or longest side. The Pythagoreans, however, thought in terms of actual square figures. Hence, the following illustration of this theorem reflects this formula in geometric terms.

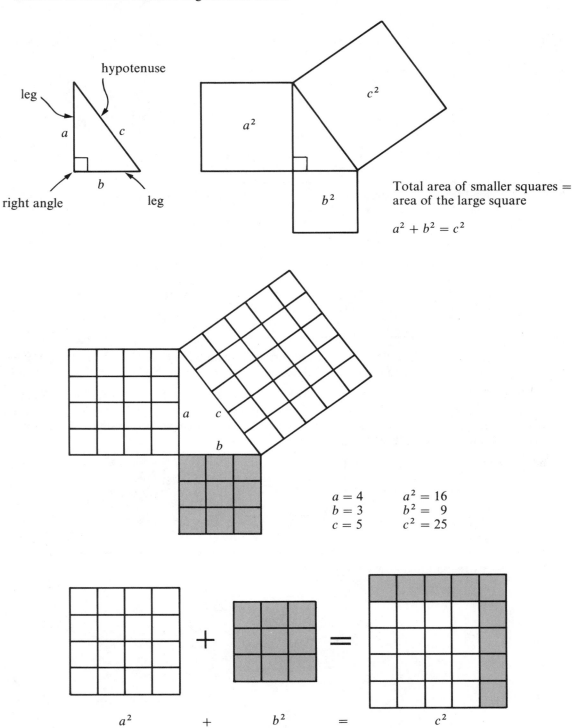

Total area of smaller squares = area of the large square

$$a^2 + b^2 = c^2$$

$a = 4$	$a^2 = 16$
$b = 3$	$b^2 = 9$
$c = 5$	$c^2 = 25$

This particular illustration shows the famous triangle with sides of 3, 4, and 5. This triangle was known throughout a long period of the history of man, several thousand years before the Pythagoreans. This particular example is also connected with odd number sums. Notice that $16 = 1 + 3 + 5 + 7$ and 9 is the next odd number. Therefore,

$$(1 + 3 + 5 + 7) + 9 = 1 + 3 + 5 + 7 + 9$$
$$4^2 + 9 = 5^2$$
$$16 + 9 = 25$$

---

5. Draw a right triangle with sides of 6, 8, and 10 units. Each unit could be 1 centimeter. Draw squares on each side of the triangle. Check to see if the area of the larger square equals the sum of the other squares. Remember this property is true only for right triangles.

Mathematicians have long been interested in whole numbers that can be the measures of the sides of a right triangle. Thus, we have seen $(3, 4, 5)$ and $(6, 8, 10)$ are the measures of the sides of a right triangle. In fact, there are many triples of numbers that can be sides of a right triangle. The triple $(6, 8, 10)$ is a multiple of $(3, 4, 5)$. Any other multiple of $(3, 4, 5)$ would also be a Pythagorean Triple.

---

6. Verify that $(30, 40, 50)$ is a Pythagorean Triple. In other words, verify that $30^2 + 40^2 = 50^2$.

7. Show that $(6, 7, 10)$ is not a Pythagorean Triple. In other words, show that $6^2 + 7^2 \neq 10^2$.

Let's look for a table of triples of whole numbers that can be measures of the sides of a right triangle. The fact that $4^2 + 3^2 = 5^2$ fits into the pattern of the sum of successive odd numbers gives us a clue. Notice that $16 = 4^2$ and is the sum of the first 4 odd numbers. Also, notice that $9 = 3^2$ and is the 5th odd number. Thus, $16 + 9 = (1 + 3 + 5 + 7) + 9 = 5^2$. Since there are many more odd numbers that are also squares, the Pythagorean relationship will happen again, in fact, infinitely many more times. The next odd number that is a square is 25 (also the next square that is an odd number is 25). Since 25 is the 13th odd number (add 1 and divide by 2, $25 + 1 = 26$ and $26/2 = 13$), we have

$$1 + 3 + 5 + \cdots + 23 + 25 = 13^2$$
$$(1 + 3 + 5 + \cdots + 23) + 25 = 13^2$$
$$12^2 + 25 = 13^2$$
$$12^2 + 5^2 = 13^2$$

This gives us the Pythagorean Triple $(5, 12, 13)$.

---

8. Find the next occurrence of an odd square and state the corresponding Pythagorean Triple.

9. Given that 81 is an odd square, find the sum

$$1 + 3 + 5 + \cdots + 79 + 81$$

Find the sum

$$1 + 3 + 5 + \cdots + 79$$

Show that $(1 + 3 + 5 + \cdots + 79) + 81 = 40^2 + 9^2 =$ a square.

The Pythagorean Triples $(3, 4, 5)$, $(5, 12, 13)$, $(7, 24, 25)$, and $(9, 40, 41)$ belong to a class of triples called primitive triples since they are not multiples of any other triple. Look at these particular primitive triples to see if there is a pattern that will enable you to predict the next entry.

Pythagorean Triples

3	4	5
5	12	13
7	24	25
9	40	41
___	___	___

It's easy to predict the next entry in the first column, it's just the next odd number, 11. The third column is always one more than the middle column. But what is the value in the middle column? Notice that each number in the middle column is a multiple of 4.

$$4 = 4 \cdot 1$$
$$12 = 4 \cdot 3$$
$$24 = 4 \cdot 6$$
$$40 = 4 \cdot 10$$

Notice that the triangular numbers have now appeared.

10. Predict the three numbers in the missing triple in the table above.

11. Complete the table below.

Pythagorean Triples

n	First leg of right triangle	Second leg of right triangle	Hypotenuse of right triangle	Sum of the squares of the legs	Square of hypotenuse
1	3	$4 = 4 \cdot 1$	$5 = 4 + 1$	$3^2 + 4^2 = 9 + 16 = 25$	$5^2 = 25$
2	5	$12 = 4 \cdot 3$	$13 = 12 + 1$	$5^2 + 12^2 = 25 + 144 = 169$	$13^2 = 169$
3	7	$24 = 4 \cdot 6$	$25 = 24 + 1$	$7^2 + 24^2 = 49 + 576 = 625$	$25^2 = 625$
4	9	$40 = 4 \cdot 10$	$41 = 40 + 1$	$9^2 + 40^2 = 81 + 1600 = 1681$	$41^2 = 1681$
5	11	$60 = 4 \cdot 15$	$61 = $ ___ $+ 1$	$11^2 + 60^2 = 121 + 3600 = 3721$	$61^2 = $ ___
6	___	___ $= 4 \cdot$ ___	___ $= $ ___ $+ 1$	___ $= $ ___ $= $ ___	___ $= $ ___
7	___	___ $= $ ___	___ $= $ ___	___ $= $ ___ $= $ ___	___ $= $ ___
8	___	___ $= $ ___	___ $= $ ___	___ $= $ ___ $= $ ___	___ $= $ ___
⋮					
n	$2n + 1$	$4 \cdot T_n$	$4 \cdot T_n + 1$	see formula below	

The Pythagorean Theorem suggests the following formula for the table above.

$$(2n + 1)^2 + (4 \cdot T_n)^2 = (4 \cdot T_n + 1)^2$$

Verify this formula for $n = 1$, $n = 2$, $n = 3$, and $n = 10$.

The following table of these particular primitive Pythagorean Triples has some interesting properties.

Pythagorean Triples		
3	4	5
5	12	13
7	24	25
9	40	41
11	60	61
⋮	⋮	⋮

For example, two numbers are odd, one is even. One of the numbers is divisible by 3, 4, or 5 (this is true of other primitive triples, such as (8, 15, 17)). Other properties are revealed in the exercises below.

---

12. Find the sum of each circled pair of numbers in the table of triples below. What sequence of numbers is generated?

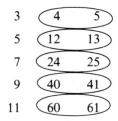

13. Add all four of the numbers in each circled group below and divide each sum by 8. What sequence of numbers is generated?

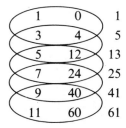

14. Add the numbers in the first and third columns and divide the sum by 2. What sequence of numbers is generated?

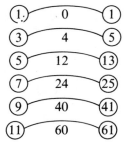

15. Find the value of the determinant of each group of circled numbers. What sequence of numbers is formed?

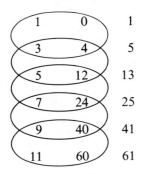

1	0	1
3	4	5
5	12	13
7	24	25
9	40	41
11	60	61

16. Add the numbers in each row and divide the sum by 2. Compare the results with the sequence of hexagonal numbers.

1	0	1
3	4	5
5	12	13
7	24	25
9	40	41
11	60	61

17. Verify that T_6, T_7, and $\sqrt{T_{49}}$ form a Pythagorean Triple.

18. Verify that T_{n-1}, $\sqrt{n^3}$, and T_n form a Pythagorean Triple for $n = 2$, $n = 3$, and $n = 4$.

19. Verify that n, n^2, and $\sqrt{2 \cdot T_{n^2}}$ form a Pythagorean Triple for $n = 1$, $n = 2$, and $n = 3$.

4 Higher Dimensional Figurate Numbers

4.1 TETRAHEDRAL NUMBERS

A tetrahedron is a pyramid with a triangular base. It is a three-dimensional figure. Each of the faces of a tetrahedron is a triangle.

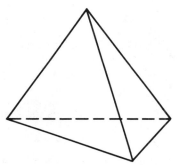

Tetrahedron

A tetrahedral number is the number of dots in the form of a tetrahedron composed from layers of triangular numbers.

1 ◯

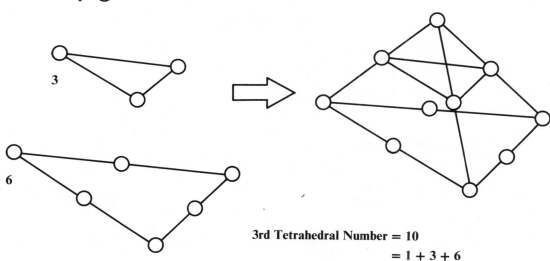

3rd Tetrahedral Number = 10

$$= 1 + 3 + 6$$

Notice that the tetrahedral numbers are equal to sums of triangular numbers.

1st tetrahedral number $= 1$

2nd tetrahedral number $= 1 + 3 = 4$

3rd tetrahedral number $= 1 + 3 + 6 = 10$

$$\vdots$$

nth tetrahedral number $= 1 + 3 + 6 + \cdots + T_n = t_n$

The notation T_n means the nth triangular number and t_n means the nth tetrahedral number.

---

1. Find the 4th tetrahedral number. Draw a sketch of the diagram for this number.

2. Find the 5th, 6th, 7th, and 8th tetrahedral numbers.

3. Verify the formula $t_n = t_{n-1} + T_n$ for $n = 2$, $n = 3$, $n = 4$, and $n = 5$.

4. Examine Pascal's Triangle and try to find the tetrahedral numbers. Circle the tetrahedral numbers that line up in a row or column.

```
                        1
                    1       1
                1       2       1
            1       3       3       1
        1       4       6       4       1
    1       5      10      10       5       1
1       6      15      20      15       6       1
1   7      21      35      35      21       7       1
1   8      28      56      70      56      28       8       1
```

5. If the 20th tetrahedral number is 1540, what is the 21st tetrahedral number? Use the formula $t_n = t_{n-1} + T_n$.

Recall from Chapter 2 the "hockey stick" property inherent in Pascal's Triangle. The numbers in the handle of the hockey stick add up to the number in the head of the stick.

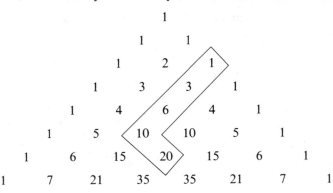

This is an illustration of the property that

$$1 + 3 + 6 + 10 + \cdots + T_n = t_n$$

6. Illustrate that the sum of the first 5 triangular numbers is equal to the 5th tetrahedral number by drawing the appropriate hockey stick.

$$
\begin{array}{ccccccccccccc}
 & & & & & & 1 & & & & & & \\
 & & & & & 1 & & 1 & & & & & \\
 & & & & 1 & & 2 & & 1 & & & & \\
 & & & 1 & & 3 & & 3 & & 1 & & & \\
 & & 1 & & 4 & & 6 & & 4 & & 1 & & \\
 & 1 & & 5 & & 10 & & 10 & & 5 & & 1 & \\
1 & & 6 & & 15 & & 20 & & 15 & & 6 & & 1 \\
\end{array}
$$

$$1 \quad 7 \quad 21 \quad 35 \quad 35 \quad 21 \quad 7 \quad 1$$

$$1 + 3 + 6 + 10 + 15 = \underline{\hspace{1cm}}$$

The following general formula for the nth tetrahedral number is formed from the property of adjacent numbers given in Chapter 1.

$$N = P \cdot \frac{R - C + 1}{C}$$

Note that N = the next number to be found in a row, P = the previous number in the row, R = the number of the row, and C = the column position of N in the row. If we want a formula for t_n, then $C = 3$, $R = n + 2$, $P = T_{n+1}$, and, therefore,

$$t_n = T_{n+1} \cdot \frac{(n + 2) - 3 + 1}{3}$$

$$= T_{n+1} \cdot \frac{n}{3}$$

$$= \frac{n}{3} \cdot \frac{(n + 1)(n + 2)}{2}$$

$$= \frac{n(n + 1)(n + 2)}{6}$$

Thus, to find the 5th tetrahedral number, we use the information that it is in the 7th row $(5 + 2)$, it is in the 3rd column position in Pascal's Triangle, and the previous number in the 7th row is $T_6 = 21$. Thus,

$$t_5 = N = P \cdot \frac{R - C + 1}{C}$$

$$= T_6 \cdot \frac{7 - 3 + 1}{3}$$

$$= 21 \cdot \frac{5}{3}$$

$$= 35$$

or, using the formula directly

$$t_n = \frac{n(n + 1)(n + 2)}{6}$$

$$t_5 = \frac{5(5 + 1)(5 + 2)}{6}$$

$$= \frac{5(6)(7)}{6}$$

$$= 35$$

---

7. Use the formula above to find $t_1, t_2, t_3, t_{20}, t_{100}$.

Furthermore, since $1 + 3 + 6 + 10 + \cdots + T_n = t_n$, it follows that

$$1 + 3 + 6 + 10 + \cdots + T_n = \frac{n(n + 1)(n + 2)}{6}$$

---

8. (a) Find the sum of the triangular numbers

$$1 + 3 + 6 + 10 + 15 + 21 + 28 + 36 + 45 + 55 + 66 = \underline{\quad}$$

(b) Find the sum of the triangular numbers

$$1 + 3 + 6 + 10 + \cdots + T_{100} = \underline{\quad}$$

Notice that the basic rule of Pascal's Triangle itself can predict the next tetrahedral number in the sequence when we know the previous one. For example, $t_5 = t_4 + T_5$ or $35 = 20 + 15$.

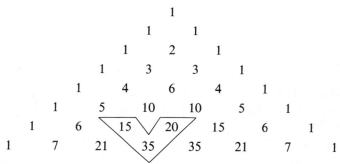

In general, we have

$$t_n = t_{n-1} + T_n$$

---

9. Verify the above formula for $n = 2$, $n = 3$, $n = 4$, and $n = 5$.

The formula above is equivalent to $t_n - t_{n-1} = T_n$. Now, consider the formula $t_n - t_{n-2} = ?$.

---

10. Find the values of $t_n - t_{n-2}$ for $n = 3$, $n = 4$, $n = 5$, and $n = 6$. What sequence of numbers is generated?

11. Perform the following operations. Extend each sequence by predicting the next two formulas. What sequence of numbers is generated in each case?

$$\frac{3}{3} \cdot 1 = \qquad\qquad \frac{3}{1} \cdot 1 =$$

$$\frac{4}{3} \cdot 3 = \qquad\qquad \frac{4}{2} \cdot 3 =$$

$$\frac{5}{3} \cdot 6 = \qquad\qquad \frac{5}{3} \cdot 6 =$$

$$\frac{6}{3} \cdot 10 = \qquad\qquad \frac{6}{4} \cdot 10 =$$

$$\underline{\qquad} = \qquad\qquad \underline{\qquad} =$$

$$\underline{\qquad} = \qquad\qquad \underline{\qquad} =$$

The sequence above suggests the formula

$$t_n = \frac{(n + 2)}{3} \cdot T_n$$

This formula is slightly different from the earlier formula,

$$t_n = T_{n+1} \cdot \frac{n}{3}$$

but they are equivalent, since they both lead to

$$t_n = \frac{n(n + 1)(n + 2)}{6}$$

12. **(a)** Evaluate the following determinants. What sequence of numbers is generated?

$$\begin{vmatrix} 1 & 1 \\ 2 & 4 \end{vmatrix} =$$

$$\begin{vmatrix} 2 & 4 \\ 3 & 10 \end{vmatrix} =$$

$$\begin{vmatrix} 3 & 10 \\ 4 & 20 \end{vmatrix} =$$

Write the next three determinants in this sequence and evaluate them.

(b) These determinants suggest that

$$n \cdot t_{n+1} - (n + 1) \cdot t_n = 2 \cdot t_n$$

Verify this formula for $n = 1$, $n = 2$, $n = 3$, and $n = 4$.

13. Perform the indicated operations in each group of numbers circled in Pascal's Triangle below. Then divide each result by 2. What sequence of numbers is generated?

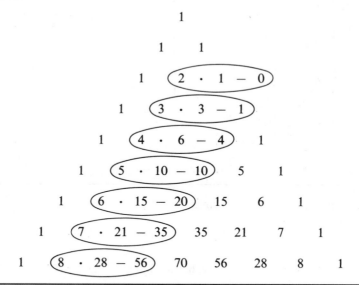

Now, let's look at two interesting arrays of numbers that lead to a remarkable relationship between the triangular and tetrahedral numbers. These arrays relate to the geometrical problem concerning rectangles with the same perimeters, called **isoperimetric rectangles**.

Array 1						**Array 2**				
1	2	3	4	5	⋯	1	2	3	4	5 ⋯
1	2	3	4	5		2	4	6	8	10
1	2	3	4	5		3	6	9	12	15
1	2	3	4	5		4	8	12	16	20
1	2	3	4	5		5	10	15	20	25
⋮						⋮				

14. Describe the numbers in the second array above.

15. Add the numbers in each group indicated below. What sequence of numbers is generated?

Array 1

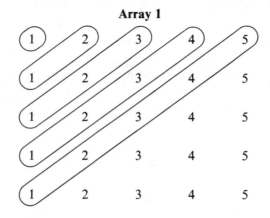

16. Extend the array above by adding two more rows and two more columns. Add the numbers in these new slanting diagonals and fit them into the sequence you have established.

17. Add the numbers in each group indicated below. What sequence of numbers is generated?

Array 2

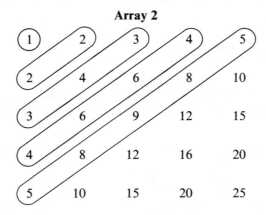

18. Describe the sequence of numbers circled below.

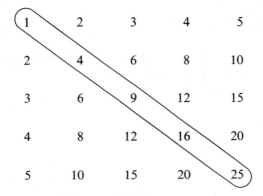

19. Extend the arrays above by adding two more rows and two more columns. Find the results you need to extend the sequences that have been established.

The sequences of the two preceding arrays suggest the following formulas.

$$t_1 = 1 \cdot 1^2$$
$$t_3 = 1 \cdot 2^2 + 2(2^2 - 1^2)$$
$$t_5 = 1 \cdot 3^2 + 2(3^2 - 1^2) + 2(3^2 - 2^2)$$
$$t_7 = 1 \cdot 4^2 + 2(4^2 - 1^2) + 2(4^2 - 2^2) + 2(4^2 - 3^2)$$
$$\vdots$$
$$t_{2n-1} = 1 \cdot n^2 + 2(n^2 - 1^2) + 2(n^2 - 2^2) + 2(n^2 - 3^2) + \cdots + 2(n^2 - (n-1)^2)$$

---

20. Verify the first four of the above formulas. Let $n = 5$ and verify the general formula.

The following geometrical problem not only leads to the relationship between tetrahedral numbers and the triangular numbers, it also produces the array of the multiples of the counting numbers we have been examining.

In this problem, let's consider rectangles made up of unit squares. For example, here is a rectangle that is 3 units long and 2 units wide.

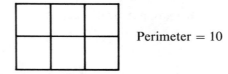

Perimeter = 10

3 by 2 Unit Square Rectangle

The perimeter of this rectangle is the sum of the lengths of its four sides. Therefore, the perimeter is 10 (10 = 3 + 2 + 3 + 2). Let's call the rectangle above a 3 by 2 rectangle. It will be counted differently from a 2 by 3 rectangle, even though the perimeters of both rectangles are the same.

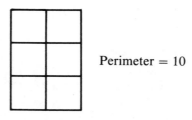

Perimeter = 10

2 by 3 Rectangle

The problem is finding other unit square rectangles whose perimeter is 10. In this case, there are two more, the 4 by 1 rectangle and the 1 by 4 rectangle.

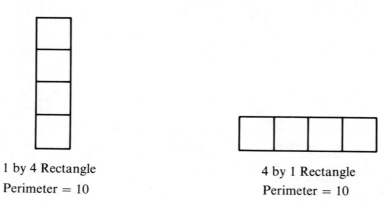

1 by 4 Rectangle
Perimeter = 10

4 by 1 Rectangle
Perimeter = 10

Now, let's collect all of these rectangles and find their total area.

All unit square rectangles whose perimeter = 10

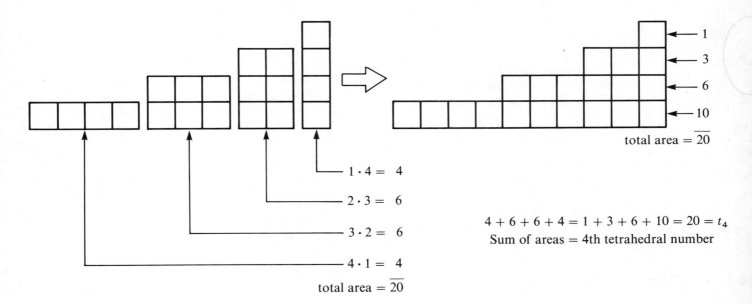

$1 \cdot 4 = 4$

$2 \cdot 3 = 6$

$3 \cdot 2 = 6$

$4 \cdot 1 = 4$

total area = $\overline{20}$

total area = $\overline{20}$

$4 + 6 + 6 + 4 = 1 + 3 + 6 + 10 = 20 = t_4$

Sum of areas = 4th tetrahedral number

The numbers representing the areas of the four rectangles whose perimeter is 10 are found in the array below.

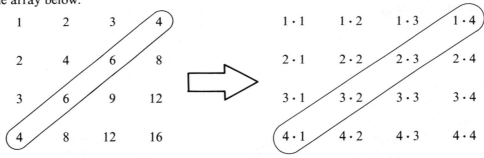

---

21. Find the rectangles whose perimeter is 8. Draw them as shown previously and find their total area. What tetrahedral number represents the total area?

22. Find all rectangles whose perimeter is 12. Draw them as shown previously and find their total area. What tetrahedral number represents the total area?

23. Extend the table below to include those rectangles whose perimeter is 12.

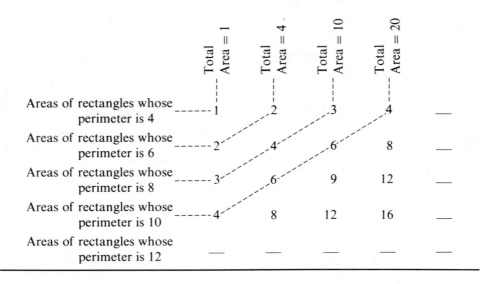

	Total Area = 1	Total Area = 4	Total Area = 10	Total Area = 20	
Areas of rectangles whose perimeter is 4	1	2	3	4	—
Areas of rectangles whose perimeter is 6	2	4	6	8	—
Areas of rectangles whose perimeter is 8	3	6	9	12	—
Areas of rectangles whose perimeter is 10	4	8	12	16	—
Areas of rectangles whose perimeter is 12	—	—	—	—	—

4.2 SQUARE PYRAMIDS

The sum of a sequence of n triangular numbers corresponds to the nth tetrahedral number. Now let's consider the square numbers. The sum of the squares corresponds to the geometrical figure called a square pyramid. The following diagrams show the first four square pyramidal numbers.

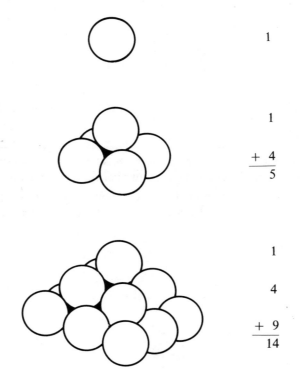

1

$$\begin{array}{r} 1 \\ + \ 4 \\ \hline 5 \end{array}$$

$$\begin{array}{r} 1 \\ 4 \\ + \ 9 \\ \hline 14 \end{array}$$

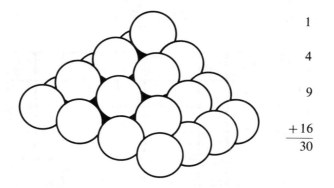

$$\begin{array}{r} 1 \\ 4 \\ 9 \\ +\,16 \\ \hline 30 \end{array}$$

The diagram below shows the first five square numbers.

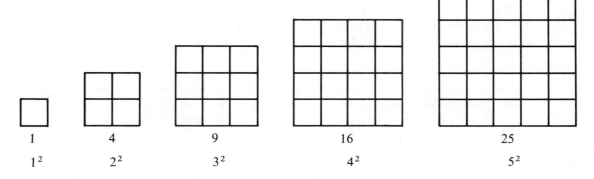

Now let's consider the sum of these numbers.

$$1 + 4 + 9 + 16 + 25 = 55$$

To find a formula for the sum of an arbitrary number of squares and to show this relationship in Pascal's Triangle, we put the square numbers together.

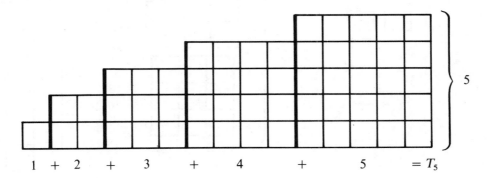

Study the associated rectangle. The dimensions of this rectangle are 5 by T_5.

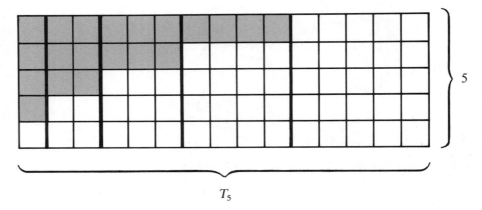

The area of the rectangle $= 5 \cdot T_5$. The area of the unshaded section $= 1 + 4 + 9 + 16 + 25$. The area of the shaded section $= 20$. Thus,

$$1 + 4 + 9 + 16 + 25 = 5 \cdot T_5 - 20$$

---

1. The diagrams below suggest a pattern for finding the sum of the first n square numbers. Extend the pattern by including two more diagrams and two more equations.

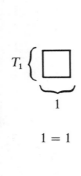

T_1

1

$1 = 1$

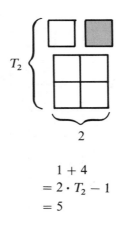

T_2

2

$$1 + 4$$
$$= 2 \cdot T_2 - 1$$
$$= 5$$

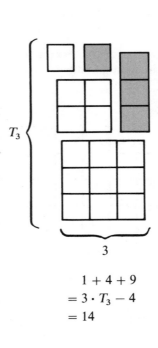

T_3

3

$$1 + 4 + 9$$
$$= 3 \cdot T_3 - 4$$
$$= 14$$

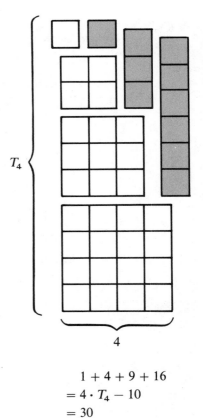

T_4

4

$$1 + 4 + 9 + 16$$
$$= 4 \cdot T_4 - 10$$
$$= 30$$

n	$1^2 + 2^2 + 3^2 + \cdots + n^2 = n \cdot T_n - t = $ **Total**
1	$1^2 = 1 \cdot 1 - 0 = 1$
2	$1^2 + 2^2 = 2 \cdot 3 - 1 = 5$
3	$1^2 + 2^2 + 3^2 = 3 \cdot 6 - 4 = 14$
4	$1^2 + 2^2 + 3^2 + 4^2 = 4 \cdot 10 - 10 = 30$
5	
6	

The numbers in the preceding table in the column labeled t are 0, 1, 4, 10, 20, 35, 56,..., the tetrahedral numbers, and the numbers in the column labeled "Total" are 1, 5, 14, 30,..., the square pyramidal numbers.

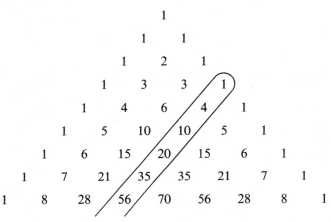

The tetrahedral numbers called t in the formula $n \cdot T_n - t$ are shown above.

2. Multiply and subtract the numbers indicated in Pascal's Triangle below. In each case verify that the result is equal to the sum of the squares. Recall that this result was found in the previous table.

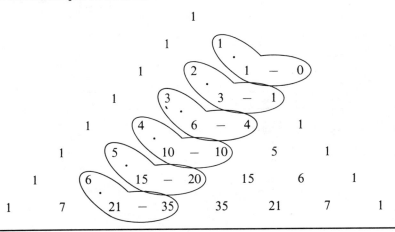

The preceding discussion and exercise suggest a formula for the nth square pyramidal number. Let s_n be the notation for the nth square pyramidal number, then

$$s_n = n \cdot T_n - t_{n-1}$$

Note: s_n represents the nth square pyramidal number, T_n represents the nth triangular number, and t_{n-1} represents the $(n-1)$th tetrahedral number. For example, if $n = 3$, the above formula states

$$
\begin{aligned}
s_3 &= 3 \cdot T_3 - t_2 \\
&= 3 \cdot 6 - 4 \\
&= 18 - 4 \\
&= 14
\end{aligned}
$$

Notice that 14 is the sum of the first three square numbers.

$$
\begin{aligned}
s_3 &= 1^2 + 2^2 + 3^2 \\
&= 1 + 4 + 9 \\
&= 14
\end{aligned}
$$

---

3. Verify the formula $s_n = n \cdot T_n - t_{n-1}$ for $n = 2$, $n = 4$, and $n = 5$.

4. Find s_{100}. $\left(\text{Recall } t_n = \dfrac{n(n+1)(n+2)}{6} \text{ and } T_n = \dfrac{n(n+1)}{2}.\right)$

5. Complete the table below.

n	T_n	s_n	$\dfrac{s_n}{T_n}$
1	1	1	$\dfrac{1}{1} = \dfrac{3}{3}$
2	3	5	$\dfrac{5}{3} = \dfrac{5}{3}$
3	6	14	$\dfrac{14}{6} = \dfrac{7}{3}$
4	10	30	$\dfrac{30}{10} = \dfrac{9}{3}$
5	15	55	$\dfrac{55}{15} = $ _____
6	_____	_____	_____ $=$ _____

The table in the previous exercise suggests that

$$\frac{s_n}{T_n} = \frac{2n+1}{3}$$

where $2n + 1$ is the $(n + 1)$th odd number. Thus,

$$s_n = T_n \cdot \frac{2n+1}{3}$$

or, equivalently,

$$s_n = \frac{n(n+1)(2n+1)}{6}$$

6. Verify that

$$1^2 + 2^2 + 3^2 + 4^2 + 5^2 = \frac{5(5 + 1)(2 \cdot 5 + 1)}{6}$$

7. Verify that

$$s_n = \frac{n(n + 1)(2n + 1)}{6}$$

for $n = 1$, $n = 2$, $n = 3$, and $n = 4$.

8. Find s_{100} using this formula.

9. Add the numbers in each group encircled in Pascal's Triangle below. What sequence of numbers is generated? Compare each sum in this sequence with the sequence for the sum of squares.

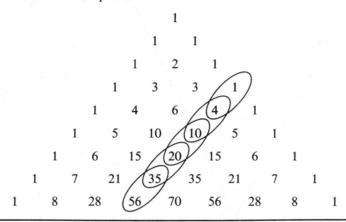

Recall that in our discussion of polygonal numbers we found that each square number is the sum of two consecutive triangular numbers. The exercise above suggests that each square pyramidal number is the sum of two consecutive tetrahedral numbers. That is,

$$s_n = t_n + t_{n-1}$$

10. Verify the formulas

$$S_n = T_n + T_{n-1}$$

and

$$s_n = t_n + t_{n-1}$$

for $n = 2$, $n = 3$, and $n = 4$.

11. Add these two sequences term by term. What sequence of numbers is generated?

	1	4	10	20	35	56	84		$\cdots$
+	1	4	10	20	35	56	84	120	$\cdots$

12. Find the length of the hypotenuse in each of the right triangles shown below. What sequence of numbers is generated?

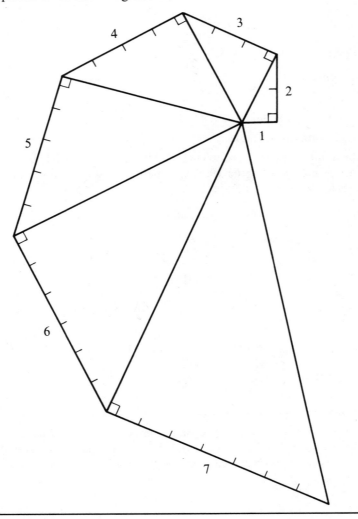

4.3 OTHER PYRAMIDAL NUMBERS

The sum of a sequence of n pentagonal numbers corresponds to the nth pentagonal pyramidal number. Recall the pentagonal numbers are $1, 5, 12, 22, 35, 51, \ldots$. Thus, the pentagonal pyramidal numbers are

$p_1 = 1$
$p_2 = 1 + 5 = 6$
$p_3 = 1 + 5 + 12 = 18$
$p_4 = 1 + 5 + 12 + 22 = 40$
$p_5 = 1 + 5 + 12 + 22 + 35 = 75$
$\vdots$

1. Find p_6.

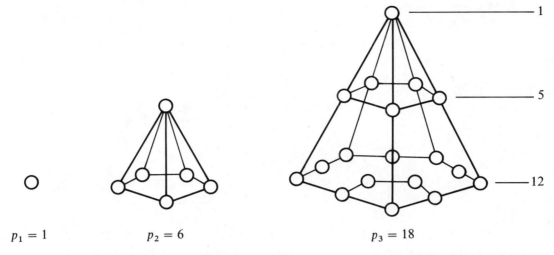

$p_1 = 1$ $p_2 = 6$ $p_3 = 18$

In general, $p_n = 1 + 5 + 12 + \cdots + P_n$. Furthermore, in Section 3.3 we found that the sum of the pentagonal numbers is given by the formula:

$$1 + 5 + 12 + \cdots + P_n = n \cdot T_n$$

Thus,

$$p_n = n \cdot T_n$$

Note: p_n represents the nth pentagonal pyramidal number, P_n represents the nth pentagonal number, and T_n represents the nth triangular number.

---

2. Complete the following table.

n	T_n	$n \cdot T_n = p_n$
1	1	$1 \cdot 1 = 1$
2	3	$2 \cdot 3 = 6$
3	6	$3 \cdot 6 = 18$
4	10	$4 \cdot 10 = $ _____
5	15	_____ $\cdot$ _____ = _____
6	_____	_____ $\cdot$ _____ = _____
7	_____	_____ $\cdot$ _____ = _____
8	_____	_____ $\cdot$ _____ = _____
9	_____	_____ $\cdot$ _____ = _____
10	_____	_____ $\cdot$ _____ = _____

3. Multiply the numbers encircled in each group in Pascal's Triangle below. What sequence of numbers is generated?

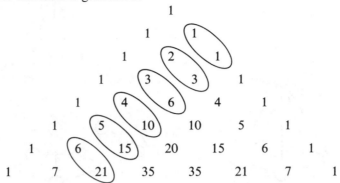

4. Find p_{100}.

The next formula states that the nth pentagonal pyramidal number is equal to the sum of the nth square pyramidal number and the $(n - 1)$th tetrahedral number.

$$p_n = s_n + t_{n-1}$$

5. Verify the formula above for $n = 2$, $n = 3$, and $n = 4$.

6. Verify the formula $P_n = S_n + T_{n-1}$ for $n = 2$, $n = 3$, and $n = 4$.

7. Verify the formula

$$p_n = t_n + 2 \cdot t_{n-1}$$

for $n = 2$, $n = 3$, and $n = 4$.

Let's look at a chart of the pyramidal numbers.

Tetrahedral t_n	Square pyramidal s_n	Pentagonal pyramidal p_n	Hexagonal pyramidal h_n
1	1	1	___
4	5	6	___
10	14	18	___
20	30	40	___
35	___	___	___
___	___	___	___

Each row of numbers consists of entries that differ by a constant amount. The difference is always a tetrahedral number of the previous row. Thus, in the 4th row the constant difference is 10, the tetrahedral number in the 3rd row. Therefore, the 4th hexagonal pyramidal number is equal to $p_4 + t_3 = 40 + 10 = 50$. In general, if h_n represents the nth hexagonal pyramidal number, then

$$h_n = p_n + t_{n-1}$$

8. Fill in the missing entries of the previous table. Use the fact that the constant difference in consecutive entries in each row is the tetrahedral number of the previous row.

The foregoing table suggests the formulas below.

$$n\text{th tetrahedral number} = T_n + t_{n-1}$$
$$n\text{th square pyramidal number} = n\text{th tetrahedral number} + t_{n-1}$$
$$n\text{th pentagonal pyramidal number} = n\text{th square pyramidal number} + t_{n-1}$$
$$n\text{th hexagonal pyramidal number} = n\text{th pentagonal pyramidal number} + t_{n-1}$$

---

9. Predict a formula for the nth heptagonal pyramidal number.
10. Predict a formula for the nth octagonal pyramidal number.
11. Complete the table below.

Tetrahedral t_n	Square pyramidal s_n	Pentagonal pyramidal p_n	Hexagonal pyramidal h_n
$1 = 1$	$1 = 1$	$1 = 1$	$1 = 1$
$4 = 3 + 1$	$5 = 3 + 2 \cdot 1$	$6 = 3 + 3 \cdot 1$	$7 = 3 + 4 \cdot 1$
$10 = 6 + 4$	$14 = 6 + 2 \cdot 4$	$18 = 6 + 3 \cdot 4$	$22 = 6 + 4 \cdot 4$
$20 = 10 + 10$	$30 = 10 + 2 \cdot 10$	$40 = 10 + 3 \cdot 10$	$50 = 10 + 4 \cdot 10$
$35 = 15 + 20$	$55 = 15 + 2 \cdot 20$	$75 = 15 + 3 \cdot 20$	$95 = 15 + 4 \cdot 20$
$56 = \underline{\quad} + \underline{\quad}$	$91 = \underline{\quad} + 2 \cdot \underline{\quad}$	$126 = \underline{\quad} + 3 \cdot \underline{\quad}$	$161 = \underline{\quad} + 4 \cdot \underline{\quad}$
$\underline{\quad} = \underline{\quad} + \underline{\quad}$	$\underline{\quad} = \underline{\quad} + 2 \cdot \underline{\quad}$	$\underline{\quad} = \underline{\quad} + 3 \cdot \underline{\quad}$	$\underline{\quad} = \underline{\quad} + 4 \cdot \underline{\quad}$
$\vdots$			
$t_n = T_n + t_{n-1}$	$s_n = T_n + 2 \cdot t_{n-1}$	$p_n = T_n + \underline{\quad} \cdot t_{n-1}$	$h_n = T_n + \underline{\quad} \cdot t_{n-1}$

From the preceding table we observe the following general formulas for pyramidal numbers.

$$n\text{th tetrahedral number} = T_n + t_{n-1} = t_n$$
$$n\text{th square pyramidal number} = T_n + 2 \cdot t_{n-1} = t_n + t_{n-1}$$
$$n\text{th pentagonal pyramidal number} = T_n + 3 \cdot t_{n-1} = t_n + 2 \cdot t_{n-1}$$
$$n\text{th hexagonal pyramidal number} = T_n + 4 \cdot t_{n-1} = t_n + 3 \cdot t_{n-1}$$

---

12. Using the formulas given above find each of the following.

　　The 10th square pyramidal number
　　The 10th pentagonal pyramidal number
　　The 10th hexagonal pyramidal number

13. Predict the formula for the nth heptagonal pyramidal number.
14. Predict the formula for the nth octagonal pyramidal number.

Verify each of the following formulas for $n = 1$, $n = 2$, and $n = 3$.

15. $n \cdot t_{n+1} = (n + 3)t_n$
16. $n \cdot s_{n+1} = (n + 3)s_n + T_n$
17. $n \cdot p_{n+1} = (n + 3)p_n + 2T_n$
18. $n \cdot h_{n+1} = (n + 3)h_n + 3T_n$

19. Verify the following formulas.

$$s_1 = t_1^2$$
$$s_1 + s_2 = t_2^2 - t_1 \cdot t_3$$
$$s_1 + s_2 + s_3 = t_3^2 - t_2 \cdot t_4$$
$$s_1 + s_2 + s_3 + s_4 = t_4^2 - t_3 \cdot t_5$$
$$s_1 + s_2 + s_3 + s_4 + s_5 = t_5^2 - t_4 \cdot t_6$$

20. Verify the formula $s_n^2 - s_{n+1} \cdot s_{n-1} = n \cdot s_n + t_{n-1}$ for $n = 2$, $n = 3$, and $n = 4$.

21. Verify the formulas

$$t_n = \frac{1}{6}n(n + 1)(n + 2)$$

$$s_n = \frac{1}{6}n(n + 1)(2n + 1)$$

$$p_n = \frac{1}{6}n(n + 1)(3n + 0)$$

$$h_n = \frac{1}{6}n(n + 1)(4n - 1)$$

for $n = 1$, $n = 2$, and $n = 3$.

22. Verify the formulas

$$t_n = \frac{n + 1}{6}(2T_n + n)$$

$$s_n = \frac{n + 1}{6}(2S_n + n)$$

$$p_n = \frac{n + 1}{6}(2P_n + n)$$

$$h_n = \frac{n + 1}{6}(2H_n + n)$$

for $n = 1$, $n = 2$, $n = 3$, $n = 4$, and $n = 5$.

23. Show that $s_{24} = S_{70}$.

24. Show that $t_2 = S_2$ and $t_{48} = S_{140}$.

25. Verify these formulas.

$$t_1 = 1 \cdot T_1$$
$$t_3 = 3 \cdot T_2 + s_1$$
$$t_5 = 5 \cdot T_3 + s_2$$
$$t_7 = 7 \cdot T_4 + s_3$$

26. Verify the following formulas

$$T_{n-1} + T_n + T_{n+1} = 3 \cdot T_n + s_1$$
$$T_{n-2} + T_{n-1} + T_n + T_{n+1} + T_{n+2} = 5 \cdot T_n + s_2$$
$$t_{n+3} - t_{n-4} = 7 \cdot T_n + s_3$$
$$t_{n+4} - t_{n-5} = 9 \cdot T_n + s_4$$

for $n = 6$ and $n = 7$.

4.4 CUBIC NUMBERS AND OTHER PRISMOIDAL NUMBERS

Continuing our discussion of three-dimensional figures, let's discuss another type of figurate number besides the pyramidal numbers previously examined. These numbers are the hexahedral numbers or simply cubes. The cubic numbers are easy to visualize and to compute.

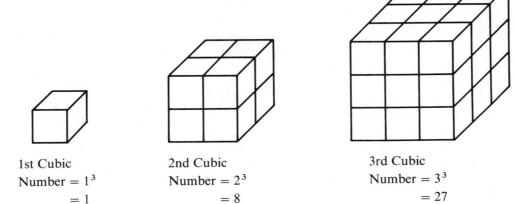

| 1st Cubic
Number $= 1^3$
$= 1$ | 2nd Cubic
Number $= 2^3$
$= 8$ | 3rd Cubic
Number $= 3^3$
$= 27$ |

Let c_n represent the nth cubic number. Then $c_1 = 1$, $c_2 = 8$, and $c_3 = 27$; that is, $c_n = n^3$.

---

1. Complete the following table.

n	$n^3 = c_n$	$n^3 = n \cdot S_n$
1	$1^3 = c_1 = 1$	$1^3 = 1 \cdot 1$
2	$2^3 = c_2 = 8$	$2^3 = 2 \cdot 4$
3	$3^3 = c_3 = 27$	$3^3 = 3 \cdot 9$
4		
5		
6		
7		
8		
9		
10		

Each cubic number can be written as the product of six and a specific tetrahedral number plus a few extra unit cubes. The formula is

$$n^3 = 6 \cdot t_{n-1} + n$$

---

2. Complete the following table.

n	$6 \cdot t_{n-1} + n = n^3$
1	$6 \cdot 0 + 1 =$ _____
2	$6 \cdot 1 + 2 =$ _____
3	$6 \cdot 4 + 3 =$ _____
4	$6 \cdot 10 + 4 =$ _____
5	$6 \cdot 20 + 5 =$ _____
6	$6 \cdot 35 +$ _____ $=$ _____
7	$6 \cdot$ _____ $+$ _____ $=$ _____
8	_____ $=$ _____
9	_____ $=$ _____
10	_____ $=$ _____

Also, we have

$$n^3 = t_n + 4 \cdot t_{n-1} + t_{n-2} \qquad \text{(six tetrahedral numbers—four of one type)}$$

---

3. Perform the following computations and extend the sequence to include two more formulas.

n	$t_n + 4 \cdot t_{n-1} + t_{n-2} = n^3$
3	$10 + 4 \cdot 4 + 1 =$ _____
4	$20 + 4 \cdot 10 + 4 =$ _____
5	$35 + 4 \cdot 20 + 10 =$ _____
6	$56 + 4 \cdot 35 + 20 =$ _____
7	
8	

Adjusting this last formula to accommodate our knowledge of pyramidal numbers, we have

$$c_n = p_n + t_{n-1} + s_{n-1} \qquad \text{(A cube is equal to the sum of a pentagonal, a tetrahedral, and a square pyramidal number.)}$$

4. Perform the following computations and extend the sequence to include two more formulas.

n	$p_n + t_{n-1} + s_{n-1} = n^3$
2	$6 + 1 + 1 = \rule{1cm}{0.4pt}$
3	$18 + 4 + 5 = \rule{1cm}{0.4pt}$
4	$40 + 10 + 14 = \rule{1cm}{0.4pt}$
5	$75 + 20 + 30 = \rule{1cm}{0.4pt}$
6	$126 + 35 + 55 = \rule{1cm}{0.4pt}$
7	
8	

5. Perform the following computations and extend the sequence to include two more formulas. What sequence of numbers is generated?

$$\rule{1cm}{0.4pt} = 1$$
$$\rule{1cm}{0.4pt} = 6 + 3 - 1$$
$$\rule{1cm}{0.4pt} = 15 + 10 + 6 - 3 - 1$$
$$\rule{1cm}{0.4pt} = 28 + 21 + 15 + 10 - 6 - 3 - 1$$
$$\rule{1cm}{0.4pt} = \rule{0.5cm}{0.4pt} + \rule{0.5cm}{0.4pt} + \rule{0.5cm}{0.4pt} + \rule{0.5cm}{0.4pt} + \rule{0.5cm}{0.4pt} - \rule{0.5cm}{0.4pt} - \rule{0.5cm}{0.4pt} - \rule{0.5cm}{0.4pt} - \rule{0.5cm}{0.4pt}$$
$$\rule{1cm}{0.4pt} = \rule{0.5cm}{0.4pt} + \rule{0.5cm}{0.4pt} + \rule{0.5cm}{0.4pt} + \rule{0.5cm}{0.4pt} + \rule{0.5cm}{0.4pt} - \rule{0.5cm}{0.4pt} - \rule{0.5cm}{0.4pt} - \rule{0.5cm}{0.4pt} - \rule{0.5cm}{0.4pt} - \rule{0.5cm}{0.4pt}$$

When viewed in two dimensions, an interesting relationship between the cubic numbers and the triangular numbers is revealed.

6. Study the next diagrams and complete the table.

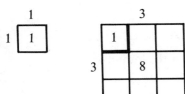
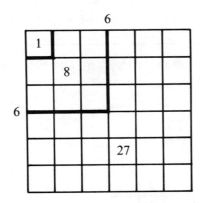
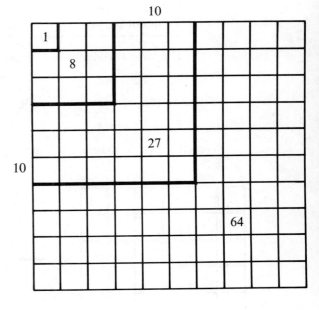

$$1^2 = 1 \cdot 1 = 1^3$$
$$= 1 = 1$$
$$3^2 = 3 \cdot 3 = 1^3 + 2^3$$
$$= 1 + 8 = 9$$
$$6^2 = 6 \cdot 6 = 1^3 + 2^3 + 3^3$$
$$= 1 + 8 + 27 = 36$$
$$10^2 = 10 \cdot 10 = 1^3 + 2^3 + 3^3 + 4^3$$
$$= 1 + 8 + 27 + 64 = \underline{\quad}$$
$$15^2 = 15 \cdot 15 = \underline{\quad} + \underline{\quad} + \underline{\quad} + \underline{\quad} + \underline{\quad}$$
$$= \underline{\quad} + \underline{\quad} + \underline{\quad} + \underline{\quad} + \underline{\quad} = \underline{\quad}$$

In general, we have

$$T_n^2 = 1^3 + 2^3 + 3^3 + \cdots + n^3$$

Note: This formula states that the square of the nth triangular number is equal to the sum of the first n cubic numbers. (Sums of cubic numbers generate hypercubic numbers of four dimensions. For more on this topic see Section 4.5.)

7. Verify the formula above for $n = 6$.

Another way of stating the general formula is as follows.

$$(1 + 2 + 3 + \cdots + n)^2 = 1^3 + 2^3 + 3^3 + \cdots + n^3$$

Also, since $T_n = \frac{1}{2}n(n + 1)$, we have

$$1^3 + 2^3 + 3^3 + \cdots + n^3 = \left[\frac{1}{2}n(n + 1)\right]^2$$

8. Use the formula above to find the sum of the first 10 cubic numbers. Find the sum of the first 100 cubic numbers.

The same two-dimensional diagrams showing 1^2, 3^2, 6^2, and 10^2 also suggest the formula

$$T_n^2 - T_{n-1}^2 = n^3$$

For example,

$$T_3^2 - T_2^2 = 3^3$$

is pictured in the diagram below.

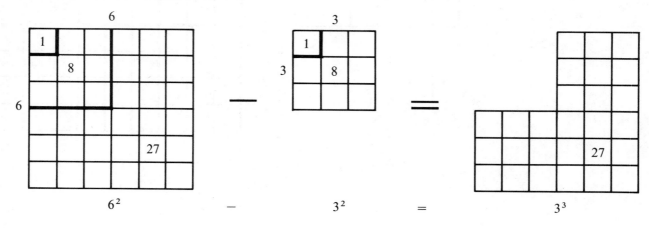

9. Draw the diagram equation for $T_4^2 - T_3^2 = 4^3$.

10. Verify the formula

$$1^3 + 2^3 + 3^3 + \cdots + n^3 = \frac{1}{2}(T_{n^2} + n^3)$$

for $n = 1$, $n = 2$, $n = 3$, and $n = 4$.

11. Verify the formulas

$$n^2 = 2 \cdot T_{n-1} + n$$

and

$$n^3 = 2n \cdot T_{n-1} + n^2$$

and

$$n^3 = 2(1 + 5 + 12 + \cdots + P_{n-1}) + 2 \cdot T_{n-1} + S_n$$

for $n = 2$, $n = 3$, and $n = 4$.

12. Verify the following formulas and write the next two equations.

$$2^3 = (2 \cdot 2) + (2 + 2)$$
$$3^3 = (6 \cdot 3) + (6 + 3)$$
$$4^3 = (12 \cdot 4) + (12 + 4)$$
$$\underline{} = (20 \cdot 5) + (20 + 5)$$
$$6^3 = \underline{}$$

13. Perform the following operations. Extend the sequence by predicting the next two formulas. What sequence of numbers is generated?

$$1 \cdot (1 + 0) =$$
$$2 \cdot (3 + 1) =$$
$$3 \cdot (6 + 3) =$$
$$4 \cdot (10 + 6) =$$
$$\underline{} =$$
$$\underline{} =$$

14. Let c_n represent the nth cubic number. Verify the formula

$$c_n - c_{n-1} = S_n + 2 \cdot T_{n-1} + S_{n-1}$$

for $n = 2$, $n = 3$, and $n = 4$.

The cubic numbers belong to the larger class of prismoidal numbers.

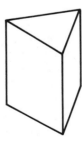

Triangular
prism

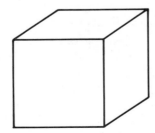

Square
prism

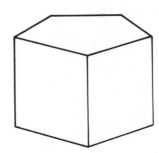

Pentagonal
prism

The first three triangular prismoidal numbers are shown below.

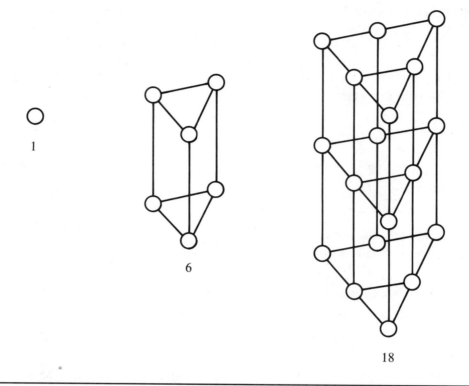

15. Draw the fourth triangular prismoidal number.
16. Verify that the triangular prismoidal numbers are given by the formula

$$n \cdot T_n$$

17. Compare the sequence of triangular prismoidal numbers to the sequence of pentagonal pyramidal numbers. What do you notice?

4.5 FIGURATE NUMBERS OF THE FOURTH DIMENSION

The sums of the 2-dimensional polygonal numbers generate the 3-dimensional pyramidal numbers. Likewise, the sums of the 3-dimensional pyramidal numbers generate 4-dimensional figurate numbers. The simplest of these are the pentatopes. A pentatopal number is formed by adding layers of tetrahedral numbers. The 4th pentatopal number is given by $t_1 + t_2 + t_3 + t_4$.

Sums of tetrahedral numbers can easily be found in Pascal's Triangle using the "hockey stick" rule.

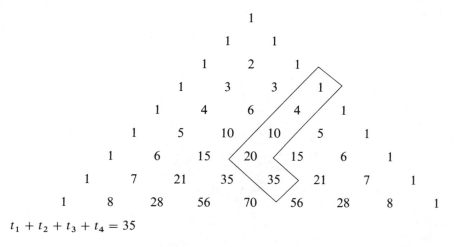

$$t_1 + t_2 + t_3 + t_4 = 35$$

---

1. Find the 5th pentatopal number.

Using the property for adjacent numbers in Pascal's Triangle we can find a general formula for the nth pentatopal number as follows.

$$n\text{th pentatopal number} = t_{n+1} \cdot \frac{n}{4}$$

$$= \frac{n(n + 1)(n + 2)(n + 3)}{24}$$

$$= \mathbb{P}_n$$

Note: $\mathbb{P}_n$ represents the nth pentatopal number and t_{n+1} represents the $(n + 1)$th tetrahedral number.

---

2. Use this formula to find the 10th pentatopal number.

The nth pentatopal number can also be expressed in terms of triangular numbers as follows.

$$\mathbb{P}_n = \frac{1}{6} T_n \cdot T_{n+2}$$

---

3. Verify the formula above for $n = 1$, $n = 2$, and $n = 3$.

---

4. Subtract the smaller number from the larger number in each of the circled groups below. What sequence of numbers is generated?

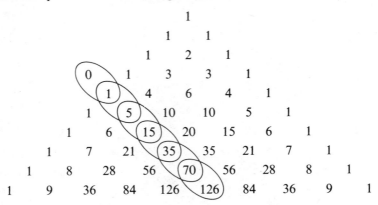

5. Subtract the smaller number from the larger number in each of the circled groups below. What sequence of numbers is generated?

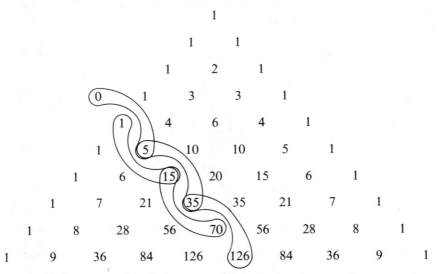

6. Develop the next three rows of the following number triangle.

```
            1
         3     6
     10    15    21
   28   36    45   55
```

Divide the elements in the column indicated below by 3. What sequence of numbers is generated?

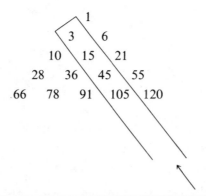

Hexatopal numbers can be found by adding layers of square pyramidal numbers. The 4th hexatopal number is given by

$$s_1 + s_2 + s_3 + s_4$$

and as we saw in a previous exercise:

$$s_1 + s_2 + s_3 + s_4 = t_4^2 - t_3 \cdot t_5$$

In general,

$$n\text{th hexatopal number} = s_1 + s_2 + s_3 + \cdots + s_n$$
$$= t_n^2 - t_{n-1} \cdot t_{n+1}$$
$$= \mathbb{H}_n$$

Note: $\mathbb{H}_n$ represents the nth hexatopal number, s_n represents the nth square pyramidal number, and t_n represents the nth tetrahedral number.

7. Find the first 4 hexatopal numbers.

8. Add these two sequences term by term. What sequence of numbers is generated?

$$
\begin{array}{ccccccc}
 & 1 & 5 & 15 & 35 & 70 & 126 & \cdots \\
+ \quad 1 & 5 & 15 & 35 & 70 & 126 & 210 & \cdots \\
\end{array}
$$

9. Complete the table below.

1	= ___	1		= ___
4 + 1	= ___	4 + 2 · 1		= ___
10 + 5	= ___	10 + 2 · 5		= ___
20 + 15	= ___	20 + 2 · 15		= ___
35 + 35	= ___	35 + 2 · 35		= ___
___ + ___	= ___	___ + 2 · ___		= ___
___ + ___	= ___	___ + ___		= ___

Describe the sequences of numbers generated.

10. Evaluate the following determinants. What sequence of numbers is formed?

$$\begin{vmatrix} 1 & 0 \\ 4 & 1 \end{vmatrix} =$$

$$\begin{vmatrix} 4 & 1 \\ 10 & 4 \end{vmatrix} =$$

$$\begin{vmatrix} 10 & 4 \\ 20 & 10 \end{vmatrix} =$$

Write the next three determinants in this sequence and evaluate them.

These determinants suggest that

$$t_n^2 - t_{n+1} \cdot t_{n-1} = n\text{th hexatopal number} = \mathbb{H}_n$$

11. Complete the tables below. Notice the patterns with hexatopal numbers, $\mathbb{H}_n$.

n	Tetrahedral numbers t_n	Square pyramidal numbers s_n	Pentagonal pyramidal numbers p_n	Hexagonal pyramidal numbers h_n
1	$\begin{vmatrix} 1 & 1 \\ 3 & 4 \end{vmatrix} = 1$	$\begin{vmatrix} 1 & 1 \\ 3 & 5 \end{vmatrix} = 2 = 2 \cdot 1$	$\begin{vmatrix} 1 & 1 \\ 3 & 6 \end{vmatrix} = 3 = 3 \cdot 1$	$\begin{vmatrix} 1 & 1 \\ 3 & 7 \end{vmatrix} = 4 = 4 \cdot 1$
2	$\begin{vmatrix} 3 & 4 \\ 6 & 10 \end{vmatrix} = 6$	$\begin{vmatrix} 3 & 5 \\ 6 & 14 \end{vmatrix} = 12 = 2 \cdot 6$	$\begin{vmatrix} 3 & 6 \\ 6 & 18 \end{vmatrix} = 18 = 3 \cdot 6$	$\begin{vmatrix} 3 & 7 \\ 6 & 22 \end{vmatrix} = 24 = 4 \cdot 6$
3	$\begin{vmatrix} 6 & 10 \\ 10 & 20 \end{vmatrix} = 20$	$\begin{vmatrix} 6 & 14 \\ 10 & 30 \end{vmatrix} = 40 = 2 \cdot 20$	$\begin{vmatrix} 6 & 18 \\ 10 & 40 \end{vmatrix} = 60 = 3 \cdot 20$	$\begin{vmatrix} 6 & 22 \\ 10 & 50 \end{vmatrix} = 80 = 4 \cdot 20$
4	$\begin{vmatrix} 10 & 20 \\ 15 & 35 \end{vmatrix} = 50$	$\begin{vmatrix} 10 & 30 \\ 15 & 55 \end{vmatrix} = 100 =$	$\begin{vmatrix} 10 & 40 \\ 15 & 75 \end{vmatrix} =$	$\begin{vmatrix} 10 & 50 \\ 15 & 95 \end{vmatrix} = 200 =$
5	$=$	$=$	$=$	$=$
6	$=$	$=$	$=$	$=$
⋮				
n	$\begin{vmatrix} T_n & t_n \\ T_{n+1} & t_{n+1} \end{vmatrix} = \mathbb{H}_n$	$\begin{vmatrix} T_n & s_n \\ T_{n+1} & s_{n+1} \end{vmatrix} = 2 \cdot \mathbb{H}_n$	$\begin{vmatrix} T_n & p_n \\ T_{n+1} & p_{n+1} \end{vmatrix} = \underline{\quad}$	$\begin{vmatrix} T_n & h_n \\ T_{n+1} & h_{n+1} \end{vmatrix} = \underline{\quad}$

The nth hexatopal number can also be expressed in terms of triangular numbers as follows.

$$n\text{th hexatopal number} = \frac{1}{3} T_n \cdot T_{n+1}$$

12. Verify the formula above for $n = 1$, $n = 2$, $n = 3$, and $n = 4$.

The hexatopal numbers are not neatly nested in Pascal's Triangle, but the simplexes in each dimension are. See the chart below.

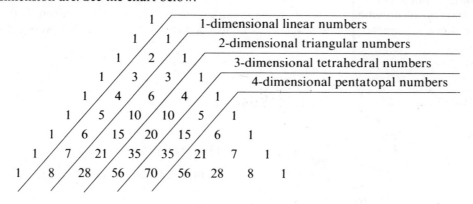

1-dimensional linear numbers
2-dimensional triangular numbers
3-dimensional tetrahedral numbers
4-dimensional pentatopal numbers

---

13. Predict the sequence of 5-dimensional simplexal numbers.

14. Complete the tables below.

2-dimensional triangular numbers	3-dimensional tetrahedral numbers	4-dimensional pentatopal numbers	5-dimensional simplexal numbers
$\begin{vmatrix} 1 & 1 \\ 2 & 3 \end{vmatrix} = 1$	$\begin{vmatrix} 1 & 1 \\ 2 & 4 \end{vmatrix} = 2 = 2\cdot 1$	$\begin{vmatrix} 1 & 1 \\ 2 & 5 \end{vmatrix} = 3 = 3\cdot 1$	$\begin{vmatrix} 1 & 1 \\ 2 & 6 \end{vmatrix} = 4 = 4\cdot 1$
$\begin{vmatrix} 2 & 3 \\ 3 & 6 \end{vmatrix} = 3$	$\begin{vmatrix} 2 & 4 \\ 3 & 10 \end{vmatrix} = 8 = 2\cdot 4$	$\begin{vmatrix} 2 & 5 \\ 3 & 15 \end{vmatrix} = 15 = 3\cdot 5$	$\begin{vmatrix} 2 & 6 \\ 3 & 21 \end{vmatrix} = 24 = 4\cdot 6$
$\begin{vmatrix} 3 & 6 \\ 4 & 10 \end{vmatrix} = 6$	$\begin{vmatrix} 3 & 10 \\ 4 & 20 \end{vmatrix} = 20 = 2\cdot 10$	$\begin{vmatrix} 3 & 15 \\ 4 & 35 \end{vmatrix} = 45 = 3\cdot 15$	$\begin{vmatrix} 3 & 21 \\ 4 & 56 \end{vmatrix} = 84 = 4\cdot 21$
$\begin{vmatrix} 4 & 10 \\ 5 & 15 \end{vmatrix} = 10$	$\begin{vmatrix} 4 & 20 \\ 5 & 35 \end{vmatrix} =$	$\begin{vmatrix} 4 & 35 \\ 5 & 70 \end{vmatrix} =$	$\begin{vmatrix} 4 & 56 \\ 5 & 126 \end{vmatrix} =$
$=$	$=$	$=$	$=$
$=$	$=$	$=$	$=$

Recall from our discussion of simplexes in Chapter 1, that subspaces of a triangle consist of 3 points, 3 line segments, and 1 triangle. Let's call this the (3, 3, 1) sequence. The subspaces for a tetrahedron consist of 4 points, 6 line segments, 4 triangles, and 1 tetrahedron. Let's call this the (4, 6, 4, 1) sequence. These sequences will also be called "strings," as they were called in Chapter 2.

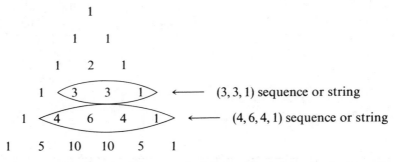

Using these sequences, we can also generate the triangular and tetrahedral numbers. To describe this we need to use the operation called "string multiplication" introduced in Chapter 2. For example, to multiply the strings $(1, 2, 1)$ and $(3, 3, 1)$ we write

$$(1, 2, 1) \bullet (3, 3, 1) = 1 \cdot 3 + 2 \cdot 3 + 1 \cdot 1$$
$$= 3 + 6 + 1$$
$$= 10$$

Multiplying strings involves the multiplication of corresponding elements in the two strings and adding the products to give the final result. The strings above give a result of 10 and $10 = T_4$. These strings are found in Pascal's Triangle as shown below.

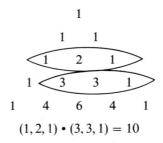

$$(1, 2, 1) \bullet (3, 3, 1) = 10$$

---

15. Multiply the two strings shown in Pascal's Triangle.

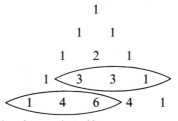

What triangular number is generated?

16. Multiply each circled string below by (3, 3, 1). What sequence of numbers is generated?

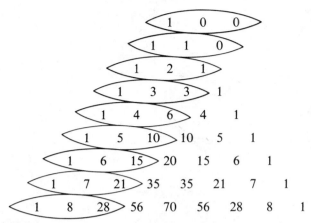

17. Multiply the two strings shown in Pascal's Triangle.

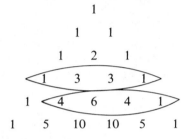

What tetrahedral number is generated?

18. Multiply each circled string below by (4, 6, 4, 1). What sequence of numbers is generated?

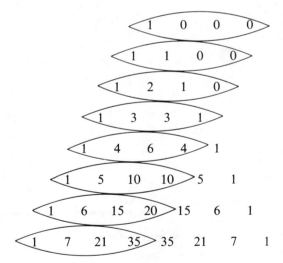

19. Multiply each circled string below by $(5, 10, 10, 5, 1)$. What sequence of numbers is generated?

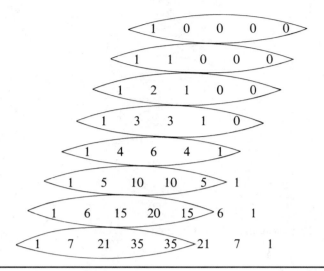

The string product $(1, 4, 6) \cdot (3, 3, 1) = 1 \cdot 3 + 4 \cdot 3 + 6 \cdot 1$, which gives a final result of 21. Examine the intermediate values above: $1 \cdot 3 = 3$, $4 \cdot 3 = 12$, and $6 \cdot 1 = 6$. These numbers tell us how many dots exist at the three vertices, on the 3 sides, and in the one triangular interior, respectively, of T_6.

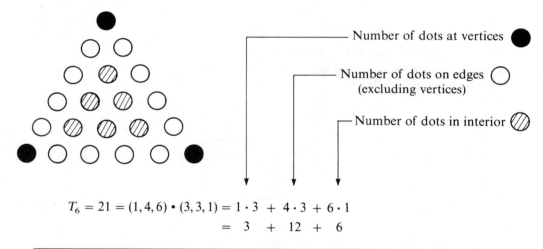

$$T_6 = 21 = (1, 4, 6) \cdot (3, 3, 1) = 1 \cdot 3 + 4 \cdot 3 + 6 \cdot 1$$
$$= 3 + 12 + 6$$

20. Without a picture, predict how many dots are at the vertices, on the edges, and in the interior of the triangular number T_7.

Draw a picture of T_7 and verify your answers.

In a similar manner, we can analyze the tetrahedral number $t_5 = 35$. Its string product is
$$t_5 = 35 = (1, 3, 3, 1) \cdot (4, 6, 4, 1) = 1 \cdot 4 + 3 \cdot 6 + 3 \cdot 4 + 1 \cdot 1$$
$$= 4 + 18 + 12 + 1$$

The numbers 4, 18, 12, and 1 are the number of dots at the vertices, the number of dots on the edges, the number of dots on the faces, and the number of dots in the interior of the tetrahedron, respectively.

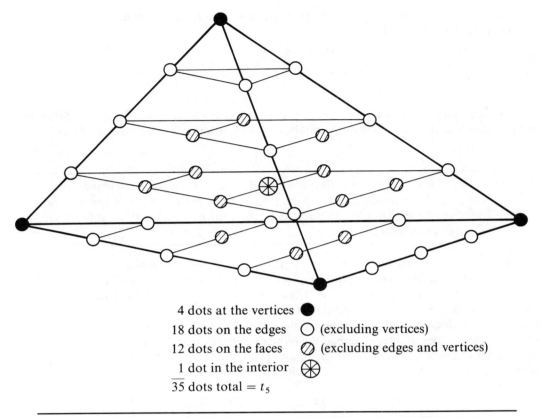

4 dots at the vertices ●
18 dots on the edges ○ (excluding vertices)
12 dots on the faces ⊘ (excluding edges and vertices)
1 dot in the interior ⊛
$\overline{35 \text{ dots total}} = t_5$

---

21. Without a picture, predict how many dots are at the vertices, on the edges, on the faces, and in the interior of the tetrahedral number $t_6 = 56$.

The string product $(1, 4, 6, 4, 1) \bullet (5, 10, 10, 5, 1)$ represents the 6th pentatopal number of four dimensions. Furthermore, the intermediate results can be interpreted similarly, as before.

$$126 = (1, 4, 6, 4, 1) \bullet (5, 10, 10, 5, 1)$$
$$= 1 \cdot 5 + 4 \cdot 10 + 6 \cdot 10 + 4 \cdot 5 + 1 \cdot 1$$
$$= 5 + 40 + 60 + 20 + 1$$

The numbers 5, 40, 60, 20, and 1 are the number of dots at the vertices, the number of dots on the edges, the number of dots on the triangular faces, the number of dots in the tetrahedral solids, and the number of dots in the interior of the pentatope, respectively.

---

22. Predict how many dots are at the vertices, on the edges, on the faces, in the tetrahedral solids, and in the interior of the 5th pentatopal number, 70.

From Chapter 1 recall that a cube has 8 vertices, 12 edges, 6 faces, and 1 cube. These numbers result from the string operation

$$(2^3, 2^2, 2^1, 2^0) \bullet (1, 3, 3, 1) = 2^3 \cdot 1 + 2^2 \cdot 3 + 2^1 \cdot 3 + 2^0 \cdot 1$$
$$= 8 + 12 + 6 + 1$$
$$= 27$$

A square, on the other hand, has 4 vertices, 4 edges, and 1 square. These numbers result from the following string operation.

$$(2^2, 2^1, 2^0) \bullet (1, 2, 1) = 2^2 \cdot 1 + 2^1 \cdot 2 + 2^0 \cdot 1$$
$$= \quad 4 \quad + \quad 4 \quad + \quad 1$$
$$= 9$$

In the products above there are powers of two, numbers from the rows of Pascal's Triangle, and powers of three that represent the total number of subspaces in each figure, $27 = 3^3$, $9 = 3^2$.

---

23. A hypercube (4-dimensional) is composed of vertices, edges, faces (squares), cubes, and one hypercube. Extending the concept presented above, predict the number of each kind of subspace comprising the hypercube. What is the total number of subspaces?

Imagine a cube that is painted over its entire surface. Suppose it is a 3-inch cube and is cut into its 27 ($27 = 3^3$) smaller unit cubes. How many of the 1-inch cubes have 0 painted faces? How many of the 1-inch cubes have just 1 painted face? How many of the 1-inch cubes have just 2 painted faces? How many of the 1-inch cubes have just 3 painted faces? There are, of course, no 1-inch cubes with 4 or more painted faces. The answers to these questions correspond to the number of interior cubes, the number of cubes in the faces of the original cube, the number of cubes on the edges of the original cube, and the number of cubes at the vertices of the original cube. In the case of the 3-inch cube, we have the following:

Dot Diagram of 3^3

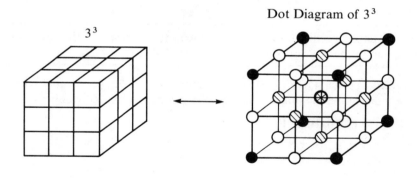

3^3

8 cubes painted on 3 faces (8 vertices)	●
12 cubes painted on 2 faces (12 edges)	○
6 cubes painted on 1 face (6 faces)	◌
1 cube painted on 0 faces (1 cube)	✪ (interior)

$\overline{27}$

---

24. Given a 4-inch cube that is painted over its entire surface, and then cut into 64 unit cubes ($64 = 4^3$), find

(a) the number of cubes painted on 3 faces

(b) the number of cubes painted on 2 faces

(c) the number of cubes painted on 1 face

(d) the number of cubes painted on 0 faces.

We can obtain the results to the previous exercise by using a string operation. In this case, we will use the string $(8, 12, 6, 1)$. These numbers are the number of subspaces in a cube and, incidentally, are produced in the string operation $(2^3, 2^2, 2^1, 2^0) \cdot (1, 3, 3, 1) = 8 + 12 + 6 + 1$. For the 4-inch cube we use the intermediate results of the following string operation.

$$(2^0, 2^1, 2^2, 2^3) \cdot (8, 12, 6, 1) = 2^0 \cdot 8 + 2^1 \cdot 12 + 2^2 \cdot 6 + 2^3 \cdot 1$$
$$= 8 \;+\; 24 \;+\; 24 \;+\; 8$$

The numbers 8, 24, 24, and 8 are the answers to the questions asked in the above exercise. Suppose we draw a dot diagram of the cubic number 64. There are 8 dots at the vertices, 24 dots on the edges, 24 dots on the faces, and 8 dots in the interior of the cube.

For a 5-inch cube we use the following string product.

$$(3^0, 3^1, 3^2, 3^3) \cdot (8, 12, 6, 1) = 3^0 \cdot 8 + 3^1 \cdot 12 + 3^2 \cdot 6 + 3^3 \cdot 1$$
$$= 8 \;+\; 36 \;+\; 54 \;+\; 27$$
$$= 125$$
$$= 5^3$$

The numbers 8, 36, 54, and 27 are the number of cubes painted on 3 faces, painted on 2 faces, painted on 1 face, and those not painted on any face of a 5-inch cube. Summarizing

Use $(1^0, 1^1, 1^2, 1^3) \cdot (8, 12, 6, 1)$ for a 3-inch cube.

Use $(2^0, 2^1, 2^2, 2^3) \cdot (8, 12, 6, 1)$ for a 4-inch cube.

Use $(3^0, 3^1, 3^2, 3^3) \cdot (8, 12, 6, 1)$ for a 5-inch cube.

---

25. Predict the string product to use for a 6-inch cube.

Given a 6-inch cube painted over its entire surface and then cut into unit cubes, find

(a) the number of cubes painted on 3 faces

(b) the number of cubes painted on 2 faces

(c) the number of cubes painted on 1 face

(d) the number of cubes painted on 0 faces

26. Recall that squares are composed of the subspaces consisting of 4 vertices, 4 edges, and 1 square. Use the string $(4, 4, 1)$ to develop the necessary string operations to give the number dots at the vertices, on the edges, and inside the various dot diagrams of squares of increasing size.

27. Develop the same kind of string operations for hypercubes.

28. Using the previous results show that the first 5 hypercubic numbers are: $1^4, 2^4, 3^4, 4^4$, and 5^4.

29. Complete the table below.

n	$(T_n + T_{n-1})^2$	$=$	$T_{n^2} + T_{n^2-1}$	$=$	n^4
2	$(3 + 1)^2 = $ ____	$=$	$10 + \quad 6 = $ ____	$=$	$2^4 = $ ____
3	$(6 + 3)^2 = $ ____	$=$	$45 + \quad 36 = $ ____	$=$	$3^4 = $ ____
4	$(10 + 6)^2 = $ ____	$=$	$136 + \quad 120 = $ ____	$=$	$4^4 = $ ____
5	(____ + ____)$^2 = $ ____	$=$	____ + ____ $= $ ____	$=$	____ $= $ ____

4.6 FINITE DIFFERENTIATION AND INTEGRATION

The difference between the 12th triangular number and the 11th triangular number is 12. The difference between the 7th triangular number and the 6th triangular number is 7. In general, the formula is

$$T_n - T_{n-1} = n$$

Look at the sequence of triangular numbers and record the successive differences. The following pattern emerges.

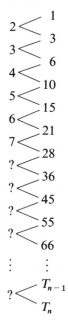

1. Complete the sequence of differences above.

The column of numbers you completed is called a **difference sequence** for the sequence of triangular numbers. This particular difference sequence is the sequence of counting numbers. The difference between consecutive counting numbers is always the number 1. Study the following chart.

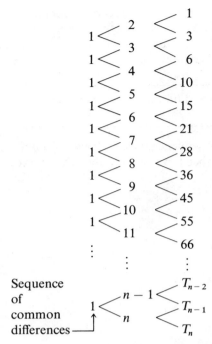

The chart above shows that it takes two difference sequences to arrive at a sequence of **common differences**. If you start with a given sequence (like the triangular numbers) and arrive at a sequence of common differences in a fixed number of steps (like that shown above, two steps), the process is called **finite differentiation**.

2. Start with the sequence of tetrahedral numbers and find the difference sequences until you arrive at a sequence of common differences.

3. Do the same with the sequence of square numbers.

4. Do the same with the sequence of pentagonal numbers.

5. Find the difference sequences indicated in the chart below. What do you notice?

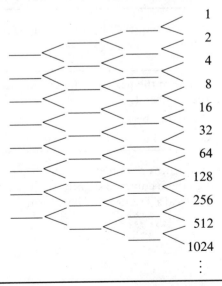

Notice that in the previous exercise you will never arrive at a sequence of common differences. The sequence you started with is the sequence of powers of two and it belongs to a special class of sequences called **geometric sequences**. These sequences do not lead to a sequence of common differences through the process of finite differentiation.

---

6. Start with the sequence of Fibonacci numbers and find the first three difference sequences. What do you notice?

Suppose the triangular numbers form a difference sequence for another set of numbers. Assuming this new set of numbers begins with the number 1, we can find the other numbers in the set by consecutive additions.

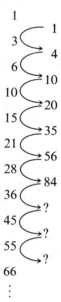

---

7. Complete the sequence above. What sequence of numbers is formed?

If you start with a sequence and arrive at a new sequence by adding successive terms (like that shown above), the process is called **integration**.

---

8. Start with the tetrahedral numbers and form the next two integrating sequences. Assume these sequences begin with the number 1.

9. Do the same with the sequence of square numbers.

10. Do the same with the sequence of pentagonal numbers.

The following table shows the difference sequences obtained when we begin with the sequence of pentatopal numbers. If we rearrange these columns slightly and include a few numbers at the heads of these columns, we get Pascal's Triangle in chart form.

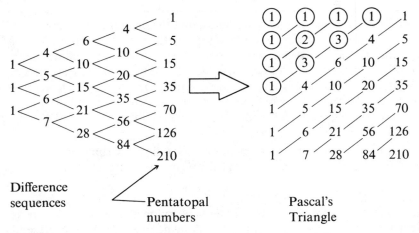

Difference sequences

Pentatopal numbers

Pascal's Triangle

Now, let's rearrange the chart form of Pascal's Triangle as follows.

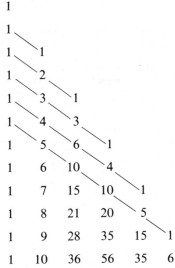

When we add the elements in each horizontal row in the previous chart we obtain the sequence of Fibonacci numbers.

$$1 = 1$$
$$1 = 1$$
$$2 = 1 + 1$$
$$3 = 1 + 2$$
$$5 = 1 + 3 + 1$$
$$8 = 1 + 4 + 3$$
$$13 = 1 + 5 + 6 + 1$$
$$21 = 1 + 6 + 10 + 4$$
$$34 = 1 + 7 + 15 + 10 + 1$$
$$55 = 1 + 8 + 21 + 20 + 5$$
$$89 = 1 + 9 + 28 + 35 + 15 + 1$$
$$144 = 1 + 10 + 36 + 56 + 35 + 6$$

Fibonacci numbers

$$F_n = F_{n-1} + F_{n-2}$$ (Recall this formula from Chapter 2.)

11. Starting with the sequence of square numbers, find the difference sequences until you arrive at a sequence of common differences. At the same time, form the next two integrating sequences assuming these sequences begin with the number 1. Put all of these sequences into a chart form like we did with Pascal's Triangle. Next, rearrange the chart displacing successive columns each by two elements as we also did with Pascal's Triangle. Finally, add the elements in each horizontal row and obtain the sequence of Fibonacci numbers (you will have to adjust the first element).

12. Starting with the sequence of pentagonal numbers, follow the same procedure as in problem 11 to obtain the sequence of Lucas numbers. Recall that

$$L_n = F_n + 2F_{n-1}$$

13. Starting with the sequence of hexagonal numbers, follow the same procedure as in problem 11 to obtain a sequence with the following property. If G_n represents the nth element of the sequence, then

$$G_n = F_n + 3F_{n-1}$$

14. Predict what the result will be if you start with the sequence of heptagonal numbers and follow the same procedure as in problem 11.

15. Starting with the sequence of cubic numbers, follow the same procedure as described in exercises 11 through 14. Verify that if G_n represents the nth number of the resulting sequence, then

$$G_n = F_{n+1} + F_n + F_{n-1} + F_{n-2} + F_{n-3}$$

In particular, verify that

$$G_4 = 5 + 3 + 2 + 1 + 1$$

and

$$G_5 = 8 + 5 + 3 + 2 + 1$$

Also, verify the following formulas.

$$G_n = F_{n+3} - F_{n-2}$$
$$G_n = 3F_{n+1} - F_n$$
$$G_n = 2F_n + 3F_{n-1}$$
$$G_n = F_{n+1} + L_n$$

For more information about the technique of finite differences and the application of this technique to a variety of problem-solving experiences, including figurate numbers, we recommend *Finite Differences* by Dale Seymour and Margaret Shedd and published by Dale Seymour Publications.

We conclude this section with an application of Pascal's Triangle to the method of finite differences. If we have three numbers of a sequence, then the successive differences can be expressed as follows.

$$a - 2b + c \begin{array}{c} a-b \begin{array}{c} a \\ b \end{array} \\ b-c \begin{array}{c} b \\ c \end{array} \end{array}$$

If we have four numbers of a sequence, then

$$a - 3b + 3c - d \begin{array}{c} a-2b+c \begin{array}{c} a-b \begin{array}{c} a \\ b \end{array} \\ b-c \begin{array}{c} b \\ c \end{array} \\ b-2c+d \begin{array}{c} b-c \begin{array}{c} c \\ d \end{array} \\ c-d \begin{array}{c} c \\ d \end{array} \end{array} \end{array}$$

You can see that the coefficients of the numbers a, b, c, and d are elements from the rows of Pascal's Triangle. Thus, without forming the successive differences we can predict in advance the ultimate result. For example, if the numbers in the sequence are 9, 6, and 4, then the difference after two applications of differentiation can be predicted to be

$$(1, -2, 1) \cdot (9, 6, 4) = 1 \cdot 9 - 2 \cdot 6 + 1 \cdot 4 = 1$$

by using the 2nd row of Pascal's Triangle and the string multiplication operation of Section 2.5. To verify, we can form the successive differences.

Suppose we start with four numbers of a sequence, 8, 4, 6, 3. By using the 3rd row of Pascal's Triangle as coefficients, we can predict the difference after three applications of differentiation to be

$$(1, -3, 3, -1) \cdot (8, 4, 6, 3) = 1 \cdot 8 - 3 \cdot 4 + 3 \cdot 6 - 1 \cdot 3 = 11$$

We can verify this by forming the successive differences.

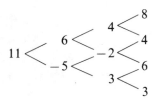

Using Pascal's Triangle predict the difference for the following sequences. Verify your results.

16. 10, 5, 3 for two applications of differentiation
17. 1, 4, 9 for two applications of differentiation
18. 2, 6, 10 for two applications of differentiation
19. 15, 7, 3, 0 for three applications of differentiation
20. 1, 2, 6, 20 for three applications of differentiation
21. 1, 3, 3, 1 for three applications of differentiation
22. 1, 1, 2, 3, 5 for four applications of differentiation

5 Counting Problems

5.1 COUNTING SUBSETS OF A SET

At Pascal's Pizza Parlor you may order one, two, or three toppings (cheese, meat, vegetarian) or you can order plain (no topping). Let's represent the pizza with all three toppings as the set $\{c, m, v\}$. The other possible pizzas that can be ordered are subsets of this set. All the possibilities are listed in the chart below.

	No topping	One topping	Two toppings	Three toppings
	∅ (plain)	$\{c\}$ $\{m\}$ $\{v\}$	$\{c, m\}$ $\{c, v\}$ $\{m, v\}$	$\{c, m, v\}$
Number of choices	1	3	3	1

The total number of different pizzas is given by $1 + 3 + 3 + 1 = 8$. Do you recognize the numbers 1, 3, 3, 1?

---

1. Suppose anchovies are added to the list of possible toppings. The pizza with all four toppings will be represented by $\{a, c, m, v\}$. Make a chart similar to the one above listing all of the different pizzas that are possible. Do you recognize the numbers generated? What is the total number of different pizzas that can be ordered when four toppings are available?

2. Complete the following chart.

Set	Number of subsets with					Total number of subsets
	0 Elements	**1 Element**	**2 Elements**	**3 Elements**	**4 Elements**	
∅						
{a}						
{a, b}						
{a, b, c}	1	3	3	1	0	8
{a, b, c, d}						
{a, b, c, d, e}						

3. Predict the total number of subsets of a set with six elements.

4. If a set has n elements, what expression represents the number of subsets?

Sets are frequently represented by Euler or Venn diagrams. In these diagrams, the points inside a circle represent the elements of a given set. Points outside the given circle are elements of another set called the **complement** of the given set. In the following diagram, all points in the rectangle belong to the **universal set**, the set of elements defined for a particular discussion. The points in the circle are elements of set A and the points outside the circle are elements of the complement of set A, denoted by A'.

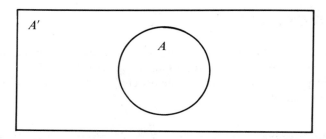

In this case, there are two subsets of the universal set: set A' and set A.

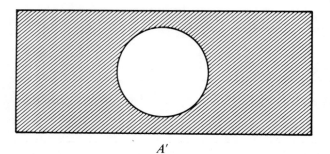

A'

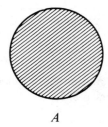

A

When two sets A and B belong to the same universal set, then an element of this universe must belong to exactly one of the following four sets:

$A \cap B$	(both A and B)
$A \cap B'$	(A but not B)
$A' \cap B$	(B but not A)
$A' \cap B'$	(neither A nor B)

The symbol $\cap$ in the expression $A \cap B$ means that the intersection of A and B is being considered and an element that is a member of the intersection of A and B is a member of A and a member of B.

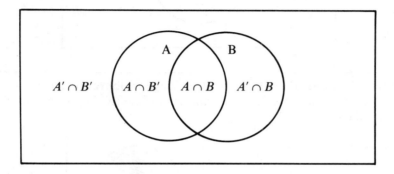

If we draw each subset separately, notice that there are two subsets that are similarly shaped.

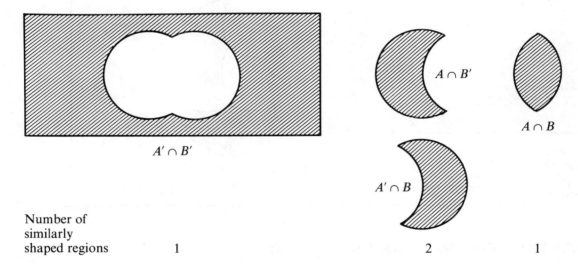

Number of similarly shaped regions	1		2	1

When three sets A, B, and C are considered in the same universal set, then an element of this universe must belong to exactly one of the following sets.

$A \cap B \cap C$	(each of the sets A, B, and C)
$A \cap B \cap C'$	(both A and B, but not C)
$A \cap B' \cap C$	(both A and C, but not B)
$A' \cap B \cap C$	(both B and C, but not A)
$A \cap B' \cap C'$	(A, but neither B nor C)
$A' \cap B \cap C'$	(B, but neither A nor C)
$A' \cap B' \cap C$	(C, but neither A nor B)
$A' \cap B' \cap C'$	(neither A nor B nor C)

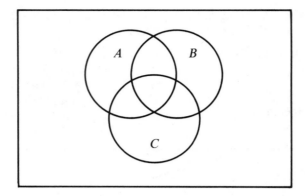

---

5. Identify each of the subsets from the Venn diagram above and label it with the appropriate set symbols. Count the number of similarly shaped regions. Do you recognize these numbers?

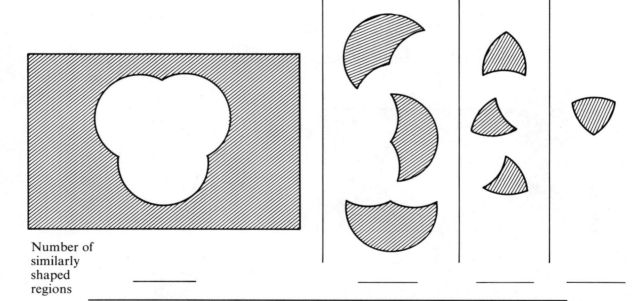

Number of
similarly
shaped
regions   _____   _____   _____   _____

5.2   COUNTING ADDENDS OF NATURAL NUMBERS

How many ways can you add two natural numbers whose sum is 5? The four possibilities are listed below.

  1 + 4   4 + 1   2 + 3   3 + 2

How many ways can you add three natural numbers whose sum is 5? The six possibilities are listed below.

  1 + 1 + 3   1 + 2 + 2
  1 + 3 + 1   2 + 1 + 2
  3 + 1 + 1   2 + 2 + 1

---

1. Find the number of ways you can add four natural numbers whose sum is 5.

The preceding information is summarized in the following table.

	1 Addend	2 Addends	3 Addends	4 Addends	5 Addends
Sums equal to five	5	1 + 4 4 + 1 2 + 3 3 + 2	1 + 1 + 3 1 + 3 + 1 3 + 1 + 1 1 + 2 + 2 2 + 1 + 2 2 + 2 + 1	1 + 1 + 1 + 2 1 + 1 + 2 + 1 1 + 2 + 1 + 1 2 + 1 + 1 + 1	1 + 1 + 1 + 1 + 1
Number of ways	1	4	6	4	1
	Total = 1 + 4 + 6 + 4 + 1 = 16				

2. Predict the number of ways you can add two natural numbers whose sum is 4.

3. Complete the following tables.

	1 Addend	2 Addends
Sums equal to two		
Number of ways		
	Total =	

	1 Addend	2 Addends	3 Addends
Sums equal to three			
Number of ways			
	Total =		

	1 Addend	2 Addends	3 Addends	4 Addends
Sums equal to four				
Number of ways				
	Total =			

	1 Addend	2 Addends	3 Addends	4 Addends	5 Addends	6 Addends
Sums equal to six						
Number of ways						
	Total =					

5.3   COUNTING LINE SEGMENTS

Two points determine a line. How many line segments will connect three points? four points?

1. Complete the table below.

	Number of points	Number of line segments
●——●	2	1
△	3	3
⊠	4	6
(5 points)	5	_____
(6 points)	6	_____

Describe the numbers found in the second column above.

If three or more points are all on the same line, they are said to be **collinear**. In the diagrams below, we will consider the points to be collinear and equally spaced. Thus, in the following diagram there are four points that are collinear and equally spaced. In this diagram there are three line segments that are one unit long, two line segments that are two units long, and one segment that is three units long.

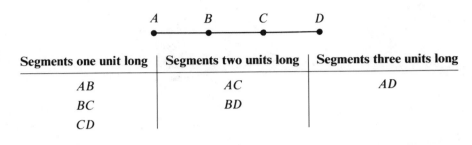

Segments one unit long	Segments two units long	Segments three units long
AB	AC	AD
BC	BD	
CD		

2. Complete the following table.

	Number of points	Number of segments having a length of:					Total
		1 unit	2 units	3 units	4 units	5 units	
	2	1					1
	3	2	1				3
	4	3	2	1			____
	5						____
	6						____

Describe the numbers you listed in the total column above.

5.4 COUNTING ANGLES

A **ray** is a part of a line. It has one endpoint and stretches infinitely far in one direction. An example of a ray is shown below.

The point P is the endpoint and the ray is named $\overrightarrow{PQ}$.

An **angle** is a figure formed by the union of two rays that have the same endpoint. The rays are called the **sides** of the angle and the common endpoint is called the **vertex** of the angle. An example of an angle is shown below.

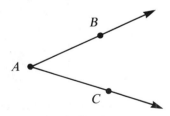

The point A is the vertex and the angle is named $\angle BAC$. Notice that the middle letter is the vertex point.

1. How many angles are there in the following figure? (Hint: There are more than three.)

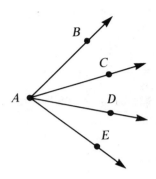

2. The angle *BAE* shown has two rays between its sides. Draw an angle with three rays between its sides and count how many angles are formed.

3. Complete the following table.

		Number of angles having					
	Number of rays	No rays between the sides	One ray between the sides	Two rays between the sides	Three rays between the sides	Four rays between the sides	Total number of angles
	2	1					1
	3	2	1				3
	4	3	2	1			6
	5						
	6						

What kind of numbers do the totals in the last column represent?

If a point is selected on a straight line, it forms two rays directed opposite from each other. The angle thus formed is called a **straight angle**.

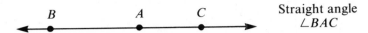

Straight angle
$\angle BAC$

If two lines intersect, then two straight angles are formed along with four other angles.

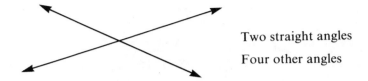

Two straight angles

Four other angles

4. Complete the following table.

	Number of straight lines	Number of angles counting straight angles	Number of angles not counting straight angles
	1	1	0
	2	6	$4 = 4 \cdot 1$
	3	15	$12 = 4 \cdot 3$
	4	_____	_____ $= 4 \cdot 6$
	5	_____	_____ $=$ ___ $\cdot$ ___

5. Describe the numbers in the last two columns of the preceding exercise.

6. In Pascal's Triangle below, circle the numbers that represent the total number of angles in each diagram of intersecting lines.

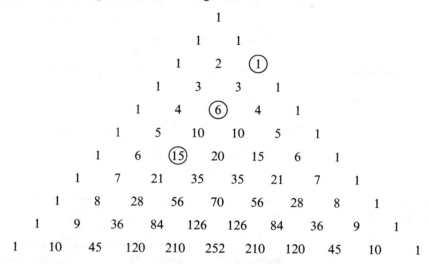

```
                              1
                          1       1
                      1       2      (1)
                  1       3       3       1
              1       4      (6)      4       1
          1       5       10      10      5       1
      1       6     (15)     20      15      6       1
  1       7       21      35      35      21      7       1
1      8       28      56      70      56      28      8       1
1     9      36      84      126     126     84      36      9      1
1    10     45     120    210    252    210    120    45     10     1
```

7. Predict the total number of angles to be found in the following diagram.

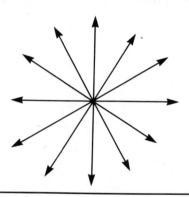

In the diagram below, there are four points on a circle that are connected with each other by line segments. At each point (vertex), 3 angles are formed. Thus, there are 12 angles with vertices on the circle.

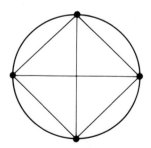

8. Complete the following table.

	Number of points on the circle	Number of angles with vertices on the circle		Total
		Number of vertices	Number of angles at each vertex	
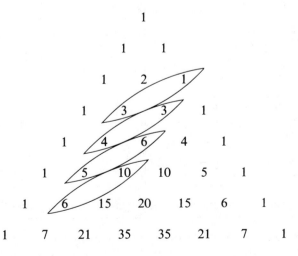	3	3	1	3
	4	4	3	12
	5	5		
	6	6		

9. Multiply the numbers encircled in Pascal's Triangle below. Compare the products to the results in the total column of the table completed in exercise 8.

```
                    1
                 1     1
              1     2     1
           1     3     3     1
        1     4     6     4     1
     1     5    10    10     5     1
  1     6    15    20    15     6     1
1     7    21    35    35    21     7     1
```

10. If seven points were placed around a circle and joined with straight lines, predict the number of angles that would be formed whose vertices would be on the circle.

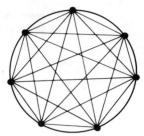

5.5 COUNTING TRIANGLES

Three noncollinear points determine a plane and, subsequently, a triangle. A line and a point not on the line determine a plane. In the table below, we want to find all of the triangles determined by a given point and two other points selected from several choices on the given line.

1. Complete the following table.

	Number of points on the line	Number of triangles
A, triangle with B, C	2	1
A, triangle with B, C, D	3	3
A •, line with B C D E	_____	_____
A •, line with B C D E F	_____	_____
A•, line with B C D E F G	_____	_____

What kind of numbers do the totals in the last column represent?

In the following diagram, there are four points on a circle that are connected with each other by line segments. Counting only the triangles with their vertices on the circle, notice that there are four of them: $\triangle ABC$, $\triangle BCD$, $\triangle CDA$, and $\triangle DAB$.

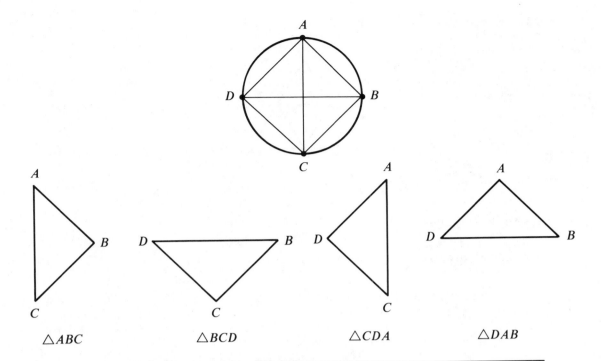

$\triangle ABC$ $\triangle BCD$ $\triangle CDA$ $\triangle DAB$

2. After completing the following table, describe the sequence of numbers you find in the last column. Predict the number of triangles you could find with vertices on the circle if you join seven points on the circle with line segments.

	Number of points on circle	Number of triangles with vertices on the circle
	3	1
	4	4
	5	10
	6	_____

How many triangles can you find in the following diagram?

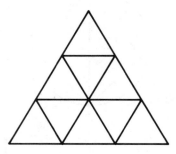

We will refer to this triangular arrangement as a 3 by 3 triangle. In the process of counting,

we will distinguish two triangular positions: position (1), △ , and position (2), ▼ . First,

we count all position (1) triangles according to levels, beginning with 1 by 1 triangles, then 2 by 2 triangles, etc. Similarly, we count all position (2) triangles. In the case of the 3 by 3 triangle, we have

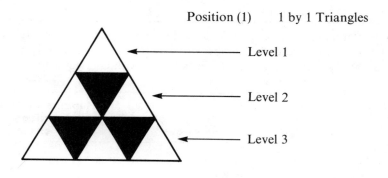

	Position (1)			Position (2)		
	Level			Level		
	1	2	3	1	2	3
1 by 1	1 + 2 + 3			1 + 2		
2 by 2	1 + 2					
3 by 3	1					

$$\begin{aligned} \text{Total} &= (1 + 2 + 3) + 2(1 + 2) + 1 \\ &= 6 \qquad\quad + 2(3) \quad + 1 \\ &= 13 \end{aligned}$$

3. Complete the following table.

		Position (1)	Position (2)	Total
	1 by 1	1		1
	1 by 1 2 by 2	1 + 2 1	1	5
	1 by 1 2 by 2 3 by 3	1 + 2 + 3 1 + 2 1	1 + 2	13
	1 by 1 2 by 2 3 by 3 4 by 4			
	1 by 1 2 by 2 3 by 3 4 by 4 5 by 5			

Each of the totals from the preceding table can be written in a way that reveals an interesting pattern of triangular numbers.

4. Complete the following table.

Given triangle	Total number of triangles
1 by 1	$1 = 1$
2 by 2	$5 = 3 + 2(1)$
3 by 3	$13 = 6 + 2(3) + 1$
4 by 4	$27 = 10 + 2(6) + 3 + 2(1)$
5 by 5	
6 by 6	

5. Using the pattern above, predict the total number of triangles to be found in a 7 by 7 triangle and an 8 by 8 triangle.

5.6   COUNTING SQUARES AND RECTANGLES

How many squares can you find in the following diagram?

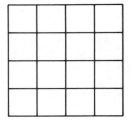

Let's refer to this grid arrangement as a 4 by 4 grid. In this grid, there are 1 by 1, 2 by 2, 3 by 3, and 4 by 4 squares. If we count the number of each type of square, we find that there are sixteen 1 by 1 squares, nine 2 by 2 squares, four 3 by 3 squares, and one 4 by 4 square. Pictured below are the four 3 by 3 squares.

 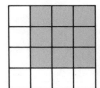 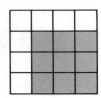

The total number of squares is given by $1 + 4 + 9 + 16 = 30$. Recall from Chapter 4 that this is a square pyramidal number. We called this number s_4 and it is located in Pascal's Triangle as shown below.

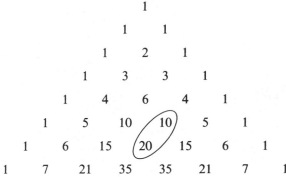

Another interesting observation involves writing the types of squares in one column and then reversing the order and writing down another column. Multiply the dimensions of the second column to give the number of each type of square in the original grid. Always start with the smallest type of square and end with the largest type.

Type of square	Number of each type of square in grid
1 by 1	$4 \cdot 4 = 16$
2 by 2	$3 \cdot 3 = 9$
3 by 3	$2 \cdot 2 = 4$
4 by 4	$1 \cdot 1 = \underline{1}$
	30 Total

---

1. Start with a 3 by 3 grid and find the total number of all squares. Find the pair of numbers in Pascal's Triangle that add up to this total.

2. Repeat with a 5 by 5 grid.

Another way of looking at the grids is to count the squares along parallel diagonals.

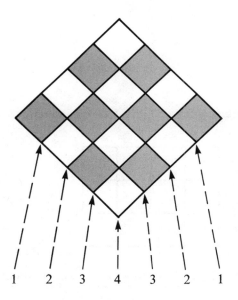

$$1 \quad 2 \quad 3 \quad 4 \quad 3 \quad 2 \quad 1$$

1 by 1: $1 + 2 + 3 + 4 + 3 + 2 + 1$
2 by 2: $1 + 2 + 3 + 2 + 1$
3 by 3: $1 + 2 + 1$
4 by 4: 1
$$\underbrace{1 + 3 + 6}_{10} + \underbrace{10 + 6 + 3 + 1}_{20} = 2(1) + 2(3) + 2(6) + 10$$
$$10 \quad + \quad 20 \quad = 30$$

3. Count the squares along parallel diagonals in the following diagram and write the sum four different ways as illustrated in the preceding paragraph.

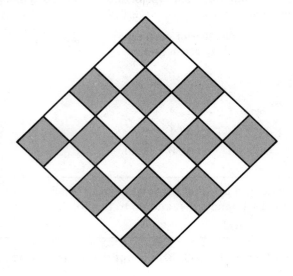

1 by 1:

2 by 2:

3 by 3:

4 by 4:

5 by 5:

4. How many rectangles are there in the following diagram?

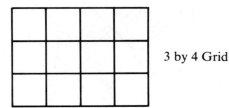

3 by 4 Grid

If T_3 and T_4 represent the third and fourth triangular numbers, find $T_3 \cdot T_4$.

In a 3 by 4 grid, there are 12 different types of rectangles to be found ($12 = 3 \cdot 4$). These twelve types are listed starting below in an orderly manner. If we count the number of each type that can be found in the grid, we find that these same numbers result when the first column is reversed and the dimensions are multiplied together.

Type of rectangle	Number of each type of rectangle in the grid
1 by 1	$4 \cdot 3 = 12$
1 by 2	$4 \cdot 2 = 8$
1 by 3	$4 \cdot 1 = 4$
2 by 1	$3 \cdot 3 = 9$
2 by 2	$3 \cdot 2 = 6$
2 by 3	$3 \cdot 1 = 3$

Type of rectangle	Number of each type of rectangle in the grid
3 by 1	$2 \cdot 3 = 6$
3 by 2	$2 \cdot 2 = 4$
3 by 3	$2 \cdot 1 = 2$
4 by 1	$1 \cdot 3 = 3$
4 by 2	$1 \cdot 2 = 2$
4 by 3	$1 \cdot 1 = \underline{1}$
	60 Total

Furthermore,

$$4 \cdot 3 + 4 \cdot 2 + 4 \cdot 1 + 3 \cdot 3 + 3 \cdot 2 + 3 \cdot 1 + 2 \cdot 3 + 2 \cdot 2 + 2 \cdot 1 + 1 \cdot 3 + 1 \cdot 2 + 1 \cdot 1$$
$$= 4(3 + 2 + 1) + 3(3 + 2 + 1) + 2(3 + 2 + 1) + 1(3 + 2 + 1)$$
$$= (3 + 2 + 1)(4 + 3 + 2 + 1)$$
$$= (6)(10)$$
$$= T_3 \cdot T_4$$
$$= 60$$

---

5. Answer the questions below for each of the following grids.

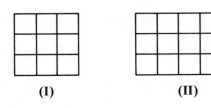   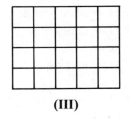

     (I)   **(II)**   **(III)**

(a) How many different rectangles can be counted in each figure?

(b) How many different types of rectangles are in each grid?

(c) List the two columns for each figure above and determine how many rectangles of each type can be found.

6. In the example (3 by 4 grid), how many 1 by 1, 2 by 2, and 3 by 3 squares can be counted? How many total squares can be counted in the 3 by 4 grid?

7. Use the information from 5(c) to determine the number of squares in each of the grids of exercise 5.

8. Generalize the above discussion to answer the following questions about a box whose dimensions are 2 by 3 by 4.

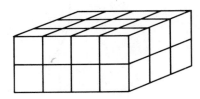

(a) How many different boxes can be counted in the figure?

(b) How many different types of boxes are there?

(c) List the two columns of numbers and determine how many boxes of each type can be found.

(d) How many 1 by 1 by 1 and 2 by 2 by 2 cubes can be counted in the given box?

5.7 COUNTING POLYGONS

In the diagram below, there are five points on a circle and these are joined by line segments.

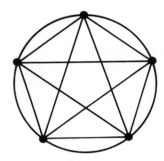

1. (a) How many line segments are there?

   (b) How many triangles can you find? (Count only those with vertices on the circle.)

   (c) How many quadrilaterals are there? (Count only those with vertices on the circle.)

   (d) How many pentagons are there? (Count only those with vertices on the circle.)

   (e) Describe where the numbers that are the answers to the above questions are located in Pascal's Triangle.

2. Draw a circle and put four points around it. Connect every point to every other point. Then answer the first three questions in exercise 1 for this new figure.

3. (a) In the figure below, how many points are there? Connect every point to every other point.

   (b) How many line segments are there?

   (c) How many triangles?

   (d) How many quadrilaterals?

   (e) How many pentagons?

   (f) How many hexagons?

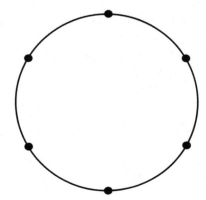

4. Complete the following table.

Number of:	Points	Line segments	Triangles	Quadrilaterals	Pentagons	Hexagons	Heptagons	Octagons	Nonagons	Decagons
	1									
	2	1								
	3	3	1							
	4	6	4	1						
	5	10	10	5	1					
	6					1				

5.8 FOUR INTERESTING PROBLEMS INVOLVING THE DIAGONALS OF POLYGONS

In this section we will look at the four problems listed below.

1. How many diagonals does a polygon have?
2. How many intersections of the diagonals are there?
3. How many regions are formed when the polygon is divided by its diagonals?
4. How many segments are formed when the diagonals are divided by their own intersection points?

The polygons we shall be working with are called "convex" polygons. In convex polygons when the diagonals are drawn, they intersect.

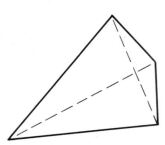

Convex Quadrilateral
(Diagonals intersect)

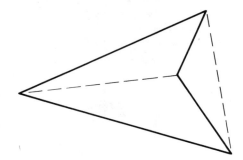

Nonconvex Quadrilateral
(Diagonals do not intersect)

Let's count the diagonals of several polygons to see if we can discover a pattern. A triangle has zero diagonals and a quadrilateral, as seen above, has two diagonals.

---

1. For each polygon, draw all of its diagonals and count them. List the results in the accompanying table.

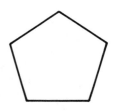 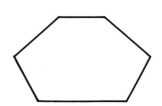  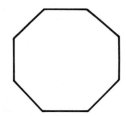

Number of sides of the polygon	3	4	5	6	7	8
Total number of diagonals	0	2				

Do you see a pattern in the numbers of diagonals? Can you predict the number of diagonals for a polygon of 9 sides? 10 sides? Add the number of sides to the number of diagonals. What sequence of numbers is generated?

If you did not see the pattern above, try adding one to each number. You should now recognize this sequence as the triangular numbers. Thus, if a polygon of n sides is given, the number of diagonals is given by one less than the appropriate triangular number. The appropriate triangular number is T_{n-2}. Thus,

$$\text{The number of diagonals of an } n\text{-sided polygon} = T_{n-2} - 1$$

---

2. (a) Find the number of diagonals in a 12-sided polygon (dodecagon).

   (b) Find the number of diagonals in a 20-sided polygon.

3. Add the encircled numbers in each group indicated in Pascal's Triangle below. What sequence of numbers is generated?

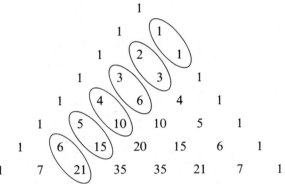

4. Subtract the pair of encircled numbers in each group indicated in Pascal's Triangle below. What sequence of numbers is generated?

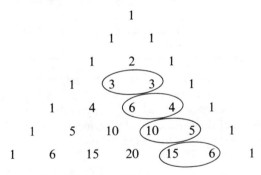

5. Perform the operations indicated in each group of numbers encircled in Pascal's Triangle below.

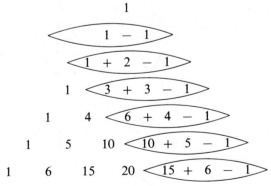

What sequence of numbers is generated?

6. (a) Develop three more rows for the following number triangle.

```
            1
        2       3
    4       5       6
7       8       9       10
```

(b) Describe the two columns of numbers indicated by the arrows.

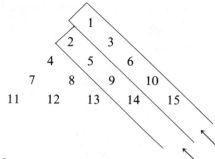

7. Find the following sums.

$1 + 1$

$2 + 2 + 1$

$3 + 3 + 2 + 1$

$4 + 4 + 3 + 2 + 1$

$5 + 5 + 4 + 3 + 2 + 1$

Continue the pattern above to find three more sums. What sequence of numbers is generated?

When counting the number of intersections of the diagonals, be careful to consider the maximum number of intersections. If more than two diagonals happen to intersect at the same point, some intersection points may be overlooked. As you draw each diagonal, count the number of times you cross other diagonals. The following system can be used to count the intersections. The case for a hexagon is illustrated below.

1. Draw all diagonals from the first vertex (as indicated by the arrow).

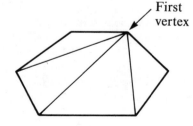

Zero intersections

2. Draw all diagonals from the second vertex and count the crossings.

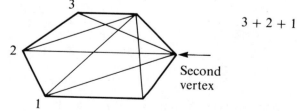

$3 + 2 + 1$

3. Draw all diagonals from the third vertex and count the crossings.

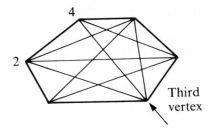

4 + 2

4. Draw all diagonals from the fourth vertex and count the crossings.

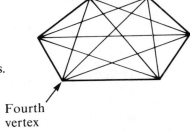

3

Third vertex

Fourth vertex

Total = 1 + 2 + 3
         2 + 4
           + 3
= 15

---

8. Using the system described above, draw the diagonals in the heptagon shown below. Verify that when you draw the diagonals from the second vertex, you get 4, 3, 2, and 1 intersections. When you draw the diagonals from the third vertex, you get 6, 4, and 2 intersections. When you draw the diagonals from the fourth vertex, you get 6 and 3 intersections. Finally, when you draw the last diagonal, you get 4 intersections. Thus, verify that the total number of intersections of the diagonals of a heptagon is:

Total = 1 + 2 + 3 + 4
          + 2 + 4 + 6
            + 3 + 6
              + 4
= 35

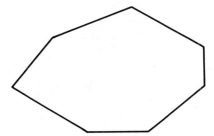

9. Examine the way the sum was written for the number of intersections of the diagonals of the hexagon and the heptagon above. Create similar sums for the pentagon and the quadrilateral.

Predict the sum for the octagon.

10. Complete the following table.

Number of sides of a polygon	4	5	6	7	8	9
Total number of intersections of the diagonals			15	35		

Do you recognize these numbers? Circle these numbers in Pascal's Triangle below.

```
                              1
                          1       1
                      1       2       1
                  1       3       3       1
              1       4       6       4       1
          1       5      10      10       5       1
      1       6      15      20      15       6       1
  1       7      21      35      35      21       7       1
1       8      28      56      70      56      28       8       1
1   9      36      84     126     126      84      36       9       1
```

There is only one intersection point for the diagonals of a quadrilateral. In the previous section, we established the number of quadrilaterals formed by sets of points around a circle. Thus, the number of quadrilaterals in an octagon, for example, which can be formed from eight points on a circle, is the same as the number of intersection points of the diagonals of an octagon. This number is 70 in both cases.

Next, we would like to count the number of regions formed in the interior of a polygon that has been divided by its diagonals. As before, you must be careful in the counting process. If three or more diagonals intersect at the same point, a region may be lost as you are counting. As each diagonal is drawn and crosses a region, it divides the region in two, creating a new region. Thus, the number of regions a diagonal crosses is equal to the number of new regions created. The case for a hexagon is illustrated below.

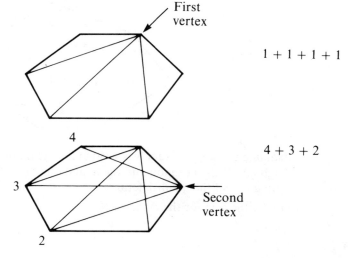

1. Draw all diagonals from the first vertex (indicated by the arrow) and count the regions.

First vertex

$1 + 1 + 1 + 1$

2. Draw all the diagonals from the second vertex and count the regions each one passes through.

Second vertex

$4 + 3 + 2$

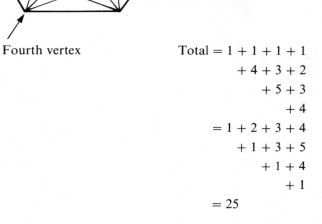

3. Draw all the diagonals from the third vertex and count the regions each one passes through.

5 + 3

Third vertex

4. Draw the last diagonal from the fourth vertex and count the regions it passes through.

4

Fourth vertex

Total = 1 + 1 + 1 + 1
    + 4 + 3 + 2
        + 5 + 3
            + 4
= 1 + 2 + 3 + 4
    + 1 + 3 + 5
        + 1 + 4
            + 1

= 25

---

11. Using the system described above, draw the diagonals in the heptagon shown below. Verify that when you draw the diagonals from the first vertex, you get 1 + 1 + 1 + 1 + 1 regions. When you draw the diagonals from the second vertex, you get 5 + 4 + 3 + 2 more regions. When you draw the diagonals from the third vertex, you get 7 + 5 + 3 more regions. When you draw the diagonals from the fourth vertex, you get 7 + 4 more regions. Finally, when you draw the last diagonal from the fifth vertex, you get 5 more new regions. Thus, verify that the total number of regions formed by the diagonals of a heptagon is (with some rearrangement of the numbers)

Total = 1 + 2 + 3 + 4 + 5
    + 1 + 3 + 5 + 7
        + 1 + 4 + 7
            + 1 + 5
                + 1

= 50

12. Examine the way the sums were written previously for the number of regions created by the diagonals of the heptagon and the hexagon. Create similar sums for the pentagon and the quadrilateral.

    Create a sum for the octagon.

13. Complete the following table.

Number of sides of the polygon	4	5	6	7	8	9
Total number of regions created by the diagonals			25	50		

14. Add the numbers encircled in Pascal's Triangle below. What sequence of numbers is generated?

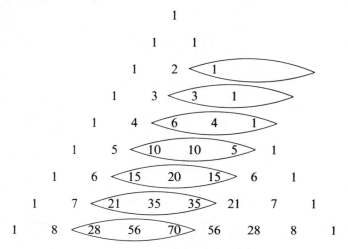

15. By completing the following table, verify that the number of diagonals + number of intersections + 1 equals the number of regions.

n sides	Diagonals + Intersections + 1 = Regions			
3	0 +	0	+ 1 =	1
4	2 +	1	+ 1 =	4
5				
6				
7				
8				

In Chapter 1, we saw Euler's Formula for polyhedra

$$V - E + F = 2$$

where V represents the number of vertices, E the number of edges, and F the number of faces of a polyhedron.

There is a similar formula for polygons and their diagonals

$$v - e + f = 1$$

where v represents the number of vertices and intersection points of the diagonals, e represents the number of sides plus the number of segments formed when the diagonals are divided by the intersection points, and f represents the number of regions formed when the polygon is divided by its diagonals. For example, consider the hexagon and its diagonals.

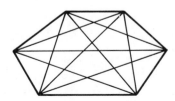

$v = 6$ vertices $+$ 15 intersection points on the diagonals $= 21$

$e = 45$ (by a direct count)

$f = 25$ regions

Thus, $v - e + f = 21 - 45 + 25 = 1$.

In the case of the heptagon, we know from our previous work that $v = 7$ vertices $+$ 35 intersection points on the diagonals $= 42$, and $f = 50$ regions. Thus, using Euler's Formula for polygons, we can solve for e.

$$v - e + f = 1$$
$$42 - e + 50 = 1$$
$$42 + 50 - 1 = e$$
$$91 = e$$

Hence, there are 91 segments and sides, or 7 sides and 84 segments.

---

16. Using Euler's Formula for polygons and your previous work in this section, complete the following table.

Sides	Diagonals	Points of intersection plus vertices	Regions	Segments plus sides
3	0	$0 + 3 = 3$	1	$0 + 3 = 3$
4	2	$1 + 4 = 5$	4	$4 + 4 = 8$
5	5	$5 + 5 = 10$	11	
6				
7				
8				
9				

17. If n represents the number of sides of the polygon, then

$$\text{Number of diagonals} = \frac{n^2 - 3n}{2}$$

$$\begin{array}{l}\text{Number of points of}\\ \text{intersection plus}\\ \text{vertices}\end{array} = \frac{n^4 - 6n^3 + 11n^2 - 6n}{24} + n$$

$$\text{Number of regions} = \frac{n^4 - 6n^3 + 23n^2 - 42n + 24}{24}$$

$$\begin{array}{l}\text{Number of segments}\\ \text{plus sides}\end{array} = \frac{n^4 - 6n^3 + 17n^2 - 24n}{12} + n$$

Using these formulas, verify the entries in the table above for $n = 3$, $n = 4$, $n = 5$, and $n = 6$.

18. Add each group of encircled numbers in Pascal's Triangle below. What sequence of numbers is generated? (Hint: Compare the sequence with the previous table.)

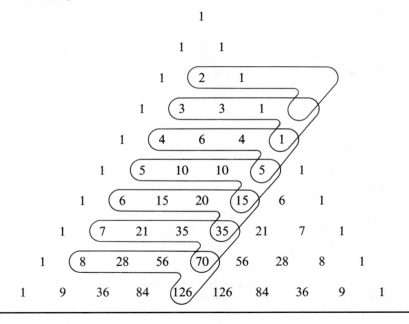

5.9 TO BE OR NOT TO BE A PATTERN

What is the maximum number of regions formed when a set of points on a circle is joined by line segments?

Investigation of this problem yields a sequence of numbers as a solution for 1, 2, 3, 4, etc., points. As the pattern develops, it suddenly changes. After five or six valid solutions, the pattern does not seem to work for subsequent values. Let's explore this problem and study this pattern.

1. Count the number of subregions formed when the circular region is divided by the line segments determined by the given points on the circle. Complete the table.

	Number of points	Number of regions
	1	1
	2	2
	3	4
	4	
	5	

On the basis of the pattern established in the preceding table, we might expect the next entry, for 6 points, to be 32 regions. This is not the case!

2. Count the regions within the circle below.

Since the answer is not 32, is there a way of predicting subsequent answers for 7, 8, 9, etc., points? To discover the pattern, first find the number of regions established by 7 points.

3. Count the regions within the circle below.

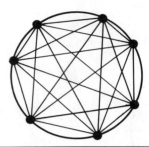

If you are not ready to predict the subsequent numbers, study Pascal's Triangle below.

4. Add the encircled numbers in Pascal's Triangle as indicated. Compare with the previous results.

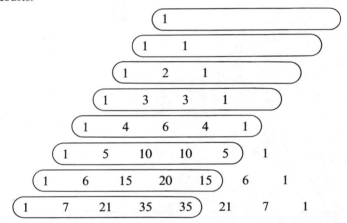

Inside each circle with *n* points on it, we have an *n*-sided polygon. We explored these polygons and their diagonals in the previous section. We counted the regions created by the diagonals in those polygons and if we now add the extra regions created by the circular arcs, we would get the results of this section.

5. Using the formula for the number of regions formed in a polygon when all of its diagonals are drawn (see the previous section), find a formula for the number of regions formed when a set of points on a circle is joined by line segments.

5.10 CUTTING UP CIRCLES

In Chapter 1, we "cut up" space. In the case of 2-dimensional space (a plane), it was cut by lines. The number of regions formed when 2-dimensional space is cut is given by the following table.

Number of lines	1	2	3	4	5	6	
Number of regions	2	4	7	11	16	22	

Recall that these numbers were located in Pascal's Triangle as shown below.

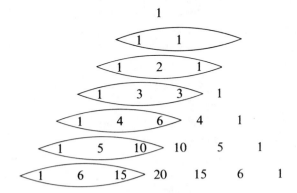

A problem similar to this is given by a circle and the regions formed by lines crossing it.

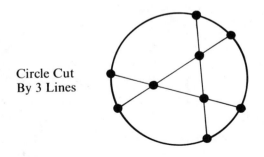

Circle Cut
By 3 Lines

7 Regions

9 Vertices (Points)

15 Edges (Straight and
curved line
segments)

1. Complete the following table by counting the number of regions, vertices, and edges for each figure.

Cut circle	Number of cutting lines	Number of vertices	Number of edges	Number of regions
	1	2	3	2
	2	5	8	4
	3	9	15	7
	4	_____	_____	_____
	5	_____	_____	_____
	6	_____	_____	_____

2. Using the information from the table of exercise 1, verify Euler's Formula for these figures. Recall that Euler's Formula is

$$v - e + f = 1$$

where v represents the number of vertices, e represents the number of edges, and f represents the number of regions.

3. In the table of exercise 1, add the number of vertices to the number of regions for each figure. What sequence of numbers is generated?

4. Count the number of vertices inside each figure shown in the table of exercise 1. What sequence of numbers is generated?

5. Compare the sequence of numbers in the vertices column of the table of exercise 1 to the number of diagonals in a polygon that we found in Section 5.8. What do you find?

6. For each figure in the table of exercise 1 add the number of vertices, edges, and regions. Find these numbers in Pascal's Triangle by doubling the sum of all the numbers in each box and subtracting one as shown below.

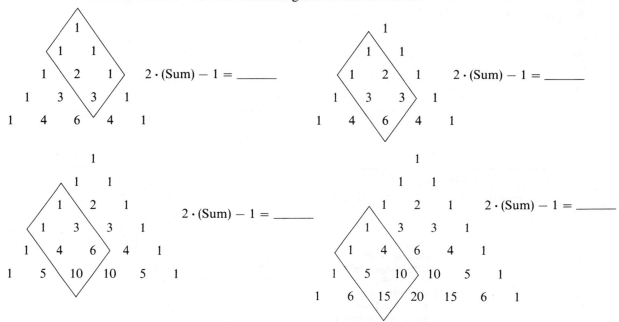

7. Develop the next three rows of the following number triangle. Describe the numbers in the column indicated by the arrows.

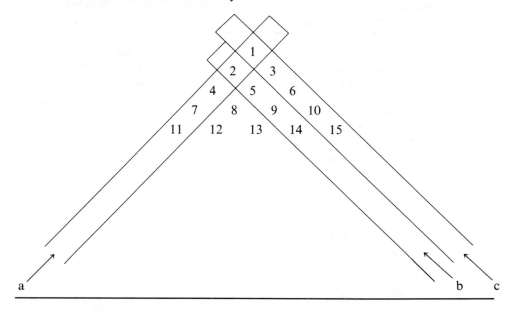

5.11 STICK DIAGRAMS

In this section, we will discover some very familiar number patterns in an unfamiliar setting.

If two line segments intersect each other, how many shorter line segments are formed? In the diagram below, there are four shorter line segments.

Suppose three line segments intersect each other; how many shorter line segments are formed? Count them in the diagram below.

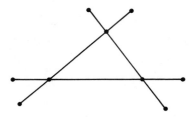

---

1. Making sure that no three lines intersect in the same point, draw four line segments that intersect each other. How many shorter line segments are formed?

   With the data from the above discussions, complete the following table.

Number of line segments	1	2	3	4		
Number of shorter line segments formed	1	4				

   From the pattern beginning to emerge in the table above, predict the number of shorter line segments formed when five line segments intersect each other. Draw a diagram and verify your prediction.

Each line segment has two endpoints. Each time a pair of line segments intersect, another point is formed. When two line segments intersect each other, how many points are there (counting the endpoints also)? In the diagram below, there are five points.

Suppose three line segments intersect each other, how many points are formed? Count them in the diagram below.

---

2. Making sure that no three lines intersect in the same point, draw four line segments that intersect each other. How many points are formed?

Using the data from the above discussions, complete the table below.

Number of line segments	1	2	3	4		
Number of points formed	2	5				

Compare the pattern of numbers beginning to emerge in the table above to the number of diagonals of a polygon found in Section 5.8. What do you discover?

Predict the number of points formed when five line segments intersect each other. Draw a diagram and verify your prediction.

Subtract one from each of the circled numbers in Pascal's Triangle below. What sequence of numbers is formed?

```
                    1
                1       1
            1       2       1
        1       3      (3)      1
      1      4      (6)     4      1
    1     5     (10)    10     5      1
  1     6    (15)    20    15     6     1
```

Three line segments that intersect each other enclose one region. How many enclosed regions are formed by the four lines that were drawn in exercise 2?

3. Complete the following table.

Stick diagram	Number of line segments	Number of shorter line segments	Number of points	Number of regions
	1	1	2	0
	2	4	5	0
	3	9	9	1
	4	16	14	3
	5	___	___	___
	6	___	___	___
	7	___	___	___

4. Using the information from the preceding table, verify Euler's Formula for stick diagrams

$$v - e + f = 1$$

where v represents the number of points (vertices), e represents the number of shorter line segments (edges), and f represents the number of regions (faces).

5. In the preceding table, add the number of shorter line segments to the number of points for each stick diagram. Do you recognize this sequence of numbers? (Hint: Divide each one by 3.)

6. For each stick diagram, add the number of shorter line segments, the number of points, and the number of regions. Find these numbers in Pascal's Triangle by adding all of the numbers in each box shown below.

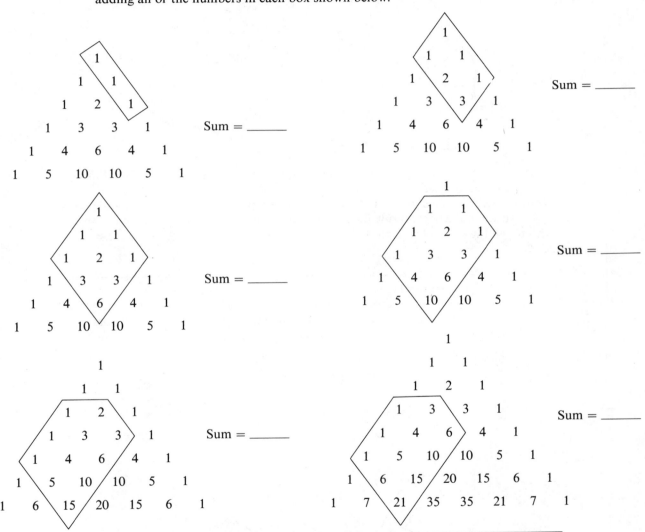

Sum = _____

Sum = _____

Sum = _____

Sum = _____

Sum = _____

Sum = _____

5.12 COUNTING PATHS

A squad of sixteen warriors enter a dungeon, a map of which follows. The Wizard had warned them that at each intersection of the corridors they should separate so that half of the group could continue their way in each direction, thus dispelling a chance encounter with an evil force that might otherwise cut off their path, entrapping them forever in the dungeon. In the Big room, they could regroup and do battle with the dormant monster therein that had cast a phantasmal spell upon the land.

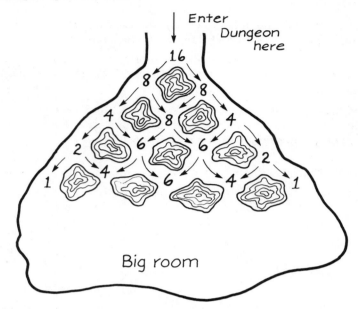

There are five entrances to the Big room. How many warriors will be coming through each entrance in the attack?

The numbers in each corridor tell us how many warriors arrive at each of those points. Thus, you can see in the bottom row the number of warriors coming through each of the five entrances to the Big room. There are 1, 4, 6, 4, and 1 warriors. Do you recognize these numbers?

---

1. In the dungeon shown below, thirty-two warriors enter and follow the same plan of attack. At each intersection of the corridors, half of the group arriving there goes in one direction and half goes in the other direction. How many warriors will be coming through each of the entrances to the Big room in this dungeon?

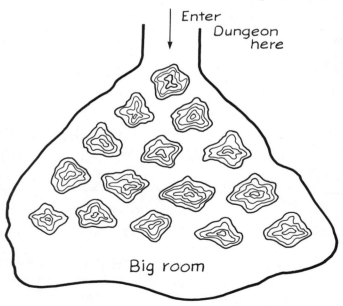

Describe the number of warriors arriving at each of the six entrances to the Big room.

2. Sixty-four marbles drop through a chute. At each junction, half of the marbles arriving there fall to the left and half fall to the right of the junction. How many marbles will stack up in the columns at the bottom?

In the dungeon pictured below, let's discover how many different paths you could take to arrive at each of the different entrances to the Big room. At each junction, you must travel either right or left; you may not back track.

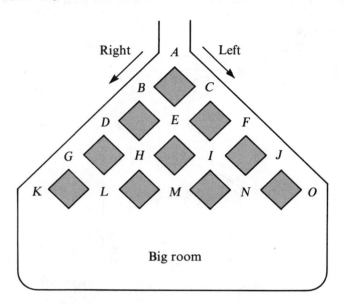

3. **(a)** In how many ways could you travel from point *A* to point *B*? point *C*? point *E*? Enter these numbers into the picture above.

(b) In how many ways could you travel from point *A* to point *D*? point *F*? Enter these numbers into the picture above.

(c) In order to get to point *H*, you had to have come from which points? How many ways could you then travel from point *A* to point *H*? Answer these same questions for point *I*. Enter these numbers into the picture above.

(d) Continue through the entire dungeon and enter the number of ways you could travel from point *A* to each point. What pattern of numbers is generated? How many ways can you travel from point *A* to each entrance of the Big room? How many different ways can you travel from point *A* to the Big room?

(e) Each of the paths from point *A* to point *H* had an equal number of moves to the right as the number of moves to the left. For instance, the path *A-B-E-I-M* could be characterized by RLLR, where R indicates a move to the right and L indicates a move to the left. Characterize each of the paths from point *A* to the Big Room in this manner. How many ways can the letters R and L be arranged in sequence, if two of each are used?

4. In the diagram below, *A* represents Al's house and *B* represents Betty's house. Al visits Betty every day. He always travels the shortest path (staying on the streets) that he can and every day of the courtship he travels a different path. How long could the courtship last?

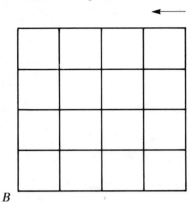

Hint: At each intersection write the number of different ways Al could arrive there.

Characterize each path with the letters H (horizontal) and V (vertical). One such path is HHHHVVVV, 4 horizontal moves and 4 vertical moves. How many ways can the letters H and V be arranged in sequence, if four of each are used?

5. How many different ways can the word PASCALS be spelled by choosing each letter along a path that zigzags back and forth, left or right, from the top to the bottom?

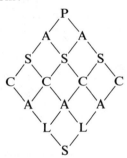

6. How many different ways can you spell LEVEL? See the diagram below. You must zigzag back and forth from top to bottom or from bottom to top.

```
        L
     E     E
  V     V     V
     E     E
        L
```

7. How many different ways can you spell NOT A TON?

5.13 THE TOWER OF HANOI

In this game, a given number of disks of diminishing size are stacked on one of three poles forming a tower. The tower of disks is then transferred to either of the two vacant poles in the fewest possible moves. A move is valid if only one disk is moved at a time and if no disk is placed on top of a smaller disk.

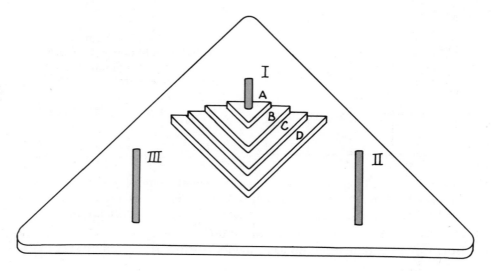

Thus, if only two disks are used in the game, the tower can be transferred in three moves. To show this, we shall label the disks A and B from the top to the bottom of the tower and number the poles I, II, and III as shown. The moves are

1. disk A to pole II
2. disk B to pole III
3. disk A to pole III

Thus, if only two disks are used, three moves are required.

---

1. Describe the moves to transfer a tower of three disks (A, B, C) from pole I to one of the other poles.

   (You can make your own disks out of cardboard, stack them up, and move them around on three different spots to simulate the game.)

   What is the fewest number of moves needed to transfer the tower of 3 disks to a vacant pole?

Originally, the Tower of Hanoi game was described using eight disks. This game was claimed to be a simplified version of yet another problem, a legendary ancient Indian problem called the Tower of Brahma. In this problem, the tower consisted of sixty-four disks of gold, and temple priests were assigned the task of transferring the disks to a vacant pole according to the rules described. This legend claimed that before the temple priests could finish their task the temple would crumble and the world would come to an end. Interestingly, this problem requires billions upon billions of moves. Allowing for one move per second, working day and night, it would require the temple priests more than one-half million millions of years to complete the task. This is a longer time than the present age of the solar system! If the priests had begun their task when the solar system was formed, they still would not be finished.

How do we know how many moves are required to transfer sixty-four disks, or eight disks, or any specific number of disks? Is there a pattern to guide us in making the moves? The answer to both questions is contained in Pascal's Triangle. First, let us analyze the tower of three disks: *A*, *B*, and *C*. It requires seven moves to transfer this tower to another pole.

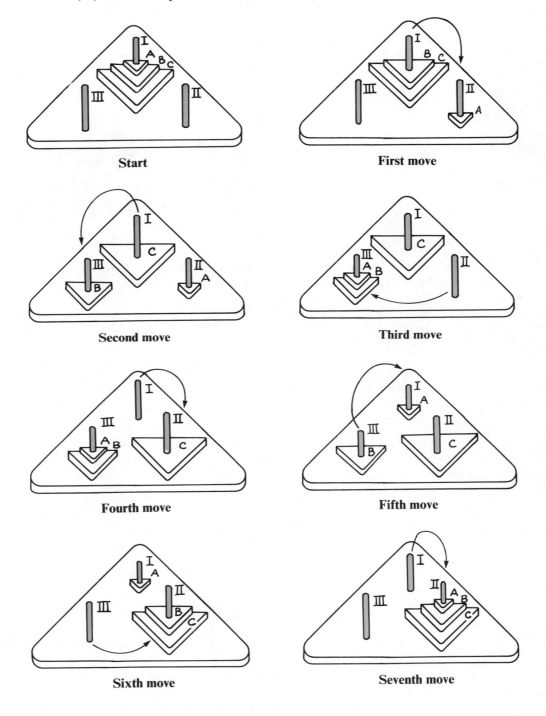

Start	First move
Second move	Third move
Fourth move	Fifth move
Sixth move	Seventh move

Notice that disk *A* is moved the most, every other time in fact, a total of 4 moves. Disk *B* is moved 2 times and disk *C* is moved only once. Thus, looking at Pascal's Triangle, we have

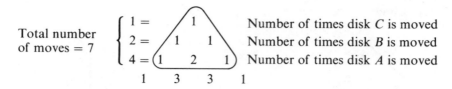

Total number of moves = 7

1 =   1   Number of times disk *C* is moved
2 =   1   1   Number of times disk *B* is moved
4 = 1   2   1 Number of times disk *A* is moved
  1   3   3   1

To find out how the disks are moved, let's line them up in the order in which they are moved.

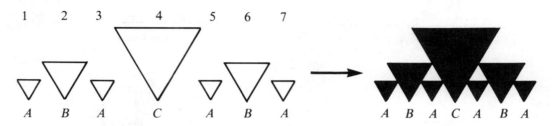

1   2   3   4   5   6   7

A   B   A   C   A   B   A   *A   B   A   C   A   B   A*

Martin Gardner, in Chapter 6 of his book *The Scientific American Book of Mathematical Puzzles and Diversions*, describes a relationship between this pattern *ABACABA* and the two games, "The Tower of Hanoi" and "The Icosian Game." The latter game has to do with tracing out a path along the edges of cubes and hypercubes as invented by the Irish mathematician, Sir William Rowan Hamilton. These paths came to be known as Hamiltonian paths. Furthermore, Gardner points out that the pattern also exists in a binary number sequence. To see this, first you write the binary numbers from 1 to 7 and label the columns *A*, *B*, and *C* as shown in the figure. Then, write opposite each binary number the letter of the column that identifies the bit "1" that is farthest to the right. The sequence of letters you get will be *ABACABA*.

Decimal	Binary			
	C	B	A	
1	0	0	1	A
2	0	1	0	B
3	0	1	1	A
4	1	0	0	C
5	1	0	1	A
6	1	1	0	B
7	1	1	1	A

2. Write the binary numbers from 1 to 15 and label the columns *A*, *B*, *C*, and *D*. Opposite each binary number write the letter of the column that identifies the bit "1" that is farthest to the right.

Gardner also observes that this same pattern can also be seen in the binary subdivisions of the inch into halves, quarters, and eighths.

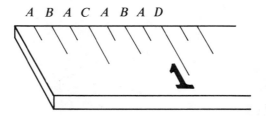

3. Draw and label the binary subdivisions of the inch into halves, quarters, eighths, and sixteenths.

The pattern of the triangular disks lined up in the order they are moved can also be seen in Pascal's Triangle. The arrangement is the same one as the one we saw when we examined the odd-even colorings of the entries in Pascal's Triangle (Section 2.9).

The odd-even pattern of Pascal's Triangle, emphasizing the binary pattern *ABACABA*

Furthermore, if you observe the chart showing the moves, you will notice that the disk labeled *A* moves clockwise around the board from pole to pole (look at the odd-numbered moves). The disk labeled *B* moves counterclockwise. The disk labeled *C* makes only one move, but moves clockwise again. In a larger tower, each successive disk moves in the opposite direction from the one previous.

You can use the odd-even pattern of Pascal's Triangle to record these moves. Suppose that each vertex of the triangular pattern represents one of the poles.

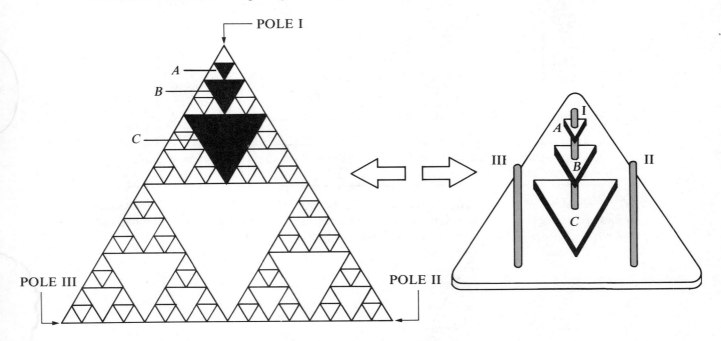

Each of the moves can be diagrammed as shown.

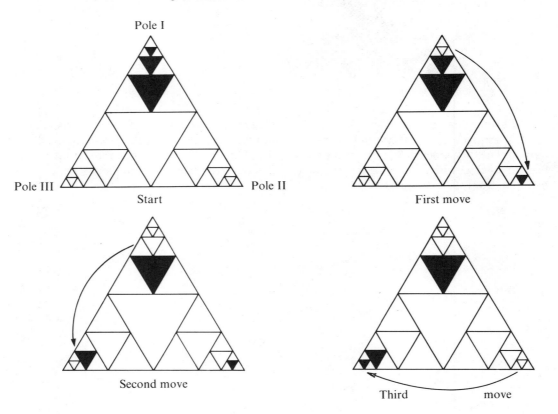

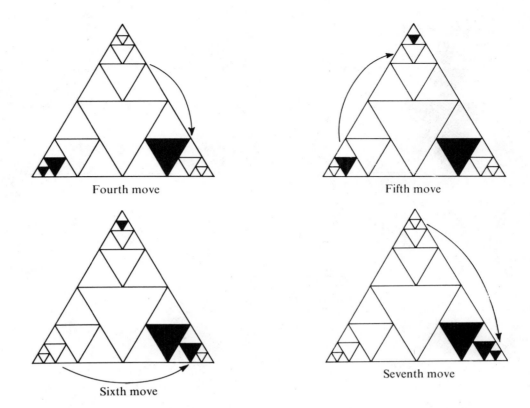

Fourth move

Fifth move

Sixth move

Seventh move

4. Construct a tower of 4 disks. How many moves are necessary to transfer these disks to one of the vacant poles?

5. If the disks are labeled A, B, C, and D, what pattern gives the proper order for the sequence of moves?

6. Shade the diagrams on the next pages to show how these moves can be made.

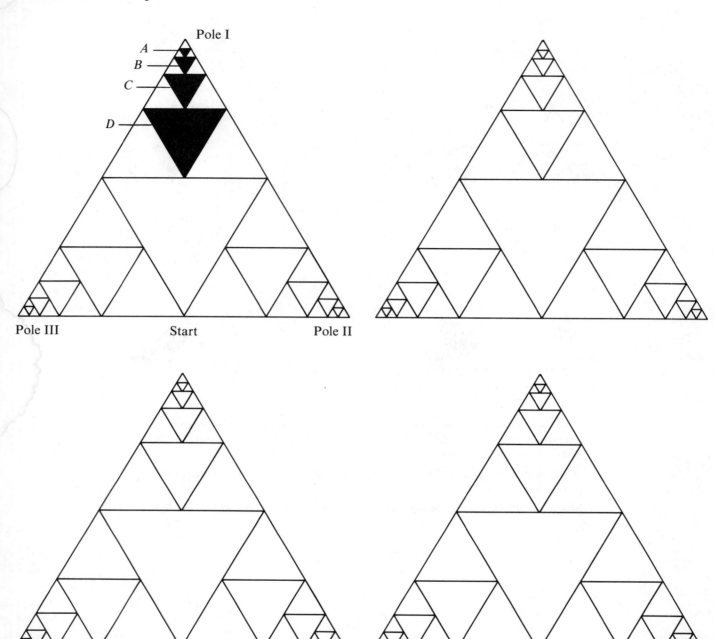

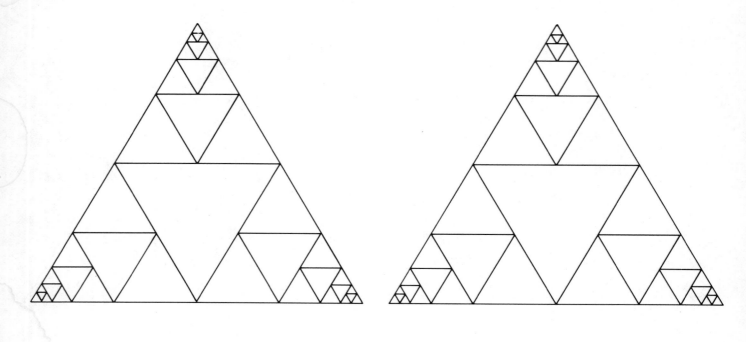

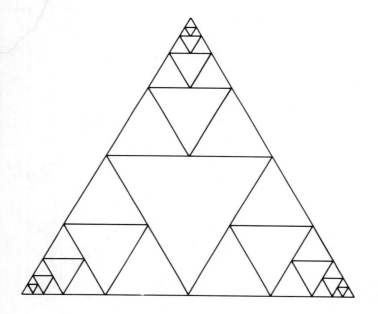
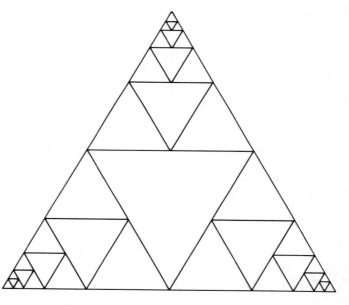

7. Enter the results for the tower consisting of 4 disks into the following table.

		Sequence of moves	**Total numbers of moves**

2 Disks

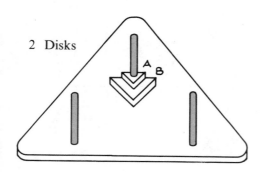

A   B   A

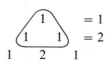

$$1 \quad 2 \quad 1$$

Sum = 1 + 2 = 3

3 Disks

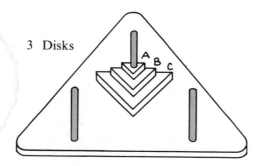

A B A C A B A

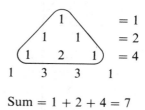

$$1 \quad 3 \quad 3 \quad 1$$

Sum = 1 + 2 + 4 = 7

4 Disks

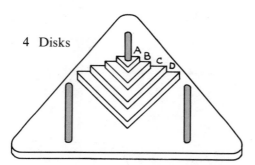

A B A _____

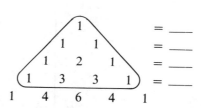

$$1 \quad 4 \quad 6 \quad 4 \quad 1$$

Sum = ___ + ___ + ___ + ___ = ___

8. Predict the number of moves required to transfer 5, 6, 7, and 8 disks to a vacant pole.

The formula for the required number of moves for a tower of *n* disks is given by

$$1 + 2 + 4 + \cdots + 2^{n-1} = 2^n - 1$$

This is a formula we have seen previously in this book. The temple priests that were attempting to transfer 64 gold disks would need to carry out

$2^{64} - 1$ moves

Since $2^{10} = 1024$ and this is approximately $1000 = 10^3$, we can estimate that 2^{64} is approximately given by

$$2^{64} = 2^{10} \cdot 2^{10} \cdot 2^{10} \cdot 2^{10} \cdot 2^{10} \cdot 2^{10} \cdot 2^4$$
$$\approx 10^3 \cdot 10^3 \cdot 10^3 \cdot 10^3 \cdot 10^3 \cdot 10^3 \cdot 2^4$$
$$= 10^{18} \cdot 2^4$$
$$= 16 \cdot 10^{18}$$

This number is 16 followed by 18 zeros!

$$16 \cdot 10^{18} = 16{,}000{,}000{,}000{,}000{,}000{,}000$$

This is 16 billion billions!

9. Estimate the number of moves required to transfer 100 disks to a vacant pole.

PRIME
FACTORIZATION CHARTS

Pascal's Triangle — Prime Factorization — To Center Number (omitting 1's)

Row 2
2 is Prime

Row 3
3 is Prime

Row 4
$4 = 2^2$
$6 = 2 \cdot 3$

Row 5
5 is Prime
$10 = 2 \cdot 5$

Row 6
$6 = 2 \cdot 3$
$15 = 3 \cdot 5$
$20 = 2^2 \cdot 5$

Row 7
7 is Prime
$21 = 3 \cdot 7$
$35 = 5 \cdot 7$

Row 8
$8 = 2^3$
$28 = 2^2 \cdot 7$
$56 = 2^3 \cdot 7$
$70 = 2 \cdot 5 \cdot 7$

Row 9
$9 = 3^2$
$36 = 2^2 \cdot 3^2$
$84 = 2^2 \cdot 3 \cdot 7$
$126 = 2 \cdot 3^2 \cdot 7$

Row 10
$10 = 2 \cdot 5$
$45 = 3^2 \cdot 5$
$120 = 2^3 \cdot 3 \cdot 5$
$210 = 2 \cdot 3 \cdot 5 \cdot 7$
$252 = 2^2 \cdot 3^2 \cdot 7$

Row 11
11 is Prime
$55 = 5 \cdot 11$
$165 = 3 \cdot 5 \cdot 11$
$330 = 2 \cdot 3 \cdot 5 \cdot 11$
$462 = 2 \cdot 3 \cdot 7 \cdot 11$

Row 12
$12 = 2^2 \cdot 3$
$66 = 2 \cdot 3 \cdot 11$
$220 = 2^2 \cdot 5 \cdot 11$
$495 = 3^2 \cdot 5 \cdot 11$
$792 = 2^3 \cdot 3^2 \cdot 11$
$924 = 2^2 \cdot 3 \cdot 7 \cdot 11$

Row 13
13 is Prime
$78 = 2 \cdot 3 \cdot 13$
$286 = 2 \cdot 11 \cdot 13$
$715 = 5 \cdot 11 \cdot 13$
$1287 = 3^2 \cdot 11 \cdot 13$
$1716 = 2^2 \cdot 3 \cdot 11 \cdot 13$

Row 14
$14 = 2 \cdot 7$
$91 = 7 \cdot 13$
$364 = 2^2 \cdot 7 \cdot 13$
$1001 = 7 \cdot 11 \cdot 13$
$2002 = 2 \cdot 7 \cdot 11 \cdot 13$
$3003 = 3 \cdot 7 \cdot 11 \cdot 13$
$3432 = 2^3 \cdot 3 \cdot 11 \cdot 13$

Row 15
$15 = 3 \cdot 5$
$105 = 3 \cdot 5 \cdot 7$
$455 = 5 \cdot 7 \cdot 13$
$1365 = 3 \cdot 5 \cdot 7 \cdot 13$
$3003 = 3 \cdot 7 \cdot 11 \cdot 13$
$5005 = 5 \cdot 7 \cdot 11 \cdot 13$
$6435 = 3^2 \cdot 5 \cdot 11 \cdot 13$

Row 16
$16 = 2^4$
$120 = 2^3 \cdot 3 \cdot 5$
$560 = 2^4 \cdot 5 \cdot 7$
$1820 = 2^2 \cdot 5 \cdot 7 \cdot 13$
$4368 = 2^4 \cdot 3 \cdot 7 \cdot 13$
$8008 = 2^3 \cdot 7 \cdot 11 \cdot 13$
$11440 = 2^4 \cdot 5 \cdot 11 \cdot 13$
$12870 = 2 \cdot 3^2 \cdot 5 \cdot 11 \cdot 13$

Row 17
17 is Prime
$136 = 2^3 \cdot 17$
$680 = 2^3 \cdot 5 \cdot 17$
$2380 = 2^2 \cdot 5 \cdot 7 \cdot 17$
$6188 = 2^2 \cdot 7 \cdot 13 \cdot 17$
$12376 = 2^3 \cdot 7 \cdot 13 \cdot 17$
$19448 = 2^3 \cdot 11 \cdot 13 \cdot 17$
$24310 = 2 \cdot 5 \cdot 11 \cdot 13 \cdot 17$

Row 18
$18 = 2 \cdot 3^2$
$153 = 3^2 \cdot 17$
$816 = 2^4 \cdot 3 \cdot 17$
$3060 = 2^2 \cdot 3^2 \cdot 5 \cdot 17$
$8568 = 2^3 \cdot 3^2 \cdot 7 \cdot 17$
$18564 = 2^2 \cdot 3 \cdot 7 \cdot 13 \cdot 17$
$31824 = 2^4 \cdot 3^2 \cdot 13 \cdot 17$
$43758 = 2 \cdot 3^2 \cdot 11 \cdot 13 \cdot 17$
$48620 = 2^2 \cdot 5 \cdot 11 \cdot 13 \cdot 17$

Row 19
19 is Prime
$171 = 3^2 \cdot 19$
$969 = 3 \cdot 17 \cdot 19$
$3\,876 = 2^2 \cdot 3 \cdot 17 \cdot 19$
$11\,628 = 2^2 \cdot 3^2 \cdot 17 \cdot 19$
$27\,132 = 2^2 \cdot 3 \cdot 7 \cdot 17 \cdot 19$
$50\,388 = 2^2 \cdot 3 \cdot 13 \cdot 17 \cdot 19$
$75\,582 = 2 \cdot 3^2 \cdot 13 \cdot 17 \cdot 19$
$92\,378 = 2 \cdot 11 \cdot 13 \cdot 17 \cdot 19$

Row 20
$20 = 2^2 \cdot 5$
$190 = 2 \cdot 5 \cdot 19$
$1\,140 = 2^2 \cdot 3 \cdot 5 \cdot 19$
$4\,845 = 3 \cdot 5 \cdot 17 \cdot 19$
$15\,504 = 2^4 \cdot 3 \cdot 17 \cdot 19$
$38\,760 = 2^3 \cdot 3 \cdot 5 \cdot 17 \cdot 19$
$77\,520 = 2^4 \cdot 3 \cdot 5 \cdot 17 \cdot 19$
$125\,970 = 2 \cdot 3 \cdot 5 \cdot 13 \cdot 17 \cdot 19$
$167\,960 = 2^3 \cdot 5 \cdot 13 \cdot 17 \cdot 19$
$184\,756 = 2^2 \cdot 11 \cdot 13 \cdot 17 \cdot 19$

Pascal's Triangle — Prime Factorization — To Center Number (omitting 1's)

Row 21

$$21 = 3 \cdot 7$$
$$210 = 2 \cdot 3 \cdot 5 \cdot 7$$
$$1\,330 = 2 \cdot 5 \cdot 7 \cdot 19$$
$$5\,985 = 3^2 \cdot 5 \cdot 7 \cdot 19$$
$$20\,349 = 3^2 \cdot 7 \cdot 17 \cdot 19$$
$$54\,264 = 2^3 \cdot 3 \cdot 7 \cdot 17 \cdot 19$$
$$116\,280 = 2^3 \cdot 3^2 \cdot 5 \cdot 17 \cdot 19$$
$$203\,490 = 2 \cdot 3^2 \cdot 5 \cdot 7 \cdot 17 \cdot 19$$
$$293\,930 = 2 \cdot 5 \cdot 7 \cdot 13 \cdot 17 \cdot 19$$
$$352\,716 = 2^2 \cdot 3 \cdot 7 \cdot 13 \cdot 17 \cdot 19$$

Row 22

$$22 = 2 \cdot 11$$
$$231 = 3 \cdot 7 \cdot 11$$
$$1\,540 = 2^2 \cdot 5 \cdot 7 \cdot 11$$
$$7\,315 = 5 \cdot 7 \cdot 11 \cdot 19$$
$$26\,334 = 2 \cdot 3^2 \cdot 7 \cdot 11 \cdot 19$$
$$74\,613 = 3 \cdot 7 \cdot 11 \cdot 17 \cdot 19$$
$$170\,544 = 2^4 \cdot 3 \cdot 11 \cdot 17 \cdot 19$$
$$319\,770 = 2 \cdot 3^2 \cdot 5 \cdot 11 \cdot 17 \cdot 19$$
$$497\,420 = 2^2 \cdot 5 \cdot 7 \cdot 11 \cdot 17 \cdot 19$$
$$646\,646 = 2 \cdot 7 \cdot 11 \cdot 13 \cdot 17 \cdot 19$$
$$705\,432 = 2^3 \cdot 3 \cdot 7 \cdot 13 \cdot 17 \cdot 19$$

Row 23

$$23 \text{ is Prime}$$
$$253 = 11 \cdot 23$$
$$1\,771 = 7 \cdot 11 \cdot 23$$
$$8\,855 = 5 \cdot 7 \cdot 11 \cdot 23$$
$$33\,649 = 7 \cdot 11 \cdot 19 \cdot 23$$
$$100\,947 = 3 \cdot 7 \cdot 11 \cdot 19 \cdot 23$$
$$245\,157 = 3 \cdot 11 \cdot 17 \cdot 19 \cdot 23$$
$$490\,314 = 2 \cdot 3 \cdot 11 \cdot 17 \cdot 19 \cdot 23$$
$$817\,190 = 2 \cdot 5 \cdot 11 \cdot 17 \cdot 19 \cdot 23$$
$$1\,144\,066 = 2 \cdot 7 \cdot 11 \cdot 17 \cdot 19 \cdot 23$$
$$1\,352\,078 = 2 \cdot 7 \cdot 13 \cdot 17 \cdot 19 \cdot 23$$

Row 24

$$24 = 2^3 \cdot 3$$
$$276 = 2^2 \cdot 3 \cdot 23$$
$$2\,024 = 2^3 \cdot 11 \cdot 23$$
$$10\,626 = 2 \cdot 3 \cdot 7 \cdot 11 \cdot 23$$
$$42\,504 = 2^3 \cdot 3 \cdot 7 \cdot 11 \cdot 23$$
$$134\,596 = 2^2 \cdot 7 \cdot 11 \cdot 19 \cdot 23$$
$$346\,104 = 2^3 \cdot 3^2 \cdot 11 \cdot 19 \cdot 23$$
$$735\,471 = 3^2 \cdot 11 \cdot 17 \cdot 19 \cdot 23$$
$$1\,307\,504 = 2^4 \cdot 11 \cdot 17 \cdot 19 \cdot 23$$
$$1\,961\,256 = 2^3 \cdot 3 \cdot 11 \cdot 17 \cdot 19 \cdot 23$$
$$2\,496\,144 = 2^4 \cdot 3 \cdot 7 \cdot 17 \cdot 19 \cdot 23$$
$$2\,704\,156 = 2^2 \cdot 7 \cdot 13 \cdot 17 \cdot 19 \cdot 23$$

Row 25

$$25 = 5^2$$
$$300 = 2^2 \cdot 3 \cdot 5^2$$
$$2\,300 = 2^2 \cdot 5^2 \cdot 23$$
$$12\,650 = 2 \cdot 5^2 \cdot 11 \cdot 23$$
$$53\,130 = 2 \cdot 3 \cdot 5 \cdot 7 \cdot 11 \cdot 23$$
$$177\,100 = 2^2 \cdot 5^2 \cdot 7 \cdot 11 \cdot 23$$
$$480\,700 = 2^2 \cdot 5^2 \cdot 11 \cdot 19 \cdot 23$$
$$1\,081\,575 = 3^2 \cdot 5^2 \cdot 11 \cdot 19 \cdot 23$$
$$2\,042\,975 = 5^2 \cdot 11 \cdot 17 \cdot 19 \cdot 23$$
$$3\,268\,760 = 2^3 \cdot 5 \cdot 11 \cdot 17 \cdot 19 \cdot 23$$
$$4\,457\,400 = 2^3 \cdot 3 \cdot 5^2 \cdot 17 \cdot 19 \cdot 23$$
$$5\,200\,300 = 2^2 \cdot 5^2 \cdot 7 \cdot 17 \cdot 19 \cdot 23$$

Row 26

$$26 = 2 \cdot 13$$
$$325 = 5^2 \cdot 13$$
$$2\,600 = 2^3 \cdot 5^2 \cdot 13$$
$$14\,950 = 2 \cdot 5^2 \cdot 13 \cdot 23$$
$$65\,780 = 2^2 \cdot 5 \cdot 11 \cdot 13 \cdot 23$$
$$230\,230 = 2 \cdot 5 \cdot 7 \cdot 11 \cdot 13 \cdot 23$$
$$657\,800 = 2^3 \cdot 5^2 \cdot 11 \cdot 13 \cdot 23$$
$$1\,562\,275 = 5^2 \cdot 11 \cdot 13 \cdot 19 \cdot 23$$
$$3\,124\,550 = 2 \cdot 5^2 \cdot 11 \cdot 13 \cdot 19 \cdot 23$$
$$5\,311\,735 = 5 \cdot 11 \cdot 13 \cdot 17 \cdot 19 \cdot 23$$
$$7\,726\,160 = 2^4 \cdot 5 \cdot 13 \cdot 17 \cdot 19 \cdot 23$$
$$9\,657\,700 = 2^2 \cdot 5^2 \cdot 13 \cdot 17 \cdot 19 \cdot 23$$
$$10\,400\,600 = 2^3 \cdot 5^2 \cdot 7 \cdot 17 \cdot 19 \cdot 23$$

Row 27

$$27 = 3^3$$
$$351 = 3^3 \cdot 13$$
$$2\,925 = 3^2 \cdot 5^2 \cdot 13$$
$$17\,550 = 2 \cdot 3^3 \cdot 5^2 \cdot 13$$
$$80\,730 = 2 \cdot 3^3 \cdot 5 \cdot 13 \cdot 23$$
$$296\,010 = 2 \cdot 3^2 \cdot 5 \cdot 11 \cdot 13 \cdot 23$$
$$888\,030 = 2 \cdot 3^3 \cdot 5 \cdot 11 \cdot 13 \cdot 23$$
$$2\,220\,075 = 3^3 \cdot 5^2 \cdot 11 \cdot 13 \cdot 23$$
$$4\,686\,825 = 3 \cdot 5^2 \cdot 11 \cdot 13 \cdot 19 \cdot 23$$
$$8\,436\,285 = 3^3 \cdot 5 \cdot 11 \cdot 13 \cdot 19 \cdot 23$$
$$13\,037\,895 = 3^3 \cdot 5 \cdot 13 \cdot 17 \cdot 19 \cdot 23$$
$$17\,383\,860 = 2^2 \cdot 3^2 \cdot 5 \cdot 13 \cdot 17 \cdot 19 \cdot 23$$
$$20\,058\,300 = 2^2 \cdot 3^3 \cdot 5^2 \cdot 17 \cdot 19 \cdot 23$$

Pascal's Triangle — Prime Factorization — To Center Number (omitting 1's)

Row 28

$$28 = 2^2 \cdot 7$$
$$378 = 2 \cdot 3^3 \cdot 7$$
$$3\,276 = 2^2 \cdot 3^2 \cdot 7 \cdot 13$$
$$20\,475 = 3^2 \cdot 5^2 \cdot 7 \cdot 13$$
$$98\,280 = 2^3 \cdot 3^3 \cdot 5 \cdot 7 \cdot 13$$
$$376\,740 = 2^2 \cdot 3^2 \cdot 5 \cdot 7 \cdot 13 \cdot 23$$
$$1\,184\,040 = 2^3 \cdot 3^2 \cdot 5 \cdot 11 \cdot 13 \cdot 23$$
$$3\,108\,105 = 3^3 \cdot 5 \cdot 7 \cdot 11 \cdot 13 \cdot 23$$
$$6\,906\,900 = 2^2 \cdot 3 \cdot 5^2 \cdot 7 \cdot 11 \cdot 13 \cdot 23$$
$$13\,123\,110 = 2 \cdot 3 \cdot 5 \cdot 7 \cdot 11 \cdot 13 \cdot 19 \cdot 23$$
$$21\,474\,180 = 2^2 \cdot 3^3 \cdot 5 \cdot 7 \cdot 13 \cdot 19 \cdot 23$$
$$30\,421\,755 = 3^2 \cdot 5 \cdot 7 \cdot 13 \cdot 17 \cdot 19 \cdot 23$$
$$37\,442\,160 = 2^4 \cdot 3^2 \cdot 5 \cdot 7 \cdot 17 \cdot 19 \cdot 23$$
$$40\,116\,600 = 2^3 \cdot 3^3 \cdot 5^2 \cdot 17 \cdot 19 \cdot 23$$

Row 29

29 is Prime
$$406 = 2 \cdot 7 \cdot 29$$
$$3\,654 = 2 \cdot 3^2 \cdot 7 \cdot 29$$
$$23\,751 = 3^2 \cdot 7 \cdot 13 \cdot 29$$
$$118\,755 = 3^2 \cdot 5 \cdot 7 \cdot 13 \cdot 29$$
$$475\,020 = 2^2 \cdot 3^2 \cdot 5 \cdot 7 \cdot 13 \cdot 29$$
$$1\,560\,780 = 2^2 \cdot 3^2 \cdot 5 \cdot 13 \cdot 23 \cdot 29$$
$$4\,292\,145 = 3^2 \cdot 5 \cdot 11 \cdot 13 \cdot 23 \cdot 29$$
$$10\,015\,005 = 3 \cdot 5 \cdot 7 \cdot 11 \cdot 13 \cdot 23 \cdot 29$$
$$20\,030\,010 = 2 \cdot 3 \cdot 5 \cdot 7 \cdot 11 \cdot 13 \cdot 23 \cdot 29$$
$$34\,597\,290 = 2 \cdot 3 \cdot 5 \cdot 7 \cdot 13 \cdot 19 \cdot 23 \cdot 29$$
$$51\,895\,935 = 3^2 \cdot 5 \cdot 7 \cdot 13 \cdot 19 \cdot 23 \cdot 29$$
$$67\,863\,915 = 3^2 \cdot 5 \cdot 7 \cdot 17 \cdot 19 \cdot 23 \cdot 29$$
$$77\,558\,760 = 2^3 \cdot 3^2 \cdot 5 \cdot 17 \cdot 19 \cdot 23 \cdot 29$$

Row 30

$$30 = 2 \cdot 3 \cdot 5$$
$$435 = 3 \cdot 5 \cdot 29$$
$$4\,060 = 2^2 \cdot 5 \cdot 7 \cdot 29$$
$$27\,405 = 3^3 \cdot 5 \cdot 7 \cdot 29$$
$$142\,506 = 2 \cdot 3^3 \cdot 7 \cdot 13 \cdot 29$$
$$593\,775 = 3^2 \cdot 5^2 \cdot 7 \cdot 13 \cdot 29$$
$$2\,035\,800 = 2^3 \cdot 3^3 \cdot 5^2 \cdot 13 \cdot 29$$
$$5\,852\,925 = 3^3 \cdot 5^2 \cdot 13 \cdot 23 \cdot 29$$
$$14\,307\,150 = 2 \cdot 3 \cdot 5^2 \cdot 11 \cdot 13 \cdot 23 \cdot 29$$
$$30\,045\,015 = 3^2 \cdot 5 \cdot 7 \cdot 11 \cdot 13 \cdot 23 \cdot 29$$
$$54\,627\,300 = 2^2 \cdot 3^2 \cdot 5^2 \cdot 7 \cdot 13 \cdot 23 \cdot 29$$
$$86\,493\,225 = 3 \cdot 5^2 \cdot 7 \cdot 13 \cdot 19 \cdot 23 \cdot 29$$
$$119\,759\,850 = 2 \cdot 3^3 \cdot 5^2 \cdot 7 \cdot 19 \cdot 23 \cdot 29$$
$$145\,422\,675 = 3^3 \cdot 5^2 \cdot 17 \cdot 19 \cdot 23 \cdot 29$$
$$155\,117\,520 = 2^4 \cdot 3^2 \cdot 5 \cdot 17 \cdot 19 \cdot 23 \cdot 29$$

Row 31

31 is Prime
$$465 = 3 \cdot 5 \cdot 31$$
$$4\,495 = 5 \cdot 29 \cdot 31$$
$$31\,465 = 5 \cdot 7 \cdot 29 \cdot 31$$
$$169\,911 = 3^3 \cdot 7 \cdot 29 \cdot 31$$
$$736\,281 = 3^2 \cdot 7 \cdot 13 \cdot 29 \cdot 31$$
$$2\,629\,575 = 3^2 \cdot 5^2 \cdot 13 \cdot 29 \cdot 31$$
$$7\,888\,725 = 3^3 \cdot 5^2 \cdot 13 \cdot 29 \cdot 31$$
$$20\,160\,075 = 3 \cdot 5^2 \cdot 13 \cdot 23 \cdot 29 \cdot 31$$
$$44\,352\,165 = 3 \cdot 5 \cdot 11 \cdot 13 \cdot 23 \cdot 29 \cdot 31$$
$$84\,672\,315 = 3^2 \cdot 5 \cdot 7 \cdot 13 \cdot 23 \cdot 29 \cdot 31$$
$$141\,120\,525 = 3 \cdot 5^2 \cdot 7 \cdot 13 \cdot 23 \cdot 29 \cdot 31$$
$$206\,253\,075 = 3 \cdot 5^2 \cdot 7 \cdot 19 \cdot 23 \cdot 29 \cdot 31$$
$$265\,182\,525 = 3^3 \cdot 5^2 \cdot 19 \cdot 23 \cdot 29 \cdot 31$$
$$300\,540\,195 = 3^2 \cdot 5 \cdot 17 \cdot 19 \cdot 23 \cdot 29 \cdot 31$$

Row 32

$$32 = 2^5$$
$$496 = 2^4 \cdot 31$$
$$4\,960 = 2^5 \cdot 5 \cdot 31$$
$$35\,960 = 2^3 \cdot 5 \cdot 29 \cdot 31$$
$$201\,376 = 2^5 \cdot 7 \cdot 29 \cdot 31$$
$$906\,192 = 2^4 \cdot 3^2 \cdot 7 \cdot 29 \cdot 31$$
$$3\,365\,856 = 2^5 \cdot 3^2 \cdot 13 \cdot 29 \cdot 31$$
$$10\,518\,300 = 2^2 \cdot 3^2 \cdot 5^2 \cdot 13 \cdot 29 \cdot 31$$
$$28\,048\,800 = 2^5 \cdot 3 \cdot 5^2 \cdot 13 \cdot 29 \cdot 31$$
$$64\,512\,240 = 2^4 \cdot 3 \cdot 5 \cdot 13 \cdot 23 \cdot 29 \cdot 31$$
$$129\,024\,480 = 2^5 \cdot 3 \cdot 5 \cdot 13 \cdot 23 \cdot 29 \cdot 31$$
$$225\,792\,840 = 2^3 \cdot 3 \cdot 5 \cdot 7 \cdot 13 \cdot 23 \cdot 29 \cdot 31$$
$$347\,373\,600 = 2^5 \cdot 3 \cdot 5^2 \cdot 7 \cdot 23 \cdot 29 \cdot 31$$
$$471\,435\,600 = 2^4 \cdot 3 \cdot 5^2 \cdot 19 \cdot 23 \cdot 29 \cdot 31$$
$$565\,722\,720 = 2^5 \cdot 3^2 \cdot 5 \cdot 19 \cdot 23 \cdot 29 \cdot 31$$
$$601\,080\,390 = 2 \cdot 3^2 \cdot 5 \cdot 17 \cdot 19 \cdot 23 \cdot 29 \cdot 31$$

Row 33

$$33 = 3 \cdot 11$$
$$528 = 2^4 \cdot 3 \cdot 11$$
$$5\,456 = 2^4 \cdot 11 \cdot 31$$
$$40\,920 = 2^3 \cdot 3 \cdot 5 \cdot 11 \cdot 31$$
$$237\,336 = 2^3 \cdot 3 \cdot 11 \cdot 29 \cdot 31$$
$$1\,107\,568 = 2^4 \cdot 7 \cdot 11 \cdot 29 \cdot 31$$
$$4\,272\,048 = 2^4 \cdot 3^3 \cdot 11 \cdot 29 \cdot 31$$
$$13\,884\,156 = 2^2 \cdot 3^3 \cdot 11 \cdot 13 \cdot 29 \cdot 31$$
$$38\,567\,100 = 2^2 \cdot 3 \cdot 5^2 \cdot 11 \cdot 13 \cdot 29 \cdot 31$$
$$92\,561\,040 = 2^4 \cdot 3^2 \cdot 5 \cdot 11 \cdot 13 \cdot 29 \cdot 31$$
$$193\,536\,720 = 2^4 \cdot 3^2 \cdot 5 \cdot 13 \cdot 23 \cdot 29 \cdot 31$$
$$354\,817\,320 = 2^3 \cdot 3 \cdot 5 \cdot 11 \cdot 13 \cdot 23 \cdot 29 \cdot 31$$
$$573\,166\,440 = 2^3 \cdot 3^2 \cdot 5 \cdot 7 \cdot 11 \cdot 23 \cdot 29 \cdot 31$$
$$818\,809\,200 = 2^4 \cdot 3^2 \cdot 5^2 \cdot 11 \cdot 23 \cdot 29 \cdot 31$$
$$1\,037\,158\,320 = 2^4 \cdot 3 \cdot 5 \cdot 11 \cdot 19 \cdot 23 \cdot 29 \cdot 31$$
$$1\,166\,803\,110 = 2 \cdot 3^3 \cdot 5 \cdot 11 \cdot 19 \cdot 23 \cdot 29 \cdot 31$$

Pascal's Triangle — Prime Factorization — To Center Number (omitting 1's)

Row 34

$$34 = 2 \cdot 17$$
$$561 = 3 \cdot 11 \cdot 17$$
$$5\,984 = 2^5 \cdot 11 \cdot 17$$
$$46\,376 = 2^3 \cdot 11 \cdot 17 \cdot 31$$
$$278\,256 = 2^4 \cdot 3 \cdot 11 \cdot 17 \cdot 31$$
$$1\,344\,904 = 2^3 \cdot 11 \cdot 17 \cdot 29 \cdot 31$$
$$5\,379\,616 = 2^5 \cdot 11 \cdot 17 \cdot 29 \cdot 31$$
$$18\,156\,204 = 2^2 \cdot 3^3 \cdot 11 \cdot 17 \cdot 29 \cdot 31$$
$$52\,451\,256 = 2^3 \cdot 3 \cdot 11 \cdot 13 \cdot 17 \cdot 29 \cdot 31$$
$$131\,128\,140 = 2^2 \cdot 3 \cdot 5 \cdot 11 \cdot 13 \cdot 17 \cdot 29 \cdot 31$$
$$286\,097\,760 = 2^5 \cdot 3^2 \cdot 5 \cdot 13 \cdot 17 \cdot 29 \cdot 31$$
$$548\,354\,040 = 2^3 \cdot 3 \cdot 5 \cdot 13 \cdot 17 \cdot 23 \cdot 29 \cdot 31$$
$$927\,983\,760 = 2^4 \cdot 3 \cdot 5 \cdot 11 \cdot 17 \cdot 23 \cdot 29 \cdot 31$$
$$1\,391\,975\,640 = 2^3 \cdot 3^2 \cdot 5 \cdot 11 \cdot 17 \cdot 23 \cdot 29 \cdot 31$$
$$1\,855\,967\,520 = 2^5 \cdot 3 \cdot 5 \cdot 11 \cdot 17 \cdot 23 \cdot 29 \cdot 31$$
$$2\,203\,961\,430 = 2 \cdot 3 \cdot 5 \cdot 11 \cdot 17 \cdot 19 \cdot 23 \cdot 29 \cdot 31$$
$$2\,333\,606\,220 = 2^2 \cdot 3^3 \cdot 5 \cdot 11 \cdot 19 \cdot 23 \cdot 29 \cdot 31$$

Row 35

$$35 = 5 \cdot 7$$
$$595 = 5 \cdot 7 \cdot 17$$
$$6\,545 = 5 \cdot 7 \cdot 11 \cdot 17$$
$$52\,360 = 2^3 \cdot 5 \cdot 7 \cdot 11 \cdot 17$$
$$324\,632 = 2^3 \cdot 7 \cdot 11 \cdot 17 \cdot 31$$
$$1\,623\,160 = 2^3 \cdot 5 \cdot 7 \cdot 11 \cdot 17 \cdot 31$$
$$6\,724\,520 = 2^3 \cdot 5 \cdot 11 \cdot 17 \cdot 29 \cdot 31$$
$$23\,535\,820 = 2^2 \cdot 5 \cdot 7 \cdot 11 \cdot 17 \cdot 29 \cdot 31$$
$$70\,607\,460 = 2^2 \cdot 3 \cdot 5 \cdot 7 \cdot 11 \cdot 17 \cdot 29 \cdot 31$$
$$183\,579\,396 = 2^2 \cdot 3 \cdot 7 \cdot 11 \cdot 13 \cdot 17 \cdot 29 \cdot 31$$
$$417\,225\,900 = 2^2 \cdot 3 \cdot 5^2 \cdot 7 \cdot 13 \cdot 17 \cdot 29 \cdot 31$$
$$834\,451\,800 = 2^3 \cdot 3 \cdot 5^2 \cdot 7 \cdot 13 \cdot 17 \cdot 29 \cdot 31$$
$$1\,476\,337\,800 = 2^3 \cdot 3 \cdot 5^2 \cdot 7 \cdot 17 \cdot 23 \cdot 29 \cdot 31$$
$$2\,319\,959\,400 = 2^3 \cdot 3 \cdot 5^2 \cdot 11 \cdot 17 \cdot 23 \cdot 29 \cdot 31$$
$$3\,247\,943\,160 = 2^3 \cdot 3 \cdot 5 \cdot 7 \cdot 11 \cdot 17 \cdot 23 \cdot 29 \cdot 31$$
$$4\,059\,928\,950 = 2 \cdot 3 \cdot 5^2 \cdot 7 \cdot 11 \cdot 17 \cdot 23 \cdot 29 \cdot 31$$
$$4\,537\,567\,650 = 2 \cdot 3 \cdot 5^2 \cdot 7 \cdot 11 \cdot 19 \cdot 23 \cdot 29 \cdot 31$$

Row 36

$$36 = 2^2 \cdot 3^2$$
$$630 = 2 \cdot 3^2 \cdot 5 \cdot 7$$
$$7\,140 = 2^2 \cdot 3 \cdot 5 \cdot 7 \cdot 17$$
$$58\,905 = 3^2 \cdot 5 \cdot 7 \cdot 11 \cdot 17$$
$$376\,992 = 2^5 \cdot 3^2 \cdot 7 \cdot 11 \cdot 17$$
$$1\,947\,792 = 2^4 \cdot 3 \cdot 7 \cdot 11 \cdot 17 \cdot 31$$
$$8\,347\,680 = 2^5 \cdot 3^2 \cdot 5 \cdot 11 \cdot 17 \cdot 31$$
$$30\,260\,340 = 2^2 \cdot 3^2 \cdot 5 \cdot 11 \cdot 17 \cdot 29 \cdot 31$$
$$94\,143\,280 = 2^4 \cdot 5 \cdot 7 \cdot 11 \cdot 17 \cdot 29 \cdot 31$$
$$254\,186\,856 = 2^3 \cdot 3^3 \cdot 7 \cdot 11 \cdot 17 \cdot 29 \cdot 31$$
$$600\,805\,296 = 2^4 \cdot 3^3 \cdot 7 \cdot 13 \cdot 17 \cdot 29 \cdot 31$$
$$1\,251\,677\,700 = 2^2 \cdot 3^2 \cdot 5^2 \cdot 7 \cdot 13 \cdot 17 \cdot 29 \cdot 31$$
$$2\,310\,789\,600 = 2^5 \cdot 3^3 \cdot 5^2 \cdot 7 \cdot 17 \cdot 29 \cdot 31$$
$$3\,796\,297\,200 = 2^4 \cdot 3^3 \cdot 5^2 \cdot 17 \cdot 23 \cdot 29 \cdot 31$$
$$5\,567\,902\,560 = 2^5 \cdot 3^2 \cdot 5 \cdot 11 \cdot 17 \cdot 23 \cdot 29 \cdot 31$$
$$7\,307\,872\,110 = 2 \cdot 3^3 \cdot 5 \cdot 7 \cdot 11 \cdot 17 \cdot 23 \cdot 29 \cdot 31$$
$$8\,597\,496\,600 = 2^3 \cdot 3^3 \cdot 5^2 \cdot 7 \cdot 11 \cdot 23 \cdot 29 \cdot 31$$
$$9\,075\,135\,300 = 2^2 \cdot 3 \cdot 5^2 \cdot 7 \cdot 11 \cdot 19 \cdot 23 \cdot 29 \cdot 31$$

Row 37

37 is Prime
$$666 = 2 \cdot 3^2 \cdot 37$$
$$7\,770 = 2 \cdot 3 \cdot 5 \cdot 7 \cdot 37$$
$$66\,045 = 3 \cdot 5 \cdot 7 \cdot 17 \cdot 37$$
$$435\,897 = 3^2 \cdot 7 \cdot 11 \cdot 17 \cdot 37$$
$$2\,324\,784 = 2^4 \cdot 3 \cdot 7 \cdot 11 \cdot 17 \cdot 37$$
$$10\,295\,472 = 2^4 \cdot 3 \cdot 11 \cdot 17 \cdot 31 \cdot 37$$
$$38\,608\,020 = 2^2 \cdot 3^2 \cdot 5 \cdot 11 \cdot 17 \cdot 31 \cdot 37$$
$$124\,403\,620 = 2^2 \cdot 5 \cdot 11 \cdot 17 \cdot 29 \cdot 31 \cdot 37$$
$$348\,330\,136 = 2^3 \cdot 7 \cdot 11 \cdot 17 \cdot 29 \cdot 31 \cdot 37$$
$$854\,992\,152 = 2^3 \cdot 3^3 \cdot 7 \cdot 17 \cdot 29 \cdot 31 \cdot 37$$
$$1\,852\,482\,996 = 2^2 \cdot 3^2 \cdot 7 \cdot 13 \cdot 17 \cdot 29 \cdot 31 \cdot 37$$
$$3\,562\,467\,300 = 2^2 \cdot 3^2 \cdot 5^2 \cdot 7 \cdot 17 \cdot 29 \cdot 31 \cdot 37$$
$$6\,107\,086\,800 = 2^4 \cdot 3^3 \cdot 5^2 \cdot 17 \cdot 29 \cdot 31 \cdot 37$$
$$9\,364\,199\,760 = 2^4 \cdot 3^2 \cdot 5 \cdot 17 \cdot 23 \cdot 29 \cdot 31 \cdot 37$$
$$12\,875\,774\,670 = 2 \cdot 3^2 \cdot 5 \cdot 11 \cdot 17 \cdot 23 \cdot 29 \cdot 31 \cdot 37$$
$$15\,905\,368\,710 = 2 \cdot 3^3 \cdot 5 \cdot 7 \cdot 11 \cdot 23 \cdot 29 \cdot 31 \cdot 37$$
$$17\,672\,631\,900 = 2^2 \cdot 3 \cdot 5^2 \cdot 7 \cdot 11 \cdot 23 \cdot 29 \cdot 31 \cdot 37$$

Pascal's Triangle — Prime Factorization — To Center Number (omitting 1's)

<u>Row 38</u>

$$38 = 2 \cdot 19$$
$$703 = 19 \cdot 37$$
$$8\,436 = 2^2 \cdot 3 \cdot 19 \cdot 37$$
$$73\,815 = 3 \cdot 5 \cdot 7 \cdot 19 \cdot 37$$
$$501\,942 = 2 \cdot 3 \cdot 7 \cdot 17 \cdot 19 \cdot 37$$
$$2\,760\,681 = 3 \cdot 7 \cdot 11 \cdot 17 \cdot 19 \cdot 37$$
$$12\,620\,256 = 2^5 \cdot 3 \cdot 11 \cdot 17 \cdot 19 \cdot 37$$
$$48\,903\,492 = 2^2 \cdot 3 \cdot 11 \cdot 17 \cdot 19 \cdot 31 \cdot 37$$
$$163\,011\,640 = 2^3 \cdot 5 \cdot 11 \cdot 17 \cdot 19 \cdot 31 \cdot 37$$
$$472\,733\,756 = 2^2 \cdot 11 \cdot 17 \cdot 19 \cdot 29 \cdot 31 \cdot 37$$
$$1\,203\,322\,288 = 2^4 \cdot 7 \cdot 17 \cdot 19 \cdot 29 \cdot 31 \cdot 37$$
$$2\,707\,475\,148 = 2^2 \cdot 3^2 \cdot 7 \cdot 17 \cdot 19 \cdot 29 \cdot 31 \cdot 37$$
$$5\,414\,950\,296 = 2^3 \cdot 3^2 \cdot 7 \cdot 17 \cdot 19 \cdot 29 \cdot 31 \cdot 37$$
$$9\,669\,554\,100 = 2^2 \cdot 3^2 \cdot 5^2 \cdot 17 \cdot 19 \cdot 29 \cdot 31 \cdot 37$$
$$15\,471\,286\,560 = 2^5 \cdot 3^2 \cdot 5 \cdot 17 \cdot 19 \cdot 29 \cdot 31 \cdot 37$$
$$22\,239\,974\,430 = 2 \cdot 3^2 \cdot 5 \cdot 17 \cdot 19 \cdot 23 \cdot 29 \cdot 31 \cdot 37$$
$$28\,781\,143\,380 = 2^2 \cdot 3^2 \cdot 5 \cdot 11 \cdot 19 \cdot 23 \cdot 29 \cdot 31 \cdot 37$$
$$33\,578\,000\,610 = 2 \cdot 3 \cdot 5 \cdot 7 \cdot 11 \cdot 19 \cdot 23 \cdot 29 \cdot 31 \cdot 37$$
$$35\,345\,263\,800 = 2^3 \cdot 3 \cdot 5^2 \cdot 7 \cdot 11 \cdot 23 \cdot 29 \cdot 31 \cdot 37$$

<u>Row 39</u>

$$39 = 3 \cdot 13$$
$$741 = 3 \cdot 13 \cdot 19$$
$$9\,139 = 13 \cdot 19 \cdot 37$$
$$82\,251 = 3^2 \cdot 13 \cdot 19 \cdot 37$$
$$575\,757 = 3^2 \cdot 7 \cdot 13 \cdot 19 \cdot 37$$
$$3\,262\,623 = 3 \cdot 7 \cdot 13 \cdot 17 \cdot 19 \cdot 37$$
$$15\,380\,937 = 3^2 \cdot 11 \cdot 13 \cdot 17 \cdot 19 \cdot 37$$
$$61\,523\,748 = 2^2 \cdot 3^2 \cdot 11 \cdot 13 \cdot 17 \cdot 19 \cdot 37$$
$$211\,915\,132 = 2^2 \cdot 11 \cdot 13 \cdot 17 \cdot 19 \cdot 31 \cdot 37$$
$$635\,745\,396 = 2^2 \cdot 3 \cdot 11 \cdot 13 \cdot 17 \cdot 19 \cdot 31 \cdot 37$$
$$1\,676\,056\,044 = 2^2 \cdot 3 \cdot 13 \cdot 17 \cdot 19 \cdot 29 \cdot 31 \cdot 37$$
$$3\,910\,797\,436 = 2^2 \cdot 7 \cdot 13 \cdot 17 \cdot 19 \cdot 29 \cdot 31 \cdot 37$$
$$8\,122\,425\,444 = 2^2 \cdot 3^3 \cdot 7 \cdot 17 \cdot 19 \cdot 29 \cdot 31 \cdot 37$$
$$15\,084\,504\,396 = 2^2 \cdot 3^3 \cdot 13 \cdot 17 \cdot 19 \cdot 29 \cdot 31 \cdot 37$$
$$25\,140\,840\,660 = 2^2 \cdot 3^2 \cdot 5 \cdot 13 \cdot 17 \cdot 19 \cdot 29 \cdot 31 \cdot 37$$
$$37\,711\,260\,990 = 2 \cdot 3^3 \cdot 5 \cdot 13 \cdot 17 \cdot 19 \cdot 29 \cdot 31 \cdot 37$$
$$51\,021\,117\,810 = 2 \cdot 3^3 \cdot 5 \cdot 13 \cdot 19 \cdot 23 \cdot 29 \cdot 31 \cdot 37$$
$$62\,359\,143\,990 = 2 \cdot 3 \cdot 5 \cdot 11 \cdot 13 \cdot 19 \cdot 23 \cdot 29 \cdot 31 \cdot 37$$
$$68\,923\,264\,410 = 2 \cdot 3^2 \cdot 5 \cdot 7 \cdot 11 \cdot 13 \cdot 23 \cdot 29 \cdot 31 \cdot 37$$

Pascal's Triangle — Prime Factorization — To Center Number (omitting 1's)

Row 40

$$
\begin{aligned}
40 &= 2^3 \cdot 5 \\
780 &= 2^2 \cdot 3 \cdot 5 \cdot 13 \\
9\,880 &= 2^3 \cdot 5 \cdot 13 \cdot 19 \\
91\,390 &= 2 \cdot 5 \cdot 13 \cdot 19 \cdot 37 \\
658\,008 &= 2^3 \cdot 3^2 \cdot 13 \cdot 19 \cdot 37 \\
3\,838\,380 &= 2^2 \cdot 3 \cdot 5 \cdot 7 \cdot 13 \cdot 19 \cdot 37 \\
18\,643\,560 &= 2^3 \cdot 3 \cdot 5 \cdot 13 \cdot 17 \cdot 19 \cdot 37 \\
76\,904\,685 &= 3^2 \cdot 5 \cdot 11 \cdot 13 \cdot 17 \cdot 19 \cdot 37 \\
273\,438\,880 &= 2^5 \cdot 5 \cdot 11 \cdot 13 \cdot 17 \cdot 19 \cdot 37 \\
847\,660\,528 &= 2^4 \cdot 11 \cdot 13 \cdot 17 \cdot 19 \cdot 31 \cdot 37 \\
2\,311\,801\,440 &= 2^5 \cdot 3 \cdot 5 \cdot 13 \cdot 17 \cdot 19 \cdot 31 \cdot 37 \\
5\,586\,853\,480 &= 2^3 \cdot 5 \cdot 13 \cdot 17 \cdot 19 \cdot 29 \cdot 31 \cdot 37 \\
12\,033\,222\,880 &= 2^5 \cdot 5 \cdot 7 \cdot 17 \cdot 19 \cdot 29 \cdot 31 \cdot 37 \\
23\,206\,929\,840 &= 2^4 \cdot 3^3 \cdot 5 \cdot 17 \cdot 19 \cdot 29 \cdot 31 \cdot 37 \\
40\,225\,345\,056 &= 2^5 \cdot 3^2 \cdot 13 \cdot 17 \cdot 19 \cdot 29 \cdot 31 \cdot 37 \\
62\,852\,101\,650 &= 2 \cdot 3^2 \cdot 5^2 \cdot 13 \cdot 17 \cdot 19 \cdot 29 \cdot 31 \cdot 37 \\
88\,732\,378\,800 &= 2^4 \cdot 3^3 \cdot 5^2 \cdot 13 \cdot 19 \cdot 29 \cdot 31 \cdot 37 \\
113\,380\,261\,800 &= 2^3 \cdot 3 \cdot 5^2 \cdot 13 \cdot 19 \cdot 23 \cdot 29 \cdot 31 \cdot 37 \\
131\,282\,408\,400 &= 2^4 \cdot 3 \cdot 5^2 \cdot 11 \cdot 13 \cdot 23 \cdot 29 \cdot 31 \cdot 37 \\
137\,846\,528\,820 &= 2^2 \cdot 3^2 \cdot 5 \cdot 7 \cdot 11 \cdot 13 \cdot 23 \cdot 29 \cdot 31 \cdot 37
\end{aligned}
$$

Row 41

$$
\begin{aligned}
41 &\text{ is Prime} \\
820 &= 2^2 \cdot 5 \cdot 41 \\
10\,660 &= 2^2 \cdot 5 \cdot 13 \cdot 41 \\
101\,270 &= 2 \cdot 5 \cdot 13 \cdot 19 \cdot 41 \\
749\,398 &= 2 \cdot 13 \cdot 19 \cdot 37 \cdot 41 \\
4\,496\,388 &= 2^2 \cdot 3 \cdot 13 \cdot 19 \cdot 37 \cdot 41 \\
22\,481\,940 &= 2^2 \cdot 3 \cdot 5 \cdot 13 \cdot 19 \cdot 37 \cdot 41 \\
95\,548\,245 &= 3 \cdot 5 \cdot 13 \cdot 17 \cdot 19 \cdot 37 \cdot 41 \\
350\,343\,565 &= 5 \cdot 11 \cdot 13 \cdot 17 \cdot 19 \cdot 37 \cdot 41 \\
1\,121\,099\,408 &= 2^4 \cdot 11 \cdot 13 \cdot 17 \cdot 19 \cdot 37 \cdot 41 \\
3\,159\,461\,968 &= 2^4 \cdot 13 \cdot 17 \cdot 19 \cdot 31 \cdot 37 \cdot 41 \\
7\,898\,654\,920 &= 2^3 \cdot 5 \cdot 13 \cdot 17 \cdot 19 \cdot 31 \cdot 37 \cdot 41 \\
17\,620\,076\,360 &= 2^3 \cdot 5 \cdot 17 \cdot 19 \cdot 29 \cdot 31 \cdot 37 \cdot 41 \\
35\,240\,152\,720 &= 2^4 \cdot 5 \cdot 17 \cdot 19 \cdot 29 \cdot 31 \cdot 37 \cdot 41 \\
63\,432\,274\,896 &= 2^4 \cdot 3^2 \cdot 17 \cdot 19 \cdot 29 \cdot 31 \cdot 37 \cdot 41 \\
103\,077\,446\,706 &= 2 \cdot 3^2 \cdot 13 \cdot 17 \cdot 19 \cdot 29 \cdot 31 \cdot 37 \cdot 41 \\
151\,584\,480\,450 &= 2 \cdot 3^2 \cdot 5^2 \cdot 13 \cdot 19 \cdot 29 \cdot 31 \cdot 37 \cdot 41 \\
202\,112\,640\,600 &= 2^3 \cdot 3 \cdot 5^2 \cdot 13 \cdot 19 \cdot 29 \cdot 31 \cdot 37 \cdot 41 \\
244\,662\,670\,200 &= 2^3 \cdot 3 \cdot 5^2 \cdot 13 \cdot 23 \cdot 29 \cdot 31 \cdot 37 \cdot 41 \\
269\,128\,937\,220 &= 2^2 \cdot 3 \cdot 5 \cdot 11 \cdot 13 \cdot 23 \cdot 29 \cdot 31 \cdot 37 \cdot 41
\end{aligned}
$$

Pascal's Triangle — Prime Factorization — To Center Number (omitting 1's)

<u>Row 42</u>

42	= 2·3·7
861	= 3·7·41
11 480	= 2^3·5·7·41
111 930	= 2·3·5·7·13·41
850 668	= 2^2·3·7·13·19·41
5 245 786	= 2·7·13·19·37·41
26 978 328	= 2^3·3^2·13·19·37·41
118 030 185	= 3^2·5·7·13·19·37·41
445 891 810	= 2·5·7·13·17·19·37·41
1 471 442 973	= 3·7·11·13·17·19·37·41
4 280 561 376	= 2^5·3·7·13·17·19·37·41
11 058 116 888	= 2^3·7·13·17·19·31·37·41
25 518 731 280	= 2^4·3·5·7·17·19·31·37·41
52 860 229 080	= 2^3·3·5·17·19·29·31·37·41
98 672 427 616	= 2^5·7·17·19·29·31·37·41
166 509 721 602	= 2·3^3·7·17·19·29·31·37·41
254 661 927 156	= 2^2·3^3·7·13·19·29·31·37·41
353 697 121 050	= 2·3·5^2·7·13·19·29·31·37·41
446 775 310 800	= 2^4·3^2·5^2·7·13·29·31·37·41
513 791 607 420	= 2^2·3^2·5·7·13·23·29·31·37·41
538 257 874 440	= 2^3·3·5·11·13·23·29·31·37·41

<u>Row 43</u>

43	is Prime
903	= 3·7·43
12 341	= 7·41·43
123 410	= 2·5·7·41·43
962 598	= 2·3·7·13·41·43
6 096 454	= 2·7·13·19·41·43
32 224 114	= 2·13·19·37·41·43
145 008 513	= 3^2·13·19·37·41·43
563 921 995	= 5·7·13·19·37·41·43
1 917 334 783	= 7·13·17·19·37·41·43
5 752 004 349	= 3·7·13·17·19·37·41·43
15 338 678 264	= 2^3·7·13·17·19·37·41·43
36 576 848 168	= 2^3·7·17·19·31·37·41·43
78 378 960 360	= 2^3·3·5·17·19·31·37·41·43
151 532 656 696	= 2^3·17·19·29·31·37·41·43
265 182 149 218	= 2·7·17·19·29·31·37·41·43
421 171 648 758	= 2·3^3·7·19·29·31·37·41·43
608 359 048 206	= 2·3·7·13·19·29·31·37·41·43
800 472 431 850	= 2·3·5^2·7·13·29·31·37·41·43
960 566 818 220	= 2^2·3^2·5·7·13·29·31·37·41·43
1 052 049 481 860	= 2^2·3·5·13·23·29·31·37·41·43

Pascal's Triangle — Prime Factorization — To Center Number (omitting 1's)

Row 44

$$44 = 2^2 \cdot 11$$
$$946 = 2 \cdot 11 \cdot 43$$
$$13\,244 = 2^2 \cdot 7 \cdot 11 \cdot 43$$
$$135\,751 = 7 \cdot 11 \cdot 41 \cdot 43$$
$$1\,086\,008 = 2^3 \cdot 7 \cdot 11 \cdot 41 \cdot 43$$
$$7\,059\,052 = 2^2 \cdot 7 \cdot 11 \cdot 13 \cdot 41 \cdot 43$$
$$38\,320\,568 = 2^3 \cdot 11 \cdot 13 \cdot 19 \cdot 41 \cdot 43$$
$$177\,232\,627 = 11 \cdot 13 \cdot 19 \cdot 37 \cdot 41 \cdot 43$$
$$708\,930\,508 = 2^2 \cdot 11 \cdot 13 \cdot 19 \cdot 37 \cdot 41 \cdot 43$$
$$2\,481\,256\,778 = 2 \cdot 7 \cdot 11 \cdot 13 \cdot 19 \cdot 37 \cdot 41 \cdot 43$$
$$7\,669\,339\,132 = 2^2 \cdot 7 \cdot 13 \cdot 17 \cdot 19 \cdot 37 \cdot 41 \cdot 43$$
$$21\,090\,682\,613 = 7 \cdot 11 \cdot 13 \cdot 17 \cdot 19 \cdot 37 \cdot 41 \cdot 43$$
$$51\,915\,526\,432 = 2^5 \cdot 7 \cdot 11 \cdot 17 \cdot 19 \cdot 37 \cdot 41 \cdot 43$$
$$114\,955\,808\,528 = 2^4 \cdot 11 \cdot 17 \cdot 19 \cdot 31 \cdot 37 \cdot 41 \cdot 43$$
$$229\,911\,617\,056 = 2^5 \cdot 11 \cdot 17 \cdot 19 \cdot 31 \cdot 37 \cdot 41 \cdot 43$$
$$416\,714\,805\,914 = 2 \cdot 11 \cdot 17 \cdot 19 \cdot 29 \cdot 31 \cdot 37 \cdot 41 \cdot 43$$
$$686\,353\,797\,976 = 2^3 \cdot 7 \cdot 11 \cdot 19 \cdot 29 \cdot 31 \cdot 37 \cdot 41 \cdot 43$$
$$1\,029\,530\,696\,964 = 2^2 \cdot 3 \cdot 7 \cdot 11 \cdot 19 \cdot 29 \cdot 31 \cdot 37 \cdot 41 \cdot 43$$
$$1\,408\,831\,480\,056 = 2^3 \cdot 3 \cdot 7 \cdot 11 \cdot 13 \cdot 29 \cdot 31 \cdot 37 \cdot 41 \cdot 43$$
$$1\,761\,039\,350\,070 = 2 \cdot 3 \cdot 5 \cdot 7 \cdot 11 \cdot 13 \cdot 29 \cdot 31 \cdot 37 \cdot 41 \cdot 43$$
$$2\,012\,616\,400\,080 = 2^4 \cdot 3 \cdot 5 \cdot 11 \cdot 13 \cdot 29 \cdot 31 \cdot 37 \cdot 41 \cdot 43$$
$$2\,104\,098\,963\,720 = 2^3 \cdot 3 \cdot 5 \cdot 13 \cdot 23 \cdot 29 \cdot 31 \cdot 37 \cdot 41 \cdot 43$$

Row 45

$$45 = 3^2 \cdot 5$$
$$990 = 2 \cdot 3^2 \cdot 5 \cdot 11$$
$$14\,190 = 2 \cdot 3 \cdot 5 \cdot 11 \cdot 43$$
$$148\,995 = 3^2 \cdot 5 \cdot 7 \cdot 11 \cdot 43$$
$$1\,221\,759 = 3^2 \cdot 7 \cdot 11 \cdot 41 \cdot 43$$
$$8\,145\,060 = 2^2 \cdot 3 \cdot 5 \cdot 7 \cdot 11 \cdot 41 \cdot 43$$
$$45\,379\,620 = 2^2 \cdot 3^2 \cdot 5 \cdot 11 \cdot 13 \cdot 41 \cdot 43$$
$$215\,553\,195 = 3^2 \cdot 5 \cdot 11 \cdot 13 \cdot 19 \cdot 41 \cdot 43$$
$$886\,163\,135 = 5 \cdot 11 \cdot 13 \cdot 19 \cdot 37 \cdot 41 \cdot 43$$
$$3\,190\,187\,286 = 2 \cdot 3^2 \cdot 11 \cdot 13 \cdot 19 \cdot 37 \cdot 41 \cdot 43$$
$$10\,150\,595\,910 = 2 \cdot 3^2 \cdot 5 \cdot 7 \cdot 13 \cdot 19 \cdot 37 \cdot 41 \cdot 43$$
$$28\,760\,021\,745 = 3 \cdot 5 \cdot 7 \cdot 13 \cdot 17 \cdot 19 \cdot 37 \cdot 41 \cdot 43$$
$$73\,006\,209\,045 = 3^2 \cdot 5 \cdot 7 \cdot 11 \cdot 17 \cdot 19 \cdot 37 \cdot 41 \cdot 43$$
$$166\,871\,334\,960 = 2^4 \cdot 3^2 \cdot 5 \cdot 11 \cdot 17 \cdot 19 \cdot 37 \cdot 41 \cdot 43$$
$$344\,867\,425\,584 = 2^4 \cdot 3 \cdot 11 \cdot 17 \cdot 19 \cdot 31 \cdot 37 \cdot 41 \cdot 43$$
$$646\,626\,422\,970 = 2 \cdot 3^2 \cdot 5 \cdot 11 \cdot 17 \cdot 19 \cdot 31 \cdot 37 \cdot 41 \cdot 43$$
$$1\,103\,068\,603\,890 = 2 \cdot 3^2 \cdot 5 \cdot 11 \cdot 19 \cdot 29 \cdot 31 \cdot 37 \cdot 41 \cdot 43$$
$$1\,715\,884\,494\,940 = 2^2 \cdot 5 \cdot 7 \cdot 11 \cdot 19 \cdot 29 \cdot 31 \cdot 37 \cdot 41 \cdot 43$$
$$2\,438\,362\,177\,020 = 2^2 \cdot 3^3 \cdot 5 \cdot 7 \cdot 11 \cdot 29 \cdot 31 \cdot 37 \cdot 41 \cdot 43$$
$$3\,169\,870\,830\,126 = 2 \cdot 3^3 \cdot 7 \cdot 11 \cdot 13 \cdot 29 \cdot 31 \cdot 37 \cdot 41 \cdot 43$$
$$3\,773\,655\,750\,150 = 2 \cdot 3^2 \cdot 5^2 \cdot 11 \cdot 13 \cdot 29 \cdot 31 \cdot 37 \cdot 41 \cdot 43$$
$$4\,116\,715\,363\,800 = 2^3 \cdot 3^3 \cdot 5^2 \cdot 13 \cdot 29 \cdot 31 \cdot 37 \cdot 41 \cdot 43$$

Pascal's Triangle — Prime Factorization — To Center Number (omitting 1's)

<u>Row 46</u>

$$
\begin{aligned}
46 &= 2 \cdot 23 \\
1\,035 &= 3^2 \cdot 5 \cdot 23 \\
15\,180 &= 2^2 \cdot 3 \cdot 5 \cdot 11 \cdot 23 \\
163\,185 &= 3 \cdot 5 \cdot 11 \cdot 23 \cdot 43 \\
1\,370\,754 &= 2 \cdot 3^2 \cdot 7 \cdot 11 \cdot 23 \cdot 43 \\
9\,366\,819 &= 3 \cdot 7 \cdot 11 \cdot 23 \cdot 41 \cdot 43 \\
53\,524\,680 &= 2^3 \cdot 3 \cdot 5 \cdot 11 \cdot 23 \cdot 41 \cdot 43 \\
260\,932\,815 &= 3^2 \cdot 5 \cdot 11 \cdot 13 \cdot 23 \cdot 41 \cdot 43 \\
1\,101\,716\,330 &= 2 \cdot 5 \cdot 11 \cdot 13 \cdot 19 \cdot 23 \cdot 41 \cdot 43 \\
4\,076\,350\,421 &= 11 \cdot 13 \cdot 19 \cdot 23 \cdot 37 \cdot 41 \cdot 43 \\
13\,340\,783\,196 &= 2^2 \cdot 3^2 \cdot 13 \cdot 19 \cdot 23 \cdot 37 \cdot 41 \cdot 43 \\
38\,910\,617\,655 &= 3 \cdot 5 \cdot 7 \cdot 13 \cdot 19 \cdot 23 \cdot 37 \cdot 41 \cdot 43 \\
101\,766\,230\,790 &= 2 \cdot 3 \cdot 5 \cdot 7 \cdot 17 \cdot 19 \cdot 23 \cdot 37 \cdot 41 \cdot 43 \\
239\,877\,544\,005 &= 3^2 \cdot 5 \cdot 11 \cdot 17 \cdot 19 \cdot 23 \cdot 37 \cdot 41 \cdot 43 \\
511\,738\,760\,544 &= 2^5 \cdot 3 \cdot 11 \cdot 17 \cdot 19 \cdot 23 \cdot 37 \cdot 41 \cdot 43 \\
991\,493\,848\,554 &= 2 \cdot 3 \cdot 11 \cdot 17 \cdot 19 \cdot 23 \cdot 31 \cdot 37 \cdot 41 \cdot 43 \\
1\,749\,695\,026\,860 &= 2^2 \cdot 3^2 \cdot 5 \cdot 11 \cdot 19 \cdot 23 \cdot 31 \cdot 37 \cdot 41 \cdot 43 \\
2\,818\,953\,098\,830 &= 2 \cdot 5 \cdot 11 \cdot 19 \cdot 23 \cdot 29 \cdot 31 \cdot 37 \cdot 41 \cdot 43 \\
4\,154\,246\,671\,960 &= 2^3 \cdot 5 \cdot 7 \cdot 11 \cdot 23 \cdot 29 \cdot 31 \cdot 37 \cdot 41 \cdot 43 \\
5\,608\,233\,007\,146 &= 2 \cdot 3^3 \cdot 7 \cdot 11 \cdot 23 \cdot 29 \cdot 31 \cdot 37 \cdot 41 \cdot 43 \\
6\,943\,526\,580\,276 &= 2^2 \cdot 3^2 \cdot 11 \cdot 13 \cdot 23 \cdot 29 \cdot 31 \cdot 37 \cdot 41 \cdot 43 \\
7\,890\,371\,113\,950 &= 2 \cdot 3^2 \cdot 5^2 \cdot 13 \cdot 23 \cdot 29 \cdot 31 \cdot 37 \cdot 41 \cdot 43 \\
8\,233\,430\,727\,600 &= 2^4 \cdot 3^3 \cdot 5^2 \cdot 13 \cdot 29 \cdot 31 \cdot 37 \cdot 41 \cdot 43
\end{aligned}
$$

<u>Row 47</u>

$$
\begin{aligned}
47 &\text{ is Prime} \\
1\,081 &= 23 \cdot 47 \\
16\,215 &= 3 \cdot 5 \cdot 23 \cdot 47 \\
178\,365 &= 3 \cdot 5 \cdot 11 \cdot 23 \cdot 47 \\
1\,533\,939 &= 3 \cdot 11 \cdot 23 \cdot 43 \cdot 47 \\
10\,737\,573 &= 3 \cdot 7 \cdot 11 \cdot 23 \cdot 43 \cdot 47 \\
62\,891\,499 &= 3 \cdot 11 \cdot 23 \cdot 41 \cdot 43 \cdot 47 \\
314\,457\,495 &= 3 \cdot 5 \cdot 11 \cdot 23 \cdot 41 \cdot 43 \cdot 47 \\
1\,362\,649\,145 &= 5 \cdot 11 \cdot 13 \cdot 23 \cdot 41 \cdot 43 \cdot 47 \\
5\,178\,066\,751 &= 11 \cdot 13 \cdot 19 \cdot 23 \cdot 41 \cdot 43 \cdot 47 \\
17\,417\,133\,617 &= 13 \cdot 19 \cdot 23 \cdot 37 \cdot 41 \cdot 43 \cdot 47 \\
52\,251\,400\,851 &= 3 \cdot 13 \cdot 19 \cdot 23 \cdot 37 \cdot 41 \cdot 43 \cdot 47 \\
140\,676\,848\,445 &= 3 \cdot 5 \cdot 7 \cdot 19 \cdot 23 \cdot 37 \cdot 41 \cdot 43 \cdot 47 \\
341\,643\,774\,795 &= 3 \cdot 5 \cdot 17 \cdot 19 \cdot 23 \cdot 37 \cdot 41 \cdot 43 \cdot 47 \\
751\,616\,304\,549 &= 3 \cdot 11 \cdot 17 \cdot 19 \cdot 23 \cdot 37 \cdot 41 \cdot 43 \cdot 47 \\
1\,503\,232\,609\,098 &= 2 \cdot 3 \cdot 11 \cdot 17 \cdot 19 \cdot 23 \cdot 37 \cdot 41 \cdot 43 \cdot 47 \\
2\,741\,188\,875\,414 &= 2 \cdot 3 \cdot 11 \cdot 19 \cdot 23 \cdot 31 \cdot 37 \cdot 41 \cdot 43 \cdot 47 \\
4\,568\,648\,125\,690 &= 2 \cdot 5 \cdot 11 \cdot 19 \cdot 23 \cdot 31 \cdot 37 \cdot 41 \cdot 43 \cdot 47 \\
6\,973\,199\,770\,790 &= 2 \cdot 5 \cdot 11 \cdot 23 \cdot 29 \cdot 31 \cdot 37 \cdot 41 \cdot 43 \cdot 47 \\
9\,762\,479\,679\,106 &= 2 \cdot 7 \cdot 11 \cdot 23 \cdot 29 \cdot 31 \cdot 37 \cdot 41 \cdot 43 \cdot 47 \\
12\,551\,759\,587\,422 &= 2 \cdot 3^2 \cdot 11 \cdot 23 \cdot 29 \cdot 31 \cdot 37 \cdot 41 \cdot 43 \cdot 47 \\
14\,833\,897\,694\,226 &= 2 \cdot 3^2 \cdot 13 \cdot 23 \cdot 29 \cdot 31 \cdot 37 \cdot 41 \cdot 43 \cdot 47 \\
16\,123\,801\,841\,550 &= 2 \cdot 3^2 \cdot 5^2 \cdot 13 \cdot 29 \cdot 31 \cdot 37 \cdot 41 \cdot 43 \cdot 47
\end{aligned}
$$

Pascal's Triangle — Prime Factorization — To Center Number (omitting 1's)

Row 48

$$
\begin{aligned}
48 &= 2^4 \cdot 3 \\
1\,128 &= 2^3 \cdot 3 \cdot 47 \\
17\,296 &= 2^4 \cdot 23 \cdot 47 \\
194\,580 &= 2^2 \cdot 3^2 \cdot 5 \cdot 23 \cdot 47 \\
1\,712\,304 &= 2^4 \cdot 3^2 \cdot 11 \cdot 23 \cdot 47 \\
12\,271\,512 &= 2^3 \cdot 3 \cdot 11 \cdot 23 \cdot 43 \cdot 47 \\
73\,629\,072 &= 2^4 \cdot 3^2 \cdot 11 \cdot 23 \cdot 43 \cdot 47 \\
377\,348\,994 &= 2 \cdot 3^2 \cdot 11 \cdot 23 \cdot 41 \cdot 43 \cdot 47 \\
1\,677\,106\,640 &= 2^4 \cdot 5 \cdot 11 \cdot 23 \cdot 41 \cdot 43 \cdot 47 \\
6\,540\,715\,896 &= 2^3 \cdot 3 \cdot 11 \cdot 13 \cdot 23 \cdot 41 \cdot 43 \cdot 47 \\
22\,595\,200\,368 &= 2^4 \cdot 3 \cdot 13 \cdot 19 \cdot 23 \cdot 41 \cdot 43 \cdot 47 \\
69\,668\,534\,468 &= 2^2 \cdot 13 \cdot 19 \cdot 23 \cdot 37 \cdot 41 \cdot 43 \cdot 47 \\
192\,928\,249\,296 &= 2^4 \cdot 3^2 \cdot 19 \cdot 23 \cdot 37 \cdot 41 \cdot 43 \cdot 47 \\
482\,320\,623\,240 &= 2^3 \cdot 3^2 \cdot 5 \cdot 19 \cdot 23 \cdot 37 \cdot 41 \cdot 43 \cdot 47 \\
1\,093\,260\,079\,344 &= 2^4 \cdot 3 \cdot 17 \cdot 19 \cdot 23 \cdot 37 \cdot 41 \cdot 43 \cdot 47 \\
2\,254\,848\,913\,647 &= 3^2 \cdot 11 \cdot 17 \cdot 19 \cdot 23 \cdot 37 \cdot 41 \cdot 43 \cdot 47 \\
4\,244\,421\,484\,512 &= 2^5 \cdot 3^2 \cdot 11 \cdot 19 \cdot 23 \cdot 37 \cdot 41 \cdot 43 \cdot 47 \\
7\,309\,837\,001\,104 &= 2^4 \cdot 11 \cdot 19 \cdot 23 \cdot 31 \cdot 37 \cdot 41 \cdot 43 \cdot 47 \\
11\,541\,847\,896\,480 &= 2^5 \cdot 3 \cdot 5 \cdot 11 \cdot 23 \cdot 31 \cdot 37 \cdot 41 \cdot 43 \cdot 47 \\
16\,735\,679\,449\,896 &= 2^3 \cdot 3 \cdot 11 \cdot 23 \cdot 29 \cdot 31 \cdot 37 \cdot 41 \cdot 43 \cdot 47 \\
22\,314\,239\,266\,528 &= 2^5 \cdot 11 \cdot 23 \cdot 29 \cdot 31 \cdot 37 \cdot 41 \cdot 43 \cdot 47 \\
27\,385\,657\,281\,648 &= 2^4 \cdot 3^3 \cdot 23 \cdot 29 \cdot 31 \cdot 37 \cdot 41 \cdot 43 \cdot 47 \\
30\,957\,699\,535\,776 &= 2^5 \cdot 3^3 \cdot 13 \cdot 29 \cdot 31 \cdot 37 \cdot 41 \cdot 43 \cdot 47 \\
32\,247\,603\,683\,100 &= 2^2 \cdot 3^2 \cdot 5^2 \cdot 13 \cdot 29 \cdot 31 \cdot 37 \cdot 41 \cdot 43 \cdot 47
\end{aligned}
$$

Row 49

$$
\begin{aligned}
49 &= 7^2 \\
1\,176 &= 2^3 \cdot 3 \cdot 7^2 \\
18\,424 &= 2^3 \cdot 7^2 \cdot 47 \\
211\,876 &= 2^2 \cdot 7^2 \cdot 23 \cdot 47 \\
1\,906\,884 &= 2^2 \cdot 3^2 \cdot 7^2 \cdot 23 \cdot 47 \\
13\,983\,816 &= 2^3 \cdot 3 \cdot 7^2 \cdot 11 \cdot 23 \cdot 47 \\
85\,900\,584 &= 2^3 \cdot 3 \cdot 7 \cdot 11 \cdot 23 \cdot 43 \cdot 47 \\
450\,978\,066 &= 2 \cdot 3^2 \cdot 7^2 \cdot 11 \cdot 23 \cdot 43 \cdot 47 \\
2\,054\,455\,634 &= 2 \cdot 7^2 \cdot 11 \cdot 23 \cdot 41 \cdot 43 \cdot 47 \\
8\,217\,822\,536 &= 2^3 \cdot 7^2 \cdot 11 \cdot 23 \cdot 41 \cdot 43 \cdot 47 \\
29\,135\,916\,264 &= 2^3 \cdot 3 \cdot 7^2 \cdot 13 \cdot 23 \cdot 41 \cdot 43 \cdot 47 \\
92\,263\,734\,836 &= 2^2 \cdot 7^2 \cdot 13 \cdot 19 \cdot 23 \cdot 41 \cdot 43 \cdot 47 \\
262\,596\,783\,764 &= 2^2 \cdot 7^2 \cdot 19 \cdot 23 \cdot 37 \cdot 41 \cdot 43 \cdot 47 \\
675\,248\,872\,536 &= 2^3 \cdot 3^2 \cdot 7 \cdot 19 \cdot 23 \cdot 37 \cdot 41 \cdot 43 \cdot 47 \\
1\,575\,580\,702\,584 &= 2^3 \cdot 3 \cdot 7^2 \cdot 19 \cdot 23 \cdot 37 \cdot 41 \cdot 43 \cdot 47 \\
3\,348\,108\,992\,991 &= 3 \cdot 7^2 \cdot 17 \cdot 19 \cdot 23 \cdot 37 \cdot 41 \cdot 43 \cdot 47 \\
6\,499\,270\,398\,159 &= 3^2 \cdot 7^2 \cdot 11 \cdot 19 \cdot 23 \cdot 37 \cdot 41 \cdot 43 \cdot 47 \\
11\,554\,258\,485\,616 &= 2^4 \cdot 7^2 \cdot 11 \cdot 19 \cdot 23 \cdot 37 \cdot 41 \cdot 43 \cdot 47 \\
18\,851\,684\,897\,584 &= 2^4 \cdot 7^2 \cdot 11 \cdot 23 \cdot 31 \cdot 37 \cdot 41 \cdot 43 \cdot 47 \\
28\,277\,527\,346\,376 &= 2^3 \cdot 3 \cdot 7^2 \cdot 11 \cdot 23 \cdot 31 \cdot 37 \cdot 41 \cdot 43 \cdot 47 \\
39\,049\,918\,716\,424 &= 2^3 \cdot 7 \cdot 11 \cdot 23 \cdot 29 \cdot 31 \cdot 37 \cdot 41 \cdot 43 \cdot 47 \\
49\,699\,896\,548\,176 &= 2^4 \cdot 7^2 \cdot 23 \cdot 29 \cdot 31 \cdot 37 \cdot 41 \cdot 43 \cdot 47 \\
58\,343\,356\,817\,424 &= 2^4 \cdot 3^3 \cdot 7^2 \cdot 29 \cdot 31 \cdot 37 \cdot 41 \cdot 43 \cdot 47 \\
63\,205\,303\,218\,876 &= 2^2 \cdot 3^2 \cdot 7^2 \cdot 13 \cdot 29 \cdot 31 \cdot 37 \cdot 41 \cdot 43 \cdot 47
\end{aligned}
$$

Pascal's Triangle — Prime Factorization — To Center Number (omitting 1's)

Row 50

$$50 = 2 \cdot 5^2$$
$$1\,225 = 5^2 \cdot 7^2$$
$$19\,600 = 2^4 \cdot 5^2 \cdot 7^2$$
$$230\,300 = 2^2 \cdot 5^2 \cdot 7^2 \cdot 47$$
$$2\,118\,760 = 2^3 \cdot 5 \cdot 7^2 \cdot 23 \cdot 47$$
$$15\,890\,700 = 2^2 \cdot 3 \cdot 5^2 \cdot 7^2 \cdot 23 \cdot 47$$
$$99\,884\,400 = 2^4 \cdot 3 \cdot 5^2 \cdot 7 \cdot 11 \cdot 23 \cdot 47$$
$$536\,878\,650 = 2 \cdot 3 \cdot 5^2 \cdot 7 \cdot 11 \cdot 23 \cdot 43 \cdot 47$$
$$2\,505\,433\,700 = 2^2 \cdot 5^2 \cdot 7^2 \cdot 11 \cdot 23 \cdot 43 \cdot 47$$
$$10\,272\,278\,170 = 2 \cdot 5 \cdot 7^2 \cdot 11 \cdot 23 \cdot 41 \cdot 43 \cdot 47$$
$$37\,353\,738\,800 = 2^4 \cdot 5^2 \cdot 7^2 \cdot 23 \cdot 41 \cdot 43 \cdot 47$$
$$121\,399\,651\,100 = 2^2 \cdot 5^2 \cdot 7^2 \cdot 13 \cdot 23 \cdot 41 \cdot 43 \cdot 47$$
$$354\,860\,518\,600 = 2^3 \cdot 5^2 \cdot 7^2 \cdot 19 \cdot 23 \cdot 41 \cdot 43 \cdot 47$$
$$937\,845\,656\,300 = 2^2 \cdot 5^2 \cdot 7 \cdot 19 \cdot 23 \cdot 37 \cdot 41 \cdot 43 \cdot 47$$
$$2\,250\,829\,575\,120 = 2^4 \cdot 3 \cdot 5 \cdot 7 \cdot 19 \cdot 23 \cdot 37 \cdot 41 \cdot 43 \cdot 47$$
$$4\,923\,689\,695\,575 = 3 \cdot 5^2 \cdot 7^2 \cdot 19 \cdot 23 \cdot 37 \cdot 41 \cdot 43 \cdot 47$$
$$9\,847\,379\,391\,150 = 2 \cdot 3 \cdot 5^2 \cdot 7^2 \cdot 19 \cdot 23 \cdot 37 \cdot 41 \cdot 43 \cdot 47$$
$$18\,053\,528\,883\,775 = 5^2 \cdot 7^2 \cdot 11 \cdot 19 \cdot 23 \cdot 37 \cdot 41 \cdot 43 \cdot 47$$
$$30\,405\,943\,383\,200 = 2^5 \cdot 5^2 \cdot 7^2 \cdot 11 \cdot 23 \cdot 37 \cdot 41 \cdot 43 \cdot 47$$
$$47\,129\,212\,243\,960 = 2^3 \cdot 5 \cdot 7^2 \cdot 11 \cdot 23 \cdot 31 \cdot 37 \cdot 41 \cdot 43 \cdot 47$$
$$67\,327\,446\,062\,800 = 2^4 \cdot 5^2 \cdot 7 \cdot 11 \cdot 23 \cdot 31 \cdot 37 \cdot 41 \cdot 43 \cdot 47$$
$$88\,749\,815\,264\,600 = 2^3 \cdot 5^2 \cdot 7 \cdot 23 \cdot 29 \cdot 31 \cdot 37 \cdot 41 \cdot 43 \cdot 47$$
$$108\,043\,253\,365\,600 = 2^5 \cdot 5^2 \cdot 7^2 \cdot 29 \cdot 31 \cdot 37 \cdot 41 \cdot 43 \cdot 47$$
$$121\,548\,660\,036\,300 = 2^2 \cdot 3^2 \cdot 5^2 \cdot 7^2 \cdot 29 \cdot 31 \cdot 37 \cdot 41 \cdot 43 \cdot 47$$
$$126\,410\,606\,437\,752 = 2^3 \cdot 3^2 \cdot 7^2 \cdot 13 \cdot 29 \cdot 31 \cdot 37 \cdot 41 \cdot 43 \cdot 47$$

Row 51

$$51 = 3 \cdot 17$$
$$1\,275 = 3 \cdot 5^2 \cdot 17$$
$$20\,825 = 5^2 \cdot 7^2 \cdot 17$$
$$249\,900 = 2^2 \cdot 3 \cdot 5^2 \cdot 7^2 \cdot 17$$
$$2\,349\,060 = 2^2 \cdot 3 \cdot 5 \cdot 7^2 \cdot 17 \cdot 47$$
$$18\,009\,460 = 2^2 \cdot 5 \cdot 7^2 \cdot 17 \cdot 23 \cdot 47$$
$$115\,775\,100 = 2^2 \cdot 3^2 \cdot 5^2 \cdot 7 \cdot 17 \cdot 23 \cdot 47$$
$$636\,763\,050 = 2 \cdot 3^2 \cdot 5^2 \cdot 7 \cdot 11 \cdot 17 \cdot 23 \cdot 47$$
$$3\,042\,312\,350 = 2 \cdot 5^2 \cdot 7 \cdot 11 \cdot 17 \cdot 23 \cdot 43 \cdot 47$$
$$12\,777\,711\,870 = 2 \cdot 3 \cdot 5 \cdot 7^2 \cdot 11 \cdot 17 \cdot 23 \cdot 43 \cdot 47$$
$$47\,626\,016\,970 = 2 \cdot 3 \cdot 5 \cdot 7^2 \cdot 17 \cdot 23 \cdot 41 \cdot 43 \cdot 47$$
$$158\,753\,389\,900 = 2^2 \cdot 5^2 \cdot 7^2 \cdot 17 \cdot 23 \cdot 41 \cdot 43 \cdot 47$$
$$476\,260\,169\,700 = 2^2 \cdot 3 \cdot 5^2 \cdot 7^2 \cdot 17 \cdot 23 \cdot 41 \cdot 43 \cdot 47$$
$$1\,292\,706\,174\,900 = 2^2 \cdot 3 \cdot 5^2 \cdot 7 \cdot 17 \cdot 19 \cdot 23 \cdot 41 \cdot 43 \cdot 47$$
$$3\,188\,675\,231\,420 = 2^2 \cdot 5 \cdot 7 \cdot 17 \cdot 19 \cdot 23 \cdot 37 \cdot 41 \cdot 43 \cdot 47$$
$$7\,174\,519\,270\,695 = 3^2 \cdot 5 \cdot 7 \cdot 17 \cdot 19 \cdot 23 \cdot 37 \cdot 41 \cdot 43 \cdot 47$$
$$14\,771\,069\,086\,725 = 3^2 \cdot 5^2 \cdot 7^2 \cdot 19 \cdot 23 \cdot 37 \cdot 41 \cdot 43 \cdot 47$$
$$27\,900\,908\,274\,925 = 5^2 \cdot 7^2 \cdot 17 \cdot 19 \cdot 23 \cdot 37 \cdot 41 \cdot 43 \cdot 47$$
$$48\,459\,472\,266\,975 = 3 \cdot 5^2 \cdot 7^2 \cdot 11 \cdot 17 \cdot 23 \cdot 37 \cdot 41 \cdot 43 \cdot 47$$
$$77\,535\,155\,627\,160 = 2^3 \cdot 3 \cdot 5 \cdot 7^2 \cdot 11 \cdot 17 \cdot 23 \cdot 37 \cdot 41 \cdot 43 \cdot 47$$
$$114\,456\,658\,306\,760 = 2^3 \cdot 5 \cdot 7 \cdot 11 \cdot 17 \cdot 23 \cdot 31 \cdot 37 \cdot 41 \cdot 43 \cdot 47$$
$$156\,077\,261\,327\,400 = 2^3 \cdot 3 \cdot 5^2 \cdot 7 \cdot 17 \cdot 23 \cdot 31 \cdot 37 \cdot 41 \cdot 43 \cdot 47$$
$$196\,793\,068\,630\,200 = 2^3 \cdot 3 \cdot 5^2 \cdot 7 \cdot 17 \cdot 29 \cdot 31 \cdot 37 \cdot 41 \cdot 43 \cdot 47$$
$$229\,591\,913\,401\,900 = 2^2 \cdot 5^2 \cdot 7^2 \cdot 17 \cdot 29 \cdot 31 \cdot 37 \cdot 41 \cdot 43 \cdot 47$$
$$247\,959\,266\,474\,052 = 2^2 \cdot 3^3 \cdot 7^2 \cdot 17 \cdot 29 \cdot 31 \cdot 37 \cdot 41 \cdot 43 \cdot 47$$

Pascal's Triangle — Prime Factorization — To Center Number (omitting 1's)

Row 52

$$52 = 2^2 \cdot 13$$
$$1\,326 = 2 \cdot 3 \cdot 13 \cdot 17$$
$$22\,100 = 2^2 \cdot 5^2 \cdot 13 \cdot 17$$
$$270\,725 = 5^2 \cdot 7^2 \cdot 13 \cdot 17$$
$$2\,598\,960 = 2^4 \cdot 3 \cdot 5 \cdot 7^2 \cdot 13 \cdot 17$$
$$20\,358\,520 = 2^3 \cdot 5 \cdot 7^2 \cdot 13 \cdot 17 \cdot 47$$
$$133\,784\,560 = 2^4 \cdot 5 \cdot 7 \cdot 13 \cdot 17 \cdot 23 \cdot 47$$
$$752\,538\,150 = 2 \cdot 3^2 \cdot 5^2 \cdot 7 \cdot 13 \cdot 17 \cdot 23 \cdot 47$$
$$3\,679\,075\,400 = 2^3 \cdot 5^2 \cdot 7 \cdot 11 \cdot 13 \cdot 17 \cdot 23 \cdot 47$$
$$15\,820\,024\,220 = 2^2 \cdot 5 \cdot 7 \cdot 11 \cdot 13 \cdot 17 \cdot 23 \cdot 43 \cdot 47$$
$$60\,403\,728\,840 = 2^3 \cdot 3 \cdot 5 \cdot 7^2 \cdot 13 \cdot 17 \cdot 23 \cdot 43 \cdot 47$$
$$206\,379\,406\,870 = 2 \cdot 5 \cdot 7^2 \cdot 13 \cdot 17 \cdot 23 \cdot 41 \cdot 43 \cdot 47$$
$$635\,013\,559\,600 = 2^4 \cdot 5^2 \cdot 7^2 \cdot 17 \cdot 23 \cdot 41 \cdot 43 \cdot 47$$
$$1\,768\,966\,344\,600 = 2^3 \cdot 3 \cdot 5^2 \cdot 7 \cdot 13 \cdot 17 \cdot 23 \cdot 41 \cdot 43 \cdot 47$$
$$4\,481\,381\,406\,320 = 2^4 \cdot 5 \cdot 7 \cdot 13 \cdot 17 \cdot 19 \cdot 23 \cdot 41 \cdot 43 \cdot 47$$
$$10\,363\,194\,502\,115 = 5 \cdot 7 \cdot 13 \cdot 17 \cdot 19 \cdot 23 \cdot 37 \cdot 41 \cdot 43 \cdot 47$$
$$21\,945\,588\,357\,420 = 2^2 \cdot 3^2 \cdot 5 \cdot 7 \cdot 13 \cdot 19 \cdot 23 \cdot 37 \cdot 41 \cdot 43 \cdot 47$$
$$42\,671\,977\,361\,650 = 2 \cdot 5^2 \cdot 7^2 \cdot 13 \cdot 19 \cdot 23 \cdot 37 \cdot 41 \cdot 43 \cdot 47$$
$$76\,360\,380\,541\,900 = 2^2 \cdot 5^2 \cdot 7^2 \cdot 13 \cdot 17 \cdot 23 \cdot 37 \cdot 41 \cdot 43 \cdot 47$$
$$125\,994\,627\,894\,135 = 3 \cdot 5 \cdot 7^2 \cdot 11 \cdot 13 \cdot 17 \cdot 23 \cdot 37 \cdot 41 \cdot 43 \cdot 47$$
$$191\,991\,813\,933\,920 = 2^5 \cdot 5 \cdot 7 \cdot 11 \cdot 13 \cdot 17 \cdot 23 \cdot 37 \cdot 41 \cdot 43 \cdot 47$$
$$270\,533\,919\,634\,160 = 2^4 \cdot 5 \cdot 7 \cdot 13 \cdot 17 \cdot 23 \cdot 31 \cdot 37 \cdot 41 \cdot 43 \cdot 47$$
$$352\,870\,329\,957\,600 = 2^5 \cdot 3 \cdot 5^2 \cdot 7 \cdot 13 \cdot 17 \cdot 31 \cdot 37 \cdot 41 \cdot 43 \cdot 47$$
$$426\,384\,982\,032\,100 = 2^2 \cdot 5^2 \cdot 7 \cdot 13 \cdot 17 \cdot 29 \cdot 31 \cdot 37 \cdot 41 \cdot 43 \cdot 47$$
$$477\,551\,179\,875\,952 = 2^4 \cdot 7^2 \cdot 13 \cdot 17 \cdot 29 \cdot 31 \cdot 37 \cdot 41 \cdot 43 \cdot 47$$
$$495\,918\,532\,948\,104 = 2^3 \cdot 3^3 \cdot 7^2 \cdot 17 \cdot 29 \cdot 31 \cdot 37 \cdot 41 \cdot 43 \cdot 47$$

Pascal's Triangle — Prime Factorization — To Center Number (omitting 1's)

<u>Row 53</u>

$$
\begin{aligned}
53 \text{ is Prime} \\
1\,378 &= 2 \cdot 13 \cdot 53 \\
23\,426 &= 2 \cdot 13 \cdot 17 \cdot 53 \\
292\,825 &= 5^2 \cdot 13 \cdot 17 \cdot 53 \\
2\,869\,685 &= 5 \cdot 7^2 \cdot 13 \cdot 17 \cdot 53 \\
22\,957\,480 &= 2^3 \cdot 5 \cdot 7^2 \cdot 13 \cdot 17 \cdot 53 \\
154\,143\,080 &= 2^3 \cdot 5 \cdot 7 \cdot 13 \cdot 17 \cdot 47 \cdot 53 \\
886\,322\,710 &= 2 \cdot 5 \cdot 7 \cdot 13 \cdot 17 \cdot 23 \cdot 47 \cdot 53 \\
4\,431\,613\,550 &= 2 \cdot 5^2 \cdot 7 \cdot 13 \cdot 17 \cdot 23 \cdot 47 \cdot 53 \\
19\,499\,099\,620 &= 2^2 \cdot 5 \cdot 7 \cdot 11 \cdot 13 \cdot 17 \cdot 23 \cdot 47 \cdot 53 \\
76\,223\,753\,060 &= 2^2 \cdot 5 \cdot 7 \cdot 13 \cdot 17 \cdot 23 \cdot 43 \cdot 47 \cdot 53 \\
266\,783\,135\,710 &= 2 \cdot 5 \cdot 7^2 \cdot 13 \cdot 17 \cdot 23 \cdot 43 \cdot 47 \cdot 53 \\
841\,392\,966\,470 &= 2 \cdot 5 \cdot 7^2 \cdot 17 \cdot 23 \cdot 41 \cdot 43 \cdot 47 \cdot 53 \\
2\,403\,979\,904\,200 &= 2^3 \cdot 5^2 \cdot 7 \cdot 17 \cdot 23 \cdot 41 \cdot 43 \cdot 47 \cdot 53 \\
6\,250\,347\,750\,920 &= 2^3 \cdot 5 \cdot 7 \cdot 13 \cdot 17 \cdot 23 \cdot 41 \cdot 43 \cdot 47 \cdot 53 \\
14\,844\,575\,908\,435 &= 5 \cdot 7 \cdot 13 \cdot 17 \cdot 19 \cdot 23 \cdot 41 \cdot 43 \cdot 47 \cdot 53 \\
32\,308\,782\,859\,535 &= 5 \cdot 7 \cdot 13 \cdot 19 \cdot 23 \cdot 37 \cdot 41 \cdot 43 \cdot 47 \cdot 53 \\
64\,617\,565\,719\,070 &= 2 \cdot 5 \cdot 7 \cdot 13 \cdot 19 \cdot 23 \cdot 37 \cdot 41 \cdot 43 \cdot 47 \cdot 53 \\
119\,032\,357\,903\,550 &= 2 \cdot 5^2 \cdot 7^2 \cdot 13 \cdot 23 \cdot 37 \cdot 41 \cdot 43 \cdot 47 \cdot 53 \\
202\,355\,008\,436\,035 &= 5 \cdot 7^2 \cdot 13 \cdot 17 \cdot 23 \cdot 37 \cdot 41 \cdot 43 \cdot 47 \cdot 53 \\
317\,986\,441\,828\,055 &= 5 \cdot 7 \cdot 11 \cdot 13 \cdot 17 \cdot 23 \cdot 37 \cdot 41 \cdot 43 \cdot 47 \cdot 53 \\
462\,525\,733\,568\,080 &= 2^4 \cdot 5 \cdot 7 \cdot 13 \cdot 17 \cdot 23 \cdot 37 \cdot 41 \cdot 43 \cdot 47 \cdot 53 \\
623\,404\,249\,591\,760 &= 2^4 \cdot 5 \cdot 7 \cdot 13 \cdot 17 \cdot 31 \cdot 37 \cdot 41 \cdot 43 \cdot 47 \cdot 53 \\
779\,255\,311\,989\,700 &= 2^2 \cdot 5^2 \cdot 7 \cdot 13 \cdot 17 \cdot 31 \cdot 37 \cdot 41 \cdot 43 \cdot 47 \cdot 53 \\
903\,936\,161\,908\,052 &= 2^2 \cdot 7 \cdot 13 \cdot 17 \cdot 29 \cdot 31 \cdot 37 \cdot 41 \cdot 43 \cdot 47 \cdot 53 \\
973\,469\,712\,824\,056 &= 2^3 \cdot 7^2 \cdot 17 \cdot 29 \cdot 31 \cdot 37 \cdot 41 \cdot 43 \cdot 47 \cdot 53
\end{aligned}
$$

Pascal's Triangle — Prime Factorization — To Center Number (omitting 1's)

Row 54

$$54 = 2 \cdot 3^3$$
$$1\,431 = 3^3 \cdot 53$$
$$24\,804 = 2^2 \cdot 3^2 \cdot 13 \cdot 53$$
$$316\,251 = 3^3 \cdot 13 \cdot 17 \cdot 53$$
$$3\,162\,510 = 2 \cdot 3^3 \cdot 5 \cdot 13 \cdot 17 \cdot 53$$
$$25\,827\,165 = 3^2 \cdot 5 \cdot 7^2 \cdot 13 \cdot 17 \cdot 53$$
$$177\,100\,560 = 2^4 \cdot 3^3 \cdot 5 \cdot 7 \cdot 13 \cdot 17 \cdot 53$$
$$1\,040\,465\,790 = 2 \cdot 3^3 \cdot 5 \cdot 7 \cdot 13 \cdot 17 \cdot 47 \cdot 53$$
$$5\,317\,936\,260 = 2^2 \cdot 3 \cdot 5 \cdot 7 \cdot 13 \cdot 17 \cdot 23 \cdot 47 \cdot 53$$
$$23\,930\,713\,170 = 2 \cdot 3^3 \cdot 5 \cdot 7 \cdot 13 \cdot 17 \cdot 23 \cdot 47 \cdot 53$$
$$95\,722\,852\,680 = 2^3 \cdot 3^3 \cdot 5 \cdot 7 \cdot 13 \cdot 17 \cdot 23 \cdot 47 \cdot 53$$
$$343\,006\,888\,770 = 2 \cdot 3^2 \cdot 5 \cdot 7 \cdot 13 \cdot 17 \cdot 23 \cdot 43 \cdot 47 \cdot 53$$
$$1\,108\,176\,102\,180 = 2^2 \cdot 3^3 \cdot 5 \cdot 7^2 \cdot 17 \cdot 23 \cdot 43 \cdot 47 \cdot 53$$
$$3\,245\,372\,870\,670 = 2 \cdot 3^3 \cdot 5 \cdot 7 \cdot 17 \cdot 23 \cdot 41 \cdot 43 \cdot 47 \cdot 53$$
$$8\,654\,327\,655\,120 = 2^4 \cdot 3^2 \cdot 5 \cdot 7 \cdot 17 \cdot 23 \cdot 41 \cdot 43 \cdot 47 \cdot 53$$
$$21\,094\,923\,659\,355 = 3^3 \cdot 5 \cdot 7 \cdot 13 \cdot 17 \cdot 23 \cdot 41 \cdot 43 \cdot 47 \cdot 53$$
$$47\,153\,358\,767\,970 = 2 \cdot 3^3 \cdot 5 \cdot 7 \cdot 13 \cdot 19 \cdot 23 \cdot 41 \cdot 43 \cdot 47 \cdot 53$$
$$96\,926\,348\,578\,605 = 3 \cdot 5 \cdot 7 \cdot 13 \cdot 19 \cdot 23 \cdot 37 \cdot 41 \cdot 43 \cdot 47 \cdot 53$$
$$183\,649\,923\,622\,620 = 2^2 \cdot 3^3 \cdot 5 \cdot 7 \cdot 13 \cdot 23 \cdot 37 \cdot 41 \cdot 43 \cdot 47 \cdot 53$$
$$321\,387\,366\,339\,585 = 3^3 \cdot 5 \cdot 7^2 \cdot 13 \cdot 23 \cdot 37 \cdot 41 \cdot 43 \cdot 47 \cdot 53$$
$$520\,341\,450\,264\,090 = 2 \cdot 3^2 \cdot 5 \cdot 7 \cdot 13 \cdot 17 \cdot 23 \cdot 37 \cdot 41 \cdot 43 \cdot 47 \cdot 53$$
$$780\,512\,175\,396\,135 = 3^3 \cdot 5 \cdot 7 \cdot 13 \cdot 17 \cdot 23 \cdot 37 \cdot 41 \cdot 43 \cdot 47 \cdot 53$$
$$1\,085\,929\,983\,159\,840 = 2^5 \cdot 3^3 \cdot 5 \cdot 7 \cdot 13 \cdot 17 \cdot 37 \cdot 41 \cdot 43 \cdot 47 \cdot 53$$
$$1\,402\,659\,561\,581\,460 = 2^2 \cdot 3^2 \cdot 5 \cdot 7 \cdot 13 \cdot 17 \cdot 31 \cdot 37 \cdot 41 \cdot 43 \cdot 47 \cdot 53$$
$$1\,683\,191\,473\,897\,752 = 2^3 \cdot 3^3 \cdot 7 \cdot 13 \cdot 17 \cdot 31 \cdot 37 \cdot 41 \cdot 43 \cdot 47 \cdot 53$$
$$1\,877\,405\,874\,732\,108 = 2^2 \cdot 3^3 \cdot 7 \cdot 17 \cdot 29 \cdot 31 \cdot 37 \cdot 41 \cdot 43 \cdot 47 \cdot 53$$
$$1\,946\,939\,425\,648\,112 = 2^4 \cdot 7^2 \cdot 17 \cdot 29 \cdot 31 \cdot 37 \cdot 41 \cdot 43 \cdot 47 \cdot 53$$

INDEX

Epilogue

Although we've offered extensive applications in this textbook, we haven't peeked and poked every facet of Pascal's Triangle. If you are seeking another area to explore and you have a decade to spare, consider the facets of Pascal's Pyramid. Each face of Pascal's Pyramid is a Pascal's Triangle.

Each number in the interior of Pascal's Pyramid is the sum of the three numbers immediately above it and each level of numbers represents the coefficients in the expansion of a trinomial, $(a + b + c)^n$. Happy exploring!

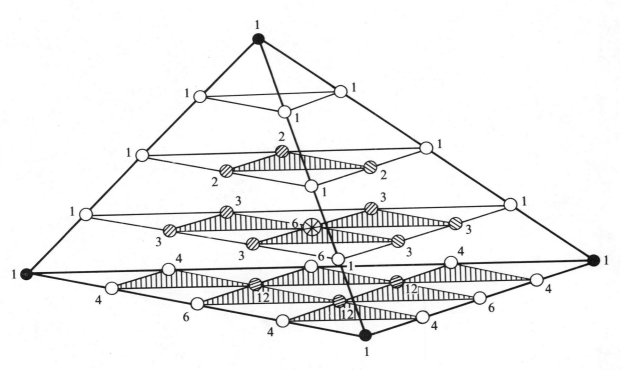

Pascal's Pyramid